The new globalism and developing countries

Note to the reader

This book is published by the United Nations University Press. The contents were prepared by the Division on Investment, Technology and Enterprise Development of the United Nations Conference on Trade and Development. The Division seeks to facilitate foreign investment to and among developing countries; foster transfer and diffusion of technology and capacity building; and stimulate enterprise development. The division undertakes global research and policy analysis aimed at promoting international dialogue among development actors and supporting intergovernmental discussions, and also provides technical assistance, primarily to developing countries, upon request. Information on the work of the Division may be obtained from the Director, Division on Investment, Technology and Enterprise Development, UNCTAD, Room E-10054, Palais des Nations, 1211 Geneva 10, Switzerland.

THE NEW GLOBALISM AND DEVELOPING COUNTRIES

Edited by John H. Dunning and Khalil A. Hamdani

**United Nations
University Press**

TOKYO • NEW YORK • PARIS

BKC 3521 - 9/3

The views expressed in this publication are those of the authors and do not necessarily reflect the views of the United Nations University or the United Nations Conference on Trade and Development.

United Nations University Press
The United Nations University, 53-70, Jingumae 5-chome,
Shibuya-ku, Tokyo 150, Japan
Tel. (03) 3499-2811   Fax: (03) 3406-7345
Telex: J25442   Cable: UNATUNIV TOKYO

UNU Office in North America
2 United Nations Plaza, Room DC2-1462-70, New York, NY 10017
Tel: (212) 963-6387   Fax: (212) 371-9454   Telex: 422311 UN UI

United Nations University Press is the publishing division of the United Nations University.

Cover design by J.-M. Antenen, Geneva

UNUP-944
ISBN 92-808-0944-X

Contents

Contents

Foreword

The globalization of business and the resulting rapid growth of economic interdependence is a supra-national phenomenon with far-reaching political, economic, social, and cultural consequences for all countries of the world. Spearheaded by the business community itself rather than by the efforts of nation states, it nevertheless profoundly influences the policies of national governments. Its impact on developing countries is undeniable and holds the Janus-like promise, for some, of greater integration, for others, of stagnation or further marginalization in the world economy.

Who stands to win or lose from the growing flows of international direct investments, cross-border trade transactions and technology transfer, and other cooperative business ventures that feed the growth of an increasingly "borderless" global economy? What have been, so far, the responses of governments, individually and collectively, nationally and regionally, to the challenges posed by the problems inherent in these developments? What strategies should developing countries consider in order to maximize for themselves the benefits of the globalization process, while minimizing its adverse effects? What is the role of the international community in support of such strategies?

These are some of the critical questions addressed by this timely and important book. They are explored by a distinguished group of social scientists, who examine the nature of the process of globalization and its numerous manifestations. They spell out the many ways in which developing regions are being affected and analyse the policy dimensions of globalization, with particular attention to its linkages with investment, trade, and science and technology flows.

For some time now, the United Nations University's research and training centres for development economics in Helsinki, Finland (UNU/ WIDER), and for the study of new technologies in Maastricht, Netherlands (UNU/INTECH), have studied various aspects of the evolving global economy, in order to help understand the complexities underlying the world's intricate traffic in goods and services. One such project, for example, re-evaluated the role direct foreign investment by transnational corporations plays as a vehicle for international economic integration. From a development perspective, it assessed the extent to which the interests of the transnationals coincide - and where they conflict - with those of the national and regional economies in which they operate.

I am very pleased that the cooperation between UNCTAD and the United Nations University, which has been evident in other areas, will be continued with the publication of this important study. It is my sincere hope that this informative and illuminating book will be of interest to a wide range of readers, stimulate public interest in the pressing problems associated with globalization processes, and encourage further research on a subject that should be of immediate interest to practitioners and scholars alike.

Heitor Gurgulino de Souza
Rector
The United Nations University

Preface

In the new globalism we witness a vision as old as time, one which began with the European age of maritime exploration five centuries ago, but which the Phoenicians, Vikings, Chinese and other great trading peoples also dreamed of: the unification of markets and of economic space on a planetary dimension.

Globalization is a complex phenomenon, fraught with contrasts. It promises to bring fully into active participation in the world economy two billion women and men in the fast-growing countries. But hundreds of millions of other individuals fear that the same forces threaten to shut them out from the promise of prosperity. They are the unemployed or low-wage earners in sectors of industrial economies that have been lagging behind in the process of change. They are, too, the poor and jobless of many developing countries that depend on a few commodities barely touched by globalization.

In this new global context for development, full of promise and threat, the role of UNCTAD must be to show how the opportunities can be seized and the challenges overcome. Through research and the building of international consensus, and through practical assistance to individual countries, UNCTAD, in cooperation with other international organizations, is contributing to the development and integration of the developing countries into the globalizing world economy.

The papers in this book examine one facet of globalization - the expansion of foreign direct investment and the internationalization of production - and its implications for developing countries. The book is the outgrowth of the United Nations Symposium on Globalization and Developing Countries, held in The Hague on 30 March 1992. Many of the contributors were participants and the papers in this book elaborate the views they first presented at the symposium. The editors, John H. Dunning and Khalil A. Hamdani, have provided structure to the volume and have ensured that the data is consistent and up to date as of 1995. The project was made possible with generous financial support of the Government of the Netherlands.

The interested reader may wish to refer to the *World Investment Report* and the *Trade and Development Report* of UNCTAD for more detailed analyses of globalization trends. Also relevant are the documentation for the ninth session of the United Nations Conference on Trade and Development, which convened in Midrand, South Africa this year from 27 April to 11 May on the agenda of promoting growth and sustainable development in a globalizing and liberalizing world economy.

Rubens Ricupero

Geneva, August 1996   Secretary-General of UNCTAD

Introduction

Khalil A. Hamdani

The world economy is globalizing, in the sense that economic activity takes place increasingly on a supranational scale, and often between entities of the same governance. There are many examples. Products which used to be manufactured in stand-alone factories, are now fabricated with parts and materials — even services — sourced in several different geographical locations: there is the world car, the world aircraft and, of course, the world sneaker. Financial operations are conducted around-the-world, around-the-clock, as matters of routine; not just by securities and trading houses, but by individuals through automatic teller machines. Perhaps the most familiar example, known to billions, is the satellite news broadcast, which can simultaneously be a bedtime story in China and an Englishman's wake-up call.

These events signal the start of a new period of economic history — a new globalism— distinct from the recent post-war period which has been dominated by internationalism. In the four decades following the Second World War, the expansion of economic activity world-wide was led primarily by nation states acting in concert through the creation of an international economic system for trade and payments, and successive rounds of multilateral tariff reduction. That era of internationalization has run its course, and has given way to a period in which firms, rather than nation states, are spearheading global economic interdependence.

A key indicator of globalization is the rapid expansion of international direct investment, which, since the mid-1980s, has grown faster than world output and trade (UNCTC, 1991). Throughout the 1990s, transnational corporations (TNCs) are likely to continue to increase their role in the world economy, in the markets for goods and services, capital and technology. Their activities are both broadening and deepening the economic interdependence of nations, to a degree that it is now commonplace to refer to the aggregate no longer as the international economy, but as a "borderless" global economy.

In the 1950s and 1960s, economic interdependence emanated mainly through the arm's- length exchange of goods and services. The transfer of technology and other intangible assets among countries was largely embodied in the exchange of intermediate and final products. Foreign direct investment (FDI) was relatively insignificant and took the form of stand-alone affiliate operations. But technological change and deregulation have given rise to global markets, and competition in the market-place has turned these trends around. Transnational corporations have penetrated foreign markets while consolidating positions in their home markets. They have also integrated their world-wide operations to reduce costs. Hence, economic interdependence is increasingly production-based, and not just trade-based (UNCTAD-DTCI, 1993). International investment has not only surged, but trade and technology transactions also take place more and more within TNCs rather than the market. A rough measure of this change in economic interdependence is the pattern in world-wide sales of TNCs from the largest home countries, which now takes place more through the sales of their affiliates than through direct exports (UN-TCMD, 1992).

With international production increasingly integrated across borders, it is apparent that many economic activities are potentially footloose and that TNCs are locationally responsive to differences in national conditions. Countries can be — and have been — confronted with outflows of entire factories, specially in low-tech assembly operations. But increasingly, relocations are also becoming more strategically motivated, focusing on particular functions such as data processing, accounting, research and development and customer assistance via remote telecommunications. The implication is that Governments must also compete with each other if they are to retain or attract international production.

Thus, competition in the market-place is leading to competition between countries. Policy makers increasingly ask: how do our national policies and institutions compare to those of other countries? If our major trading partners offer incentives and subsidies to attract FDI, can we afford not to? Globalization is therefore triggering a process of systemic convergence in which all Governments face pressures to pursue more or less similar policies to enhance their national (or regional) competitiveness, *vis-à-vis* other countries, as locations for international production. Although competitiveness-enhancing policies are not necessarily market-distorting, they can be, and this danger has prompted calls for placing competition policy on the international policy agenda.

Developing countries face a systemic convergence of a different sort: when all countries adopt similar liberalizing measures, the relative attractiveness of any potential host country will be determined by other factors. What are these factors and which are really amenable to policy intervention? Developing countries also face the challenge of competing for FDI against the developed countries, which, possessing more advanced human and physical infrastructures, offer more attractive locations for international production.

Indeed, the early signs of globalization brought forth warnings of a marginalization of developing countries. Analysts pointed to a concentration of investment in the Triad of Europe, Japan and the United States. But, in fact, an increasing number of developing countries from all regions are actively participating in globalization. Investment in developing countries has increased five-fold since the mid-1980s. In 1994 they received about as much as total world flows in 1986, and their share of world-wide investment inflows reached an unprecedented 40 per cent (UNCTAD-DTCI, 1995). Although this investment has largely flowed to only a handful of countries in Asia, their success has encouraged many other developing countries to open up their economies and enter the global competition for foreign investment. Will they succeed?

In the chapters in this volume, the current, and likely future, impact of globalization on developing nations are examined. Who are the probable winners and losers? Do investment strategies take full account of the technology dimension? Are Governments seizing the opportunities resulting from the deregulation of markets and the liberalization of trade?

Is regional integration imposing new entry barriers? Are there any winning strategies in the more competitive global economic environment of the 1990s? And how can the international community best support those strategies?

There are no simple and unambiguous answers, but the overall theme is affirmative, even optimistic. This last decade of the twentieth century offers a great many opportunities and challenges for international investment, more than any that preceded it. There are, of course, important caveats: not all countries are benefiting equally; social inequalities persist and sustainable development is an overriding challenge. None the less, the 1990s are witnessing the greening of the global economy, with an increasing number of developing countries from all regions participating actively in globalization.

The industrialization quest of developing countries has long been associated with the Lima target, which envisaged increasing their share of world manufactured output to 25 per cent by the year 2000. This target was dismissed as soon as it was proclaimed in 1975 and has since been forgotten even by its proponents. In fact, if current trends continue (and hopefully they will), the target will come near to being attained. But, if the Lima target is reached, it will perhaps have less to do with the strategies of Governments pursued in the 1970s, and more to do with the globalization of business.

At the same time, the world economy has moved on, and presence in manufacturing no longer implies a fundamental change in the international division of labour of the sort developing countries had hoped: services, not manufacturing, is the most dynamic growth sector in the world today, though increasingly the production of goods and services are interdependent of each other. Nevertheless, the Asian experience shows that traditional sources of comparative advantage can be the basis for impressive growth, and provide not only entry into the web of globalization, but a path for the later upgrading of value added and the restructuring of production along new and more competitive lines of international exchange. Transnational corporations play a key role in this process, but as important are government policies to exploit investment, trade and technology linkages and enhance dynamic comparative advantage. Such is the overarching theme of this volume.

An overview of the papers

There are ten papers, which are organized in four parts. Part I is forward-looking and speculative, and attempts in broad brush strokes to characterize the international setting of globalization and the future of the world trade and investment system in the post-Uruguay Round period. Part II adds diversity to the stylized global presentations by examining the different ways in which the three developing regions of the world are being affected by globalization.

The second half of the volume addresses the policy dimensions of globalization, and particularly the need for integrated strategies that can catalyze and reinforce — in the sense of the fabled virtuous circle — the emerging linkages between investment, trade and technology. Part III addresses investment and trade linkages. How might developing countries benefit from the globalization of production and markets? Part IV tackles investment and technology linkages: How might developing countries best create or acquire the human competencies and created assets that increasingly define competitive advantage in the global economy?

International setting

John Dunning, in chapter 1, describes the globalization process, and discusses the roles of the main actors shaping it — TNCs and Governments. The author speculates about the likely evolution of TNC activity or, as he aptly puts it, the advent of alliance capitalism. He shows how corporate alliances (hierarchical and cooperative) are the natural micro-organizational response to new technologies, competition in world markets and other globalizing forces. Through alliances, TNCs are seeking strategic assets, a new type of FDI which can also create opportunities for firms from developing countries whose Governments establish an environment conducive to alliance formation. He goes on to suggest how Governments can play a more pro-active role in upgrading their wealth-creating capabilities, a challenge in which many developing countries may have a comparative advantage, but which few can rise to without international development assistance.

Robert Lawrence, in chapter 2, examines the international institutional framework and its capacity to deal with issues arising from globalization. These issues include the linkage between investment and

5

trade, regional blocs, managed trading arrangements and integration schemes. The Uruguay Round succeeded in introducing investment provisions into the multilateral framework, but the partial treatment of international investment through separate protocols — TRIPS, TRIMS and GATS[1/] — reflected the approach of a bygone era. Although investment is slated to be taken up on the post Uruguay Round agenda, a comprehensive approach to international investment in the context of globalization inevitably means negotiating measures of deep integration, and most countries would prefer to do that in bilateral and regional arrangements, if at all. This would then suggest the coexistence of several regimes for many years. Lawrence examines the various scenarios and reaches one unambiguous conclusion: market access for developing countries means increased obligations to conform to high standards for domestic policies and institutional practices (in such areas as infant industry protection, subsidies, intellectual property rights, labour practices and environmental standards). This pressure will be felt even when there may be legitimate reasons for differentiated treatment for countries at different levels of development.

Taken together, the chapters by Dunning and Lawrence suggest that the way Governments respond to globalization, individually and collectively, is by no means irrelevant, particularly for developing countries, even though the scope and authority of national sovereignty and supranational regimes may have diminished with the emergence of a "borderless" global economy.

Regional perspectives

Linda Lim and Nathaniel Siddall, in chapter 3, examine the investment dynamism of Asia and the FDI-led development paths which the South-East Asian nations have followed to catapult themselves into the ranks of the newly-industrializing economies. Although many factors are involved, it is noteworthy that static comparative advantage of natural resources and cheap labour was the initial attraction for FDI in all the countries. The Asian miracle lay less in the ability to attract FDI, which was achieved through standard policy prescriptions and the help of external factors, and more in the ability to upgrade from resource-based and labour-based FDI, to skill-and-technology-based FDI. The key to success was the building of technological capabilities: first, by absorbing know-how transferred through FDI and, then, by applying the newly-acquired skills to develop indigenous technologies and to master more complex imported technologies. In the process, they were able not only to move up the technology ladder, but even, in some cases, to leapfrog former investors in world markets.

Daniel Chudnovsky, in chapter 4, approaches the same issues from a Latin American perspective. The initial conditions are very different from Asia, he argues: a legacy of a lost development decade and the context of macroeconomic adjustment and liberalization in many countries, calls for a new policy set to help Latin American firms restructure and regain international competitiveness. He outlines the elements of innovation policy, which should help firms operating inside the technological frontier to raise productivity by adopting modern technologies and organizational techniques, available globally, and to produce better quality goods and services for sale at home and abroad. Given the setbacks of the 1980s, he argues that powerful incentives are needed to re-start the process of technological accumulation but, in the context of globalization, when governments intervene to promote competitiveness, they should rely whenever possible on the competitive stimuli of the market to mobilize private sector capabilities, and also on the catalytic role that TNCs can play in capacity-building.

John Cantwell, in chapter 5, considers the implications of globalization for Africa. These may seem remote, but, as he notes, while development and FDI expansion in Africa are generally slower than in the other developing regions, FDI is still a catalyst for most development that does occur. Like Asia, FDI has been resource-based; but unlike Asia and more like Latin America, such investment that has entered manufacturing is import-substituting rather than export-oriented, and with less capacity for dynamic upgrading. Thus, to a degree, the lessons of both regions apply to Africa: to avoid closed strategies of the type associated with national economic independence and to look to resource-based FDI to play a more catalytic role in stimulating economic growth, particularly in areas where there are indigenous capabilities that can be quickly built up, such as in resource-based simple manufacturing industries.

Taken together, the three regional chapters emphasize the dynamics of development. Thus, the contribution of FDI extends beyond the mere bridging of a resource gap and encompasses technological spillovers essential for industrial upgrading. Equally, technology is important not only because it offers new possibilities for production, but also for learning. Capturing these dynamics is the defining characteristic of all winning strategies of globalization.

Investment and trade

Louka Katseli, in chapter 6, examines the linkages between FDI and trade, and how countries can exploit them to facilitate industrial upgrading. The process is by no means automatic, as she shows by reference to different country experiences. Governments can pursue pro-active policies that may encourage TNCs to upgrade their investments, however, as traditional sources of comparative advantage erode over time. These policies, which the East Asian countries pursued with much success, include improvements in infrastructure, skills, services and the political and business environment.

Stephen Thomsen, in chapter 7, notes the importance of market-seeking FDI in developing countries and suggests that regional integration among developing countries may hold the key to attracting greater FDI. This applies especially to the smaller and poorer developing countries, which could enlarge their effective markets by becoming attached to larger neighbours (such as Mexico, Brazil, India or South Africa). Coalitions of smaller economies can become dynamic markets in their own right, as the ASEAN experience suggests. Of course, regional integration is not a substitute for expanding international trade.

Investment and technology

Sanjaya Lall, in chapter 8, examines the linkages between FDI and technology transfer, and how countries can exploit them to facilitate technological upgrading. Again, as in the case of trade, the process is by no means automatic: success in attracting more advanced technology flows depends on the success of domestic efforts at building indigenous capabilities. He examines the process of capability development and how it is affected by different modes of technology transfer and FDI. Local capability development is both complementary to and competitive with the use of imported technologies, and the right policy mix should aim at maintaining a balanced relationship by altering the modes of technology transfer according to the level of indigenous capabilities and their potential for upgrading over time.

Seev Hirsch and Yair Aharoni, in chapter 9, examine the development options for technology-intensive industries. They note that concepts such as inward- and outward-orientation have different meanings when applied to technology, as opposed to trade; for example, an import-substituting firm could have — or be inhibited from having — an outward technology posture. Outward-orientation is specially important for technology-intensive industries, and they note that some developing countries could well pursue policies to enhance the competitive advantage of local firms to produce high technology products.

Finally, Albert Bressand, in chapter 10, examines the core policy issue in virtual reality: access to networks. Successful competition in world markets depends not only on producing a good product at a low price, but also on a variety of other factors including marketing channels, subcontracting relationships, real-time corporate link-ups and the like. Developing countries have traditionally sought greater access to trade, but efforts in that direction will not necessarily bring about greater participation in globalization unless market access strategies are rethought in terms of networking strategies which can help penetrate the linkages of deep integration. More than national efforts are needed, and Bressand concludes by proposing an agenda for North-South relinking, which gives a flavour of the kind of international cooperation signalled by globalization.

Note

1. TRIPS - Agreement on Trade-Related Aspects of Intellectual Property Rights.
    TRIMS - Agreement on Trade-Related Investment Measures.
    GATS - General Agreement on Trade in Services.

References

United Nations Centre on Transnational Corporations (UNCTC) (1991). *World Investment Report 1991: The Triad in Foreign Direct Investment*. (United Nations publication, Sales No E.91.II.A.12).

United Nations Conference on Trade and Development, Division on Transnational Corporations and Investment (UNCTAD-DTCI) (1993). *World Investment Report 1993: Transnational Corporations and Integrated International Production*. (United Nations publication, Sales No E.93.II.A.14).

_____ (1995). *World Investment Report 1995: Transnational Corporations and Competitiveness*. (United Nations publication, Sales No E.95.II.A.9).

United Nations, Transnational Corporations and Management Division (UNTCMD) (1992). *World Investment Report 1992: Transnational Corporations as Engines of Growth*. (United Nations publication, Sales No E.92.II.A.19).

Part I
International setting

1

The advent of alliance capitalism

John H. Dunning

Globalization, its meaning and the reasons for it

In many respects, the globalizing economy of the 1990s is the latest stage in the enlargement of the spatial dimension of economic activity which dates back to pre-industrial times. Essentially, its speed and direction have been conditioned by advances in transport and communications technologies, and by the actions of governments in affecting the creation, management and disposition of physical and human assets. Yet, it is only in our lifetime that the role of trade, foreign direct investment (FDI) and cross-border strategic alliances have become such critical determinants of economic progress. And, it has only been in the last 20 years that the world economy has become so structurally interdependent that the use of the word *global*, as distinct from *international*, has become justifiable.

There have already been a plethora of books, articles and newspaper stories written on the nature and extent of globalization. In the last year or so, three volumes, with the intriguing titles *Global Embrace, Global Dream* and *Global Paradox*, have seen the light of day.[1] Of the various definitions of globalization, however, my preference is for the one given by Anthony McGrew in a book jointly edited with P.G. Lewis:[2]

"Globalization refers to the multiplicity of linkages and interconnections between the states and societies which make up the present world system. It describes the process by which events, decisions, and activities in one part of the world come to have significant consequences for individuals and communities in quite distant parts of the globe. Globalization has two distinct phenomena: scope (or stretching) and intensity (or deepening). On the one hand, it defines a set of processes which embrace most of the globe or which operate world-wide; the concept therefore has a spatial connotation. ... On the other hand, it also implies an intensification of the levels of interaction, interconnectedness or *interdependence* between the states and societies which constitute the world community. Accordingly, alongside the stretching goes a deepening of global processes."

In short, then, economic globalization is a process towards the widening of the extent and form of cross-border transactions, and of the deepening of the economic interdependence between the actions of globalizing entities - be they private or public institutions or governments – located in one country, and those of related or independent entities located in other countries.

The *shallowest* form of globalization – if that is not a misnomer for the term – is where an economic entity in one country engages in arm's length trade in a single product with another economic entity in one other country. The *deepest* form of globalization – and it is here we can most easily distinguish globalization from other forms of internationalization – is where an economic entity transacts with a large number of other economic entities throughout the world; where it does so across a network of value-added chains; where these exchanges are highly coordinated to serve the world-wide interests of the globalizing entity; and where they consist of a myriad of different kinds or forms of transactions.

Thus, a typical global *firm* will own or control subsidiaries, and engage in value-added business alliances and networks in each continent and in each major country. It will source its inputs of manpower, capital, raw materials and intermediate products from wherever it is best to do so, and it will sell its goods and services in each of the main markets of the world. Similarly a *country* which is fully open to the forces of globalization is likely to be geographically diversified in its financial trading and investment relationships, and the value added associated with these relationships should constitute a significant part of its gross national product (GNP).

In practice, few firms – or for that matter countries – engage in either the *shallowest* or *deepest* forms of globalization. More important than situating entities on this continuum, however, is the almost universal trend by both firms and countries towards a more integrated cross-border organization of economic activity. As a consequence, the structure of the world economy is very different today than it was even a generation ago. We would emphasize, in particular, three features. First, the significance (and scope) of all kinds of cross-border transactions has greatly increased. For example, as a proportion of world GNP, such transactions have more than doubled since 1970. Second, the value of the foreign production of firms, that is, production financed by foreign direct investment (FDI), and that arising from cross-border strategic alliances - both of which are deeper forms of internationalization than that of arm's-length trade - now considerably exceeds that of trade. And third, there are a variety of signs that the major institutional players are changing their ways of thinking and modes of operation, and are adopting a more systemic approach to their behaviour and activities.

It is, of course, the case that the pace and pattern of globalization has been very uneven among firms, sectors and countries. Moreover, while some markets, for example, financial markets, are largely globalized, others, for example, those for technology and most kinds of labour, still remain national or regional. Since many of the features of globalization just described are principally applicable to members of the Triad nations, some scholars have argued that the term regionalization better describes the current stage of development. This may well be so; certainly, intraregional production and transactions of all kinds in Europe, America and Asia have risen faster than interregional transactions. It is also true that certain parts of the world, notably sub-Saharan Africa, have been relatively unaffected. But, like ripples in a pond, regionalization may spread outwards, initially to the immediate hinterland of the developed countries, but then further as this hinterland generates its own momentum of growth. Neither should one overlook the surge of autonomous development within certain parts of the developing world – particularly in much of East Asia and parts of Latin America. Indeed, with growth rates in the advanced countries slipping, international transactions involving developing countries have risen faster in recent years than those internal to the Triad countries.

The main causes of globalization are well known. We shall focus on just two. The first is the pressure on business enterprises – by consumers and competitors alike – continually to innovate new products and to upgrade the quality of existing goods and services. At the same time, the escalating costs of research and development (R&D), coupled with ever truncated product life cycles, are compelling corporations both to down-size the scope of their value- added activities, and to search for wider markets. Moreover, in order to exploit effectively and speedily their core competencies, firms are increasingly finding that they need to combine these competencies with those of other firms.

The second cause of globalization – which in many ways is better described as a removal of an obstacle – is the renaissance of market-oriented policies pursued by national governments and regional authorities. In the last five years alone, while more than 30 countries have abandoned central planning as the main mode of allocating scarce resources, over 80 countries have liberalized their inward FDI policies. The privatization of state owned enterprises, the liberalization and deregulation of markets – especially for services – and the removal of a bevy of structural distortions, have all worked to stimulate cross-border corporate integration, both within TNCs and between independent firms or groups of firms.

Underlying and reinforcing these two explanations for globalization and fashioning its character, have been changes in the organization of economic activity. At a *micro* level, the changes are best exemplified by the introduction of a more flexible approach to production, together with a growing appreciation by firms of the need to form close and ongoing relationships with other firms to capture fully the benefits of their own competencies. At a *macro* level, they reflect the changing costs and benefits of alternative systems for allocating scarce resources; and the demands being made by globalization on national governments and supranational regimes. At an *international* level, and of particular relevance to developing countries, has been the replacement of non-conditional sources of finance by more fragile and "quicksilver" sources of funding, for example, portfolio investment. Together with the increasing participation of developing countries in regional integration schemes and the restructuring of the gobal financial system, this is making for a convergence of macroeconomic and macro-organizational policies among national governments.

Since we are in the midst of these techno-economic and socio-institutional changes, it is premature to judge either their extent or their consequences for the world economy. But the clues we have been able to discern so far, point to a very different path of economic development than the one we have lived through over the past 20 or 30 years.

With respect to the micro-organization of business activity, there are several forces at work which are leading firms to reappraise the benefits of the Fordist or mass production system, which has been the hallmark of hierarchical capitalism for most of the twentieth century. First, improved living standards – particularly in the Triad nations – have caused consumers to reorient their spending habits. There is a greater expectancy of fault-free products, continuous product improvement, and new and innovative goods and services. At the same time, competitive pressures are demanding that firms reexamine their cost-control procedures; this spans all areas of business, from inventories to manning levels and to advertising budgets. Lean production has become the order of the day.

Second, the new technologies of the 1980s and 1990s, such as computer-aided design and manufacturing techniques, and the miniaturization of components, are not only enabling firms to exercise more rigorous quality control, but are permitting them to make use of multi-purpose machinery and equipment.

Third, contemporary technological and organizational advances are demanding a much closer synthesis, and more interactive learning, between the innovatory and production functions of the firm. Indeed, in the words of two scholars, "the factory itself is becoming a research laboratory - a setting for both product and process innovation."[3] In this new environment, knowledge and intellectual labour are being mobilized on a collective basis; and the skills and ideas of shop floor workers are being actively tapped to raise product quality and productivity. Such innovation-driven production both facilitates the functional integration of tasks and socializes the organization of production.

With respect to the macro level, two observations are in order. The first is that globalization is requiring national governments to reappraise their domestic macro-organizational policies; and, in doing so, to take a more systemic approach to the implementation of those policies. It is also demanding a reconsideration of the role of supra-national regimes, for example, WTO, IMF, OECD and the United Nations, as fashioners and sustainers of the ground rules for international transactions of one kind or another. The second is that, if individual nation states are to encompass fully the challenges of the global marketplace, their governments need not only to appreciate the distinctive characteristics of the new international division of labour, but to take more constructive and coordinated action to help cross-border markets to work efficiently.

Neither of these propositions necessarily implies that there should be less government. Nor do they endorse the view that governments should intervene more in the decision-taking process of the wealth creators of society, viz business enterprises. But what they do mean is that governments should understand and accept that, as an organizational mechanism, markets are <u>not</u> a free good; they cost resources to set up, to operate and to maintain. They also mean that governments need to recognize that the efficiency of many markets – and particularly those supplying products for global customers – is not solely determined by the transactions of the buyers and sellers in those markets, but by a host of other factors, including the actions taken by other governments, over which they may have no immediate influence or control. They mean that national governments, like firms competing in the global marketplace, need to reexamine their organizational structures, and to concentrate on only those activities which they are comparatively best able to perform. And they finally mean that, in times of disturbingly high structural unemployment, and as governments seek to attract the highest possible share of the world's "quicksilver" resources of capital, technology and managerial skills to their territories, the role of supra-national regimes may need to be re-examined if the playing field of the global competitive game is to be kept reasonably fair and level.

Modalities of globalization

A distinctive feature of globalization is the impact on the modes of undertaking cross-border business activity. For most of modern industrial history, that is, since around 1750, arm's length trade in goods, services and financial assets has been the main means of conducting international commerce. By 1914, however, FDI, which is the modality by which a package of resources and capabilities are transferred across national boundaries *within* the same firm, had already begun to assume some importance in linking national economies – particularly between the Metropolitan countries and their colonies, and between the North American and European economies. But, it was not until after the Second World War that FDI really took off as a mechanism for delivering goods and services to foreign markets; and it has only been since the 1980s that outbound TNC activity has become a significant form of international economic activity by other than a handful of the advanced industrial economies. It has also only been during the last decade that the world – and particularly the industrialized world – has witnessed such an explosive growth in mergers and acquisitions (M&As) and cooperative cross-border arrangements (such as strategic alliances) between firms. Like FDI, such mergers and acquisitions and alliances are both a cause and a consequence of globalization.

The tables provide a few statistics which portray the growth of international transactions, and reveal that the modalities of these transactions have moved from those making for *shallow* to those making for *deep* integration. First, with reference to table 1, the most noticeable feature of the contents is that world trade, world investment and the number of non-equity technology transfers and/or cross-border associations, have all increased at a faster rate than the world GNP since 1980.[4/] A separate set of data, set out in table 2, shows that, for the great majority of countries, the significance of both trade and FDI to their domestic economies has risen substantially over the last decade or more.

Next, with reference to the role of FDI and the role of TNCs in the globalizing economy, some critical statistics of the level and geographical composition of outbound and inbound FDI stocks are set out in tables 3 and 4. Table 5 makes some estimates of the role of United States FDI as a means of servicing three leading industrial markets compared with that of exports and licensing. Table 6 presents some "bullet" points about the main features of TNC activity, and table 7 sets out the reasons for the fastest growing form of FDI in the 1980s, viz by way of mergers and acquisitions.

In reviewing these data, the following seven points should be emphasized:

Table 1. World-wide foreign direct investment and selected economic indicators

(Billions of US dollars and percentage)

Indicator	Value at current prices, 1995	Annual growth rate (percent) 1981-1985[a]	1986-1990[a]	1991-1994[a]
FDI outflows	171	3	24	12
FDI outward stock	2730 [b]	5	19.8	8.8
Sales of foreign affiliates of TNCs[c]	6022 [d]	2 [e]	17.4	5.4 [b]
Current gross domestic product at factor cost	24948 [j]	2	10.8	4.3
Gross domestic investment	5681 [j]	0.4	10	4
Exports of goods and non-factor services	4707 [d]	-0.2	14.3	3.8
Royalty and fees receipts	41 [j]	0.1	21.8	10.1
Strategic alliances[h] (Number)	327 [f]	258 [g]	388 [g]	395 [i]

Source: UNCTAD, Division on Transnational Corporations and Investment, based on International Monetary Fund, balance-of-payments tape, and unpublished data provided by the World Bank, International Economics Department.

[a]   Compounded growth rate estimates, based on a semi-logarithmic regression equation.
[b]   1991-1993.
[c]   Estimated by extrapolating the worldwide sales of foreign affiliates of TNCs from Germany, Japan and the United States on the basis of the relative importance of these countreis in world-wide outward FDI stock.
[d]   1993.
[e]   1982-1985.
[f]   Average per annum 1981/1992.
[g]   Average per annum.
[h]   In high technology sectors.
[i]   1992.
[j]   1994.

Table 2. Extent to which a country is globally involved
(Percentages)

FDI TO GDP RATIO (STOCK) Inward + Outward Investment divided by GDPx2		
	1980	1993
1 Netherlands	18.3	35.8
2 Belgium/Luxembourg	5.2	27.4
3 Switzerland	18.1	27.1
4 Malaysia	13.5	24.4
5 United Kingdom	13.6	24.0
6 Australia	4.9	20.1
7 Canada	14.4	17.9
8 Sweden	3.6	15.4
9 Spain	2.8	13.7
10 France	3.2	11.4
Norway	1.2	11.4
11 Chile	1.7	10.6
12 Germany	5.5	9.1
13 South Africa	13.4	8.3
14 Finland	1.2	8.2
15 United States	5.8	7.9
16 Venezuela	1.3	7.4
17 Hungary	n.a.	7.0
18 Italy	2.0	6.4
19 Thailand	1.5	5.9
20 Austria	2.6	4.8

TRADE TO GDP RATIO Exports + Imports divided by GDPx2		
	1980	1992
1 Hong Kong	104.1	126.6
2 Singapore	206.9	123.4
3 Malaysia	44.9	62.7
4 Belgium/Luxembourg	58.0	54.1
5 Ireland	55.2	50.4
6 Netherlands	42.8	44.9
7 Taiwan, Province of China	n.a.	35.3
8 Thailand	23.5	29.7
9 Portugal	32.0	28.7
10 Hungary	n.a.	28.6
11 Switzerland	32.5	27.3
12 Austria	27.3	26.6
13 Denmark	27.0	26.0
14 Norway	30.9	24.9
15 Indonesia	23.4	24.2
16 Chile	n.a.	24.0
17 Korea, Republic of	34.2	23.9
18 Canada	24.2	23.7
19 Germany	23.2	23.4
20 New Zealand	23.3	22.9
21 Sweden	26.2	21.4
22 Venezuela	25.5	21.0
Greece	22.0	21.0
23 Finland	29.8	20.9
24 United Kingdom	22.5	19.8
25 France	18.9	17.8
26 South Africa	30.1	17.6
27 Pakistan	18.5	17.1
28 Turkey	9.8	16.6
29 Italy	22.5	15.0
30 Australia	14.3	14.6
31 Spain	13.8	14.3
32 Mexico	10.4	11.5
33 United States	9.1	8.3
34 Japan	12.7	7.8

Source: World Competitiveness Report (World Economic Forum and IMEDE) 1993, *World Development Report* (World Bank) 1994, *World Investment Report* (UNCTAD) 1995, *United Nations Statistical Yearbook 1983/1984* (United Nations) 1986.

Table 3. Stocks of outward foreign direct investment, by major home country and regions
(Billions of US dollars)

Countries/ regions	1967 Value	% of total	% of GDP	1973 Value	% of total	% of GDP	1980 Value	% of total	% of GDP	1993 Value	% of total	% of GDP
DEVELOPED	109.3	97.3	4.8	205.0	97.1	5.1	503.6	97.2	6.2	2012	96.2	10.8
United States	56.6	50.4	7.1	101.3	48.0	7.7	220.2	40.0	8.2	559.7	26.8	8.8
United Kingdom	15.8	14.1	14.5	27.5	13.0	9.1	79.2	14.8	15.2	253.4	12.1	27.0
Japan	1.5	1.3	0.9	10.3	4.9	2.5	19.6	6.6	3.4	259.8	12.4	6.2
Germany (FDR)	3.0	2.7	1.6	11.9	5.6	3.4	43.1	7.8	5.3	185.0	8.8	10.8
Switzerland	2.5	2.2	10.0	7.1	3.4	16.2	22.4	7.0	37.9	89.1	4.3	38.4
Netherlands	11.0	9.8	33.1	15.8	7.5	25.8	42.4	7.6	24.7	134.0	6.4	43.4
Canada	3.7	3.3	5.3	7.8	3.7	6.1	21.6	3.9	8.2	86.3	4.1	16.1
France	6.0	5.3	7.0	8.8	4.2	3.8	20.8	3.8	3.2	160.5	7.7	12.8
Italy	2.1	1.9	2.8	3.2	1.5	2.4	7.0	1.3	1.8	73.8	3.5	7.5
Sweden	1.7	1.5	5.7	3.0	1.4	6.1	7.2	1.3	5.8	44.6	2.1	24.0
Other	5.4	4.8	0.8	20.0	9.5	1.7	15.4	3.2	1.9	162.5	7.8	12.0
DEVELOPING	3.0	2.7	0.6	6.1	2.9	0.6	13.3	2.8	0.7	78.2	3.7	1.5
TOTAL	112.3	100.0	4.0	211.1	100.0	4.2	516.9	100.0	4.9	2090.4	100.0	8.7

Source: *World Development Report* (World Bank) various editions, *World Investment Report* (UNCTAD) various editions and Dunning (1993b).

Table 4. Stocks of inward foreign direct investment, by major host countries and regions
(Billions of US dollars)

Countries/ regions	1967 Value	% of total	% of GDP	1973 Value	% of total	% of GDP	1980 Value	% of total	% of GDP	1993 Value	% of total	% of GDP
DEVELOPED	73.2	69.4	3.2	153.7	74.0	3.8	394.1	78.0	4.7	1561	75.3	8.4
Western Europe	31.4	29.8	4.2	79.9	38.4	5.6	211.6	42.0	4.8	880.2	42.4	12.5
United Kingdom	7.9	7.5	7.2	24.1	11.6	13.9	63.0	12.5	12.0	197.1	9.5	21.0
Germany	3.6	3.4	1.9	13.1	6.3	3.8	47.9	9.5	5.8	128.0	6.2	7.5
Switzerland	2.1	2.0	8.4	4.3	2.1	9.8	14.3	2.8	14.1	36.5	1.8	15.7
United States	9.9	9.3	1.2	20.6	9.9	1.6	83.0	16.4	3.2	445.3	21.5	7.0
Other	31.9	30.2	4.2	53.2	25.6	4.2	99.5	19.7	6.5	251.8	12.1	4.7
Japan	0.6	0.6	0.3	1.6	0.8	0.4	3.3	0.7	0.3	16.9	0.8	0.4
DEVELOPING	32.3	30.6	6.4	54.4	26.1	5.4	111.2	22.0	5.4	299.8	24.0	9.9
Africa	5.6	5.3	9.0	10.2	4.9	8.7	13.1	2.6	4.1	50.1	2.4	14.1
Asia	8.3	7.8	3.9	15.3	7.4	3.6	35.8	7.1	5.0	278.6	13.4	8.7
Latin America	18.5	17.5	15.8	28.9	13.9	12.3	62.3	12.3	8.4	167.6	8.1	11.4
TOTAL	105.5	100.0	3.8	208.1	100.0	4.1	505.3	100.0	4.7	2074	100.0	8.7

Source: Same as for table 3.

Table 5. Alternative modalities of servicing Japanese, UK and German markets by US firms

JAPAN

	Affiliate sales[a]	Exports[b]	Licensed sales[c]	Total
All industries (US$ bil.)	49.7	42.8	20.9	113.4
(Per capita) (US$)	403.7	347.7	169.8	921.2
(% of total)	43.8	37.7	18.4	100.0

UK

	Affiliate sales[a]	Exports[b]	Licensed sales[c]	Total
All industries (US$ bil.)	125.3	20.8	3.2	149.3
(Per capita) (US$)	2190.5	363.6	55.9	2610.0
(% of total)	83.9	13.9	2.1	100.0

GERMANY

	Affiliate sales[a]	Exports[b]	Licensed sales[c]	Total
All industries (US$ bil.)	71.7	16.8	2.7	91.2
(Per capita) (US$)	1156.5	271.0	43.5	1471.0
(% of total)	78.6	18.4	3.0	100.0

Source: US Department of Commerce (1992a, 1992b, 1993a, and 1993b), Weinberg (1993).

[a] Affiliate sales represent sales of US manufacturing affiliates (excluding exports) in the three countries.

[b] Exports represent all exports to the three countries by all US firms (n.b. part if these may be included in affiliate sales).

[c] Licensed sales represent royalties and fees paid by unaffiliated Japanese, UK or German firms to US firms multiplied by 20 (it being assumed that royalties and fees were calculated as 5% of gross sales).

Table 6. Transnational corporations and the global economy some facts 1995

- There are 39,000 TNCs (including 4,148 from developing countries) with 270,000 affiliates (of which 119,765 are in developing countries).

- Outward FDI stock at the end of 1995 was $2.7 trillion. Of this amount, 65 per cent was accounted for by France, Germany, Japan, the United Kingdom and the United States. Developing countries accounted for about 7.8 per cent of the world-wide FDI stock.

- The sales of foreign affiliates of TNCs in 1993 was estimated to be $6 trillion (compared with $4.7 trillion of world exports).

- China was the leading developing country recipient of FDI flows in 1995. South, East and South East Asia received 65 per cent of the total flows to developing countries, and Latin America and the Caribbean 27 per cent of the total flows.

- The largest 100 TNCs (excluding those in banking and finance) are estimated to account for about one-third of global FDI.

- World-wide cross-border mergers & acquisitions of all kinds doubled in value between 1988 and 1995, and accounted for 72 per cent of FDI outflows (42 per cent in the case of majority-held M&A transactions).

- 75-80 per cent of all FDI stock in 1992 was in sectors requiring above average human skill, capital or technology intensity.

- 50-55 per cent of all FDI in 1992 was in the tertiary (service) sector.

- FDI and strategic alliances are growing faster than other forms of international transactions.

- Some 73 per cent of the stock of inward investment at the end of 1995 was in developed countries, though developing countries accounted for 32 per cent of all new FDI. Central and Eastern Europe accounted for almost 4 per cent of world-wide inflows of FDI in 1995.

- Over the period 1991-1994, FDI from privatization schemes in Central and Eastern Europe amounted to over $8.5 billion, or 49 per cent of the region's total FDI inflows. In the case of developing countries, privatizations amounted to $17.6 billion, or 6 per cent of their total FDI inflows in 1989-1994.

Source: UNCTAD 1994 and UNCTAD 1996.

Table 7. The international business environment and mergers and acquisitions in the 1980s

Forces driving mergers and acquisitions	Application to cross-border mergers and acquisitions
Growing competition, globalization and favourable government policies	To achieve internationalization and geographical market diversification and to increase market share rapidly, firms prefer to engage in mergers and acquisitions as opposed to greenfield investment as a faster way to do so. Merger-friendly government policies encouraged the wave of mergers and acquisitions of the 1980s.
Higher efficiency in the face of growing competition and globalization	To achieve scale economies and synergies in value-adding activities, firms build integrated international production networks aimed at improving efficiency of the firm as a whole. Mergers and acquisitions allow the speedy establishment of such networks.
Access to technology and reduced costs of research and development	To gain access to new technology, share the risks and costs associated with technology development and reduce the time needed for product innovation, TNCs may acquire firms engaged in research and development or merge with such firms to access their technological capabilities and resources.
Response to the Single Market programme of the European Community	The Single Market programme created competitive pressures, as well as opportunities for European Community and third-country firms for mergers and acquisitions aimed at rationalizing production and distribution of goods and services within the European Community and increasing market share.
Availability of low-cost financing options available after the financial liberalization of the 1980s in many developed countries	To take advantage of the substantial growth in the availability of credit, innovations in corporate finance and the valuation of many companies below break-up values.
New investment opportunities in developed countries during the boom period in the second half of the 1980s	To take advantage of favourable investment opportunities created by economic growth to expand into new markets or activities. Period of economic growth are also associated with a greater availability of investible funds from corporate profits or loans to finance mergers and acquisitions.

Source: UNCTAD (1994).

(i)   Inbound and outbound FDI stocks as a percentage of the GDP of virtually all countries has substantially increased over the last 25 years. Our own estimate for 1994 is that, for the world as a whole, this percentage was 9.5 per cent — and it is still rising. These data are, perhaps, the best indicators on the growth of deep cross-border economic integration.

(ii)   Outbound FDI is still predominantly accounted for by the leading industrial countries, although such investment by some developing countries, noticeably the Republic of Korea and Taiwan Province of China, is increasing quite rapidly.

(iii)   The slow-down in FDI growth between 1990 and 1992 - and this has been partially reversed in 1993 and 1994 - was partly cyclical, and reflected the recession in the United States and Europe. It was also partly a reflection of a sharp cut-back in Japanese FDI, which, *inter alia*, was a reaction to the huge outflow of such FDI in the second part of the 1980s, and to a less dynamic domestic economy.

(iv)   For the reasons set out in table 7, the mergers and acquisitions was a major form of FDI in the 1980s, but less so in the early 1990s; 1994 has, however, seen some resurgence in that activity.

(v)   Foreign direct investment is strongly concentrated in technology intensive, information intensive and growth-oriented manufacturing and service sectors. Much of the FDI by developing countries in other developing countries, however, is to seek out low-cost labour and natural resources.

(vi)   There has been a marked increase in FDI activity in developing countries since 1990. Partly this reflects the robustness and renaissance of market-oriented policies of many developing countries, for example China and India, and partly the faster rate of growth of the leading inward investors, cf that of the rest of the world. Of the FDI flows directed to developing countries, in the first half of the 1990s, China accounted for 28.2 per cent, the rest of South, East and South-East Asia for 34.5 per cent[5/] and Latin America and the Caribbean for 28.1 per cent.

(vii)   The significance of both outbound and inbound FDI in the globalizing economy varies considerably between countries. Table 5, for example, shows that, in 1989, the affiliates of United States firms in Japan accounted for only 43.8 per cent of the foreign-related sales in

Table 8. Some reasons for firms to conclude cross-border strategic business alliances

(Alliances may be aggressive or defensive, they may be market facilitating or collusory, they may be between firms along a value chain or between value chains.)

- To capture economies of synergy (e.g. by pooling of resources and capabilities, and by rationalization of production).

- To lower capital investment, to disperse or reduce fixed costs, to better exploit scale and/or scope economies, to lower unit costs by using comparative production advantages of each partner.

- As a consequence of the convergence of technologies and interdependencies among innovation processes, to spread R&D costs, to gain speedy access to new technologies.

- As a response by firms to growing competition, a shorter product cycle and a faster rate of technological obsolescence.

- To obtain reciprocal benefits from the combined use of complementary asses, to exchange patents and territories.

- To overcome government mandated trade or investment barriers.

- As a means of promoting joint R&D and design efforts with suppliers and/or customers.

- To assist the entry process of small firms into high risk, entrepreneurial ventures, especially in emerging technology sectors.

- To gain new knowledge about, or achieve quicker access to, markets and/ or to spread marketing and distribution costs, to widen market sources.

- To pre-empt or neutralize the strategy of competitors, or to advance monopoly power, as a defensive strategy to reduce competition.

- To better secure contracts from foreign governments who favour local firms, to better deal with local suppliers and/or labour unions.

- As an initial entry strategy in unfamiliar markets.

- To reduce cross-border political risks.

Source: J. H. Dunning, *Multinational Enterprises and the Global Economy*, chap. 9, p. 250.

Japan, compared with 83.9 per cent in the United Kingdom and 78.6 per cent in Germany.

Two other characteristics of the FDI of the last decade which are not demonstrated in the statistics just presented also need emphasizing. These are:

(viii) The orientation of the motivation for TNC activity has changed from that of seeking *markets* and *natural resources* to exploit better the existing competitive advantages of the investing companies, to that of acquiring *created assets* perceived necessary to *sustain and advance existing competitive advantages*.

(ix) Firms – particularly TNCs – are becoming more pluralistic in their modes of capturing the benefits of globalization, and, the way firms coordinate (that is, integrate) their trans-border activities is an amalgam of hierarchical and cooperative capitalism.

These two latter features of contemporary business activity, as well as those already identified – and especially the growth of strategic alliances – suggest that the role of FDI in the international market economy is in the process of important change. For most of the period of modern capitalism – whether FDI has been undertaken to obtain natural resources and labour, to secure or protect markets, or to promote a more cost effective distribution of its foreign activities – the main *raison d'être* of FDI has been to exploit the core competencies of the investing corporations, and to do so by internalizing cross-border intermediate product markets. Spurred by local market opportunities, much of United States direct investment in Europe in the 1960s and 1970s, and most of Japanese investment in Asia, Europe and the United States in the early 1980s, was of this kind. For the most part, too, this FDI was of a "stand alone" or discrete character in the sense that its success was judged mainly by the ability of the investing companies to exploit their home-based competitive advantages and to coordinate related intra-firm (hierarchical) value activities across national boundaries.

Since around the mid-1980s, however, the same features which have fostered globalization – and of these, technological advances and the renaissance of the market system are, perhaps, the two most important – have also impacted on both the motives of FDI and on its role in the strategy of firms. Increasingly – and as reflected especially by the dramatic increases in intra-triad M&As – firms have expanded their territorial horizons, not so much to exploit existing competitive advantages, but to

27

protect or enhance these advantages and their global market positions by acquiring, or gaining access to, new resources and capabilities. In the late 1980s, there was hardly a day when the financial press did not report a new takeover of a United States firm by a European firm – or vice versa – which was usually justified by the acquiring firm in terms of "the need to strengthen our technological or product base *vis-à-vis* our global competitors"; or, "to rationalize our cross-border production capabilities or to capture new scale or synergistic economies"; or, "to better access unfamiliar markets and distribution networks".

The critical feature of *strategic asset seeking* FDI[6/] is that the acquiring firm in a takeover, or both partners in the case of a merger, accept(s) that its (their) internal, or stand-alone, resources and capabilities are insufficient to sustain its (or their) international competitiveness, and that it (or they) need(s) to draw upon resources and capabilities of *other* firms to achieve this goal. This is one of the characteristics of the emerging "collective", "relational" or "alliance" capitalism of the 1990s. And, although by internalizing the markets for these resources and capabilities it would appear that global hierarchies are being strengthened, this is not always the case. This is because asset acquiring investment is frequently accompanied by asset shedding as firms have sought to specialize in those activities which (they perceive) will best protect or advance their core competencies. Strategic asset acquiring investment is, then, best regarded as an integral part of a restructuring of the resources and capabilities of firms, and as a response to globalization.

At the same time, it is becoming increasingly clear that FDI, while a necessary condition, is not always a sufficient condition for a successful global strategy. Indeed, FDI is not always the most efficient means of accessing foreign assets. Often, a firm does not want to acquire all the assets of a foreign firm, but only those which directly advance its competitive position. In such cases, the conclusion of inter-firm alliances to achieve a specific objective may be preferable to FDI. These alliances may serve as alternatives to vertical integration; and sometimes to horizontal or lateral diversification.

Moreover, the aforementioned shedding of value adding activities does not mean that firms now rely more on arm's length markets for the intermediate products they buy or sell. More often than not, the market imperfections which promoted the internalization in the first place still remain; indeed, the strategic need to maintain an influence over the quality and supply of inputs, or the processing of downstream activities, and the pace and direction of innovation in times of competitive pressures, is even greater (Quinn and Hilmer, 1994). So, in addition to FDI, firms have been engaging in a myriad of bilateral or multilateral cooperative arrangements, in order to capture the economic benefits which a "stand alone" strategy cannot achieve.

In practice, it is extremely difficult to assess the role of strategic alliances as part of the internationalization process of firms or, indeed, to value their outcome either from the perspective of the participants or of the countries involved. Yet, it is important that policy makers seeking to attract FDI – for example, to upgrade their competitiveness or to assist their own firms in capturing global markets – should recognize that, in some cases, the objectives may just as well be reached by the formation of cross-border alliances. Indeed, research suggests that those countries whose governments have striven to provide the right environment for alliance formation – for example, Japan, the Republic of Korea and Taiwan Province of China – are often also those which do best in the global economy.

While there are many reasons why firms conclude alliances with other firms, the great majority of those concluded over the past decade have been for four main reasons. These are:

(i)   To acquire new product or process technologies and organizational competencies – and especially those perceived necessary to advance the core competence of the acquiring firm;

(ii)   To spread the risks of high capital outlays, or reduce the time of product development;

(iii)   To capture the economies of synergy or scale; and

(iv)   To gain access to new markets or distribution channels.

It should be observed that each of these motives runs parallel to strategic asset acquiring FDI (see table 8).

As might be supposed, cross-border alliances – like FDI – are concentrated in particular industrial sectors; and, in the main, these are similar to those in which FDI is concentrated (that is the dynamic technology and information intensive product and service sectors).

Of course, cross-border strategic alliances are not the only form of cooperative arrangements. These range from very specific technical service and subcontracting agreements, to less formal – but no less binding – modes of inter-firm cooperation found in business or industrial

Figure 1. Some examples of situations in which Governments might successfully contain their own organizational costs

Government intervention	Consequences for the reduction of government related transaction costs
• The containment of interventionist policies to activities severely hampered by market failures.	• Reduces effectiveness of rent seeking special interest groups. • Increases work effort of public agents.
• A holistic approach to the coordination of complementary policies and institutional mechanisms.	• Makes policy trade-offs easier to identify and solve. • Clarifies policy makers' task and reduces problem of bounded rationality.
• An ethos of consensus and cooperation between private and public policy makers, e.g. with respect to mutually beneficial goals and the means by which goals can best be achieved.	• Reduces likelihood of sub-optimization. • Captures economies of scope in governance and increases intra-organizational information flows and learning.
• The recruitment of the most talented and well motivated individuals for public sector employment, e.g. by offering competitive working conditions and encouraging initiative and entrepreneurship.	• Reduces transaction costs of interaction between representatives of the private and public sector. • Increases knowledge of public decision takers.
• The insulation of the policy-making process from the strongest (and most undesirable) pressure groups.	• Reduces chance of uninformed or biased media coverage in forcing governments into ill advised or hasty decision.
• The presence of a national ethos or mentality of the need to be competitive and create wealth. Partly, this embraces a "commutarian" culture and partly one which encourages personal initiative, entrepreneurship scientific specialisation and competition.	• Likely to inhibit the pursuance of sub-optimal goals and to reduce bounded rationality and opportunism and use of inefficient production technologies. • Reduces the effectiveness of rent seeking by special interest groups, and relieves the policy-making process from the pressure of day-to-day politics.
• The absence of strong sectoral interest groups, e.g. farmers and left-wing labour groups, which might press for interventionist measures by governments other than those which are market facilitating.	• Favours coordination of strategies and policies of public and private organizations and reduces the sub-optimization problem in the public sector. • Reduces possibility of ideological conflicts and undue emphasis being placed on the redistribution of incomes as a (short-term) social good.

Sources: Wade (1988), Stiglitz (1989), Grestchmann (1911), Hämäläinen (1994).

districts, and also to *keiretsu*-type relationships. But, although the type of arrangements vary, all represent a kind of quasi-internalization of cross-border assets and should be considered as integral parts of the total portfolio of the firm's assets.

The evidence, then, suggests that asset acquiring FDI and cooperative arrangements are critical features of the contemporary global economy and of alliance capitalism; and that, while the first is primarily a response by Western nations to the demands of the global marketplace, the second is primarily a response by Eastern nations. But, there is plenty of casual evidence to suggest that both forms of corporate restructuring are now spreading throughout the industrialized world - and throughout parts of the industrializing world as well.[7]

The consequences of globalization

What are some of the likely consequences of globalization for economic development. One can argue that, just as globalization is qualitatively different from previous stages of internationalization, so its effects on development are distinctive.

So far in the present chapter, an optimistic view of globalization has been presented, and it is true that the structural transformation of the world now occurring does hold out great promise for the future. It is also the case that the political changes and technological advances of the last decade have provided a stronger basis for economic growth than at any other time since the mid-1940s. The world has the necessary resources, knowledge and experience. It has the technical means by which these assets can be transmitted between countries. It has the economic systems, policies, institutions and structures capable of translating human and physical resources into the goods and services which people want. Moreover, at first sight, the "organcentric" production system, with its focus on smaller production runs, multi-purpose machinery, economies of scope, and relational networking, its renewed reliance on the "putting out" of some value activities, and its greater respect for the individual in the work place appears to be particularly well suited to the needs and capabilities of developing countries, and to the linking of these with those of the flagship nations in the global economy.

Already, there are signs of the fruits of alliance capitalism in East Asia, where much of the expansion of cross-border activity has taken the form of networking by small and medium-sized firms. There is also a much greater willingness of the newly emerging TNCs from China, the Republic of Korea, Mexico and Thailand to collaborate with local firms, than was earlier demonstrated by their United States and European counterparts. One of the great promises for development which ranks at least as highly as regional integration and intra-Southern hemisphere trade and investment is the emergence of a new brand of capitalism, which blends the richness of the Confucian ethos of cooperation with that of the staunch individualistic culture of the West.

Unfortunately, however, there are down-sides to globalization. There is, in John Naisbitt's words, "a global paradox" (Naisbitt, 1994). The most immediate and visible consequences of the down-side, which all countries of the world are currently experiencing, is the increase in structural unemployment brought about by competitive pressures, the implementation of new technologies and the introduction of more market oriented systems of governance. Across the globe, for developed and developing countries alike, change is bringing economic hardship. It is transforming the life styles of people, and their expectancies of the future. Nowhere is this more clearly observed than in China and in Central and Eastern Europe, and in the dynamic, but internationally mobile, sectors of economic activity.

It has long been recognized that the invisible hand of the market is only acceptable if there is some way that the losers from market forces are compensated by the winners; and this primarily means helping the losers to adjust to political and technological change. And, as we see it, the possible Achilles heel of globalization and alliance capitalism is that they could so easily become dysfunctional if they cannot accommodate the desires of ordinary men and women looking for and willing to work; and, if they fail to equip individuals with the skills and talents necessary for the kind of jobs which are now being created.

This, indeed, is one of the most daunting challenges of the 1990s. For there can surely be little doubt that long-term unemployment is one of the most socially divisive and destabilizing forces of modern times. While an innovation led – as opposed to a Fordist – production system offers more purposeful, responsible and rewarding job opportunities for those in work, it does not help reduce unemployment, at least not in the short run. This is because the new system requires a different mix of labour skills than the one it is replacing; and to match those needs, not only do labour markets need to be more flexible, but quite huge adjustment assistance and retraining programmes are needed.

More generally, if global economic interdependence offers the prospects of higher productivity and living standards, it also more closely links national economies to exogenous financial and other disturbances. The world economy of the 1990s is intrinsically more fragile and vulnerable than that of 30, 40 or 50 years ago. No longer is it just the case that, if the United States sneezes, the world catches a cold. Economic shocks originating in any one of the five or six leading economies are now electronically and instantaneously transmitted across the globe, with possibly devastating affects on nations which may have had nothing to do with the causes of the shocks. Even being part of a micro-network of value-adding activities can bring external costs, as well as external benefits, to the participating firms. This is why a much more systemic approach to the management of macro-economic affairs, and a more educated understanding of the spatial implications of economic turbulences, needs to be high on the political agenda of national and regional governments in the next ten years.

Two further points can be made. The first is that, while the forces of globalization are leading to a convergence of the spending habits of the world's consumers, they are also exposing substantial differences in the way people think and behave. Indeed, not all countries welcome the effects of globalization, as they fear it may erode their traditional life styles. As has been observed, this leads to a global dilemma. On the one hand, the universality of such goods as the motor car, the television set, hamburgers and jeans, and such services as tourism, sport and pop-music, is leading to cultural convergence. On the other hand, most people want to remain loyal to their distinctive customs and institutions. The task of peacefully resolving this dilemma is, indeed, likely to tax the minds of both scholars and politicians well into the next century. How, for example, does one balance the advantages of sovereignty with those of interdependence, of homogeneity with diversity, of centralization with decentralization, of communitarism with individualism and so on? There is, of course, nothing new in these perplexities, but globalization has put them in a new and starker perspective, and has given their resolution a new urgency.

There seems little doubt that the end of the cold war, and the growing pressures towards economic "at-one-ness", are refocusing the attention of people towards cultural, ideological and religious issues, over which most of the wars in history have been fought. We also sense that the battle lines are being drawn not primarily between the haves and have-nots, but between groups of nations with different ways of looking at the world. The picture painted by Samuel Huntington (1993) on the future relationships between the major civilizations of the world is not an optimistic one. Our own feeling is that there is more in common among the ideologies and religions of these civilizations - at least what they preach about attitudes and conduct - than there are differences; and that a focus on these similarities, rather than on the differences, offers the best hope for global peace.

Reference has already been made to the dominant organizational system now evolving as that of alliance capitalism. This is because the unit of economic activity – the individual firm – in order to promote fully its own objectives, needs increasingly to be part of – that is, allied to – a network or web of related activities. It is believed that this concept can be extended to a global level. From the time of the Roman Empire and beyond, history is littered with the debris of once all-powerful nations. For much of the nineteenth century, the United Kingdom really did rule the economic waves. The pound sterling was the business currency of the world and the principles of the craft system were practised by all industrial countries. The mantel of economic leadership passed to the United States around 1870; and the mass, or scale, production system became the symbol of its hegemony. But, today there is no single dominant nation. Instead, as Fred Bergsten (1990) has observed, it is likely that the leadership of the world over the next century will have to be collectively shared by the European Community, Japan and the United States. Such an alliance of flagship nations, particularly if widened to embrace China – which, according to some sources, already has the second largest GNP in the world – will require all the bonding characteristics of inter-firm collaborative schemes.

The developing economies

What about the developing countries? How and where do they fit in to the future? What, indeed, does globalization mean for the trajectory of economic development? So far, little specific attention has been paid to the problems and needs of the developing world. This is partly because we believe the opportunities and challenges of globalization cut across the traditional North/South divide, and partly because, over the next 25 years, it is likely that many millions of the descendants of yesterday's impoverished generation will come to enjoy at least the basic creature comforts which the inhabitants of richer countries, so easily take for granted.

That is in the future; and, notwithstanding the possibility that the East Asian miracle might spread westwards to India and northwards to China, and that more developing countries will be drawn into North-South regional integration schemes, there would appear to be little prospect that most of the poorer countries will derive much immediate benefit from the new global economic order. Indeed, the share of new FDI that went to the least developed nations in the early 1990s was only one-half that of the 1980s (UNCTAD, 1994).

At the same time, the prospects for economic growth in the 1990s are considerably better than those actually achieved in the "lost" decade of the 1980s. The World Bank has projected that, on average, the GDP growth rate of developing countries will be 4.7 per cent per annum between 1992 and 2002, and that even in the poorest countries - excluding India and China - the rate of growth will be 3.5 per cent (World Bank, 1993a).

The World Bank offers four main reasons for their cautious optimism. The first is that the macro-economic and organizational reforms introduced in the 1980s are now starting to show results. The second is that internal supply-side sources of growth, that is, domestic savings rates, incentives to invest and the emergence of a production system less dependent on the economies of scale, are expected to improve. The third is that commodity prices are predicted to stabilize in real terms - a sharp break from their 20-year declining trend. And, the fourth cause for optimism is the increased flow of capital now being directed to the Third World. Between 1989 and 1994, for example, developing countries attracted 26.7 per cent of the FDI flows compared with 20 per cent for most of the previous decade (UNCTAD, 1995).[8/] Private portfolio flows rose even more dramatically - from $6 billion a year between 1982 and 1988 to $34 billion in 1992 (World Bank, 1993a). In recent years, too, such investments have been supplemented by new financial instruments, that is debt-equity swaps and depository receipts; and also by the setting up of new financial institutions (for example, the European Bank for Reconstruction and Development).

Overall, then, we sense that the portends for real growth in the developing world – taken as a whole – are probably better than they have been for many years. There is a huge untapped reservoir of young and energetic manpower and an equally huge unmet set of consumer needs, waiting to be activated. The development of countries like Japan and Singapore, which lack the natural resources which were the foundation of nineteenth century development, ought to provide good heart to even the poorest of countries. Increasingly, as has been seen, the key to economic prosperity in the twenty-first century lies in the ability of firms and countries to acquire and create new knowledge – and in the case of smaller developing nations, new markets.

To what extent is economic development currently being led by exogenous – mainly Triad related – globalizing forces, and to what extent is it being endogenously induced? The answer to these questions will obviously vary from country to country, depending, for example, on the size and structure of the economy, its stage of development, and the government policies it pursues. Even the larger and most prosperous developing countries, however, now accept that, "no nation in this global age can afford to be an island". The only question at issue is "how far", "with whom", "in what way" and "by what means" should developing countries engage in alliance capitalism?

It was earlier suggested that the hierarchical production system was centrifugal as it decentralized the production of labour-intensive activities to low wage countries. This resulted in a scale related division of labour, with consequences broadly similar to those arising from the resource-based division of labour in the nineteenth century. While this system aided development, it was an uneven development. It encouraged interdependence, but it was asymmetrical. All too frequently, the foreign sector was not fully integrated into the host economy; as a result, the syndrome of the dual economy began to emerge.

In both kinds of international specialization, it was the smaller economies which usually benefited the most, although both in Latin America and East Asia, regional integration schemes did lead to some intra-regional alliance capitalism. Most larger developing countries also had trading and investment links with the developed world, but, as the main objective of several of these economies – particularly in the 1970s

– was to use these links as a means of advancing their own economic autonomy, there were few genuine cross-border alliances and only a limited transfer of organizational systems.

The advent of alliance capitalism, at a time when most developing nations are modifying their internal economic strategies to benefit better from economic interdependence, is encouraging such countries to play a more pro-active role in the globalizing economy. At the same time, the extent which alliance capitalism is primarily a phenomena of the Triad nations is yet to be seen. Certainly, outside the apparel and footwear industries, the great majority of joint ventures and networks so far concluded have been between firms in the dynamic industrial or service sectors, and have involved at least one developed nation (Hagedoorn, 1993). Moreover, the experience of smaller European nations, both within and outside the European Union, suggests that their counterparts in the developing world may find it extremely difficult to create the sophisticated infrastructure which networks require.

History also suggests that the probable winners are likely to be those developing countries which can offer the best educational and communication infrastructures to foreign firms, and which are geographically close to the industrial heartland of the Triad. By the late 1990s, however, it may be expected that at least the larger and more prosperous developing countries will have built up their own internal networks; and that their firms will have established alliances with firms from developing countries in the same region. In so doing, they will take the first step towards developing-world-led globalization. Indeed, it is already occurring in the Chinese economic space of East Asia; and in the Malaysian-Thailand axis. And, as more Latin American countries adopt outward looking development strategies, it is likely to happen there too (World Bank, 1993b). By contrast, because of ethnic, religious and cultural differences, the prospects for intraregional integration in Central Asia, the Middle East and much of sub-Saharan Africa seem less promising, although such development is taking place.

Although, as has been suggested, there are aspects of flexible production systems and interactive learning which favour the resources and capabilities of developing countries, and which may lead to a revitalization of the "putting out" system of production. There are others, notably the increasing role played by costly created assets in the competitive process, and the need for a physically close and ongoing relationship between firms in dynamic sectors along the value chain,[9/] which are centripetal in their effects. Because of this, it follows that, at least for the foreseeable future, and with the possible exception of China and India, developing countries are unlikely to be the flagships of global alliance capitalism. There are reasons to suppose, however, that some at least could become hubs of regional alliance capitalism. Singapore is already bidding to be the leading financial and high technology centre and cruise gateway, and Taipei the leading regional operations centre, of South-East Asia. At the same time, United States computer firms are increasingly favouring the Caribbean as a regional centre for their software facilities.

For the poorer developing countries, most of which are far removed from the critical nodes of growth, the impact of globalization and alliance capitalism is likely to be marginal – except in so far as they may benefit from a "trickle down" affect of some kinds of subcontracting.[10/] This, however, should not be taken to mean that these countries will not benefit from other economic events in the 1990s; but rather that any such gains will be the outcome of internal economic and institutional reforms, and of the higher spending power of the faster growing nations; and, in the case of resource rich countries, the stabilization of commodity prices, the direction of resource related innovation and the emergence of new sources of supply. But, in their attempts to upgrade their wealth-creating abilities, the least developed nations will most surely have to rely mainly on aid and loans from foreign governments and international institutions.[11/] This is simply because their most pressing need is to improve their educational, legal and commercial infrastructures which, in the past at least, private investors have been unwilling to finance.

At the same time, with the introduction of more market-oriented macro-organizational policies, we would expect the threshold at which FDI becomes viable to fall. We would also like to think that such policies - and the kind of technological advances earlier described - will make it easier for both governments and firms from the poorer nations to explore the possibility of partnerships and cross-border alliances; and will promote more regional economic cooperation.

The implications of globalization for national governments

Let us now consider those consequences of the emerging global economy and alliance capitalism for national governments. The first and the most significant of these arises from the increasing ease with which competitive enhancing assets can move across national boundaries. This means that any action governments might take which affect the competitiveness of these assets cannot be divorced from the actions taken by other governments. The theory of competing governments suggests that, in the last resort, a country's citizens can respond to high taxation – or any other unacceptable government policies – by "voting with their feet" (Brennan and Buchanan, 1985), that is, by emigrating to another country. This idea can readily be extended to explain the locational choices of firms, as they may be affected by the tax and macro-organizational policies of national polities. No longer can governments assume that the firms, resources and capabilities presently located in their areas of jurisdiction are inextricably bound to those territories; nor that they are impotent to attract resources and capabilities now sited in other countries. Finally, there are suggestions that the actions of governments are becoming increasingly interdependent of each other. Governments – on behalf of their constituents, and like firms – may compete as oligopolists.[12/]

Yet, while most large TNCs have responded to the demands of globalization and alliance capitalism by reconfiguring their organizational structures and decision-taking procedures, there is little evidence that governments have elected to do so. The result is that most are singularly ill equipped to deal with the consequences of globalization. Exceptions include some East Asian administrations, which are not only taking a more holistic approach to the organization of their tasks and functions, but are replacing a "hub and spoke" hierarchical structure of governance by a "spider's web" network structure, in order to encourage more fruitful interdepartmental exchanges of information and cross-fertilization of ideas.

We would suggest that the main reason for the reluctance of governments to embrace new structures of governance is the inflexibility and intransigence of established institutional regimes, and the opposition of powerful sectoral interests within the executive branch to changing the status quo. It is, perhaps, no accident that the administrations with the least institutional impediments are those which are most successfully adapting to the needs of the global market-place. To this extent, developing nations could well have a comparative organizational advantage - particularly if their cultures are sympathetic to alliance capitalism.

The second consequence concerns the direct impact of government behaviour on the competitiveness of the firms located in their territories. This impact arises because many of the complementary assets needed by firms to create and effectively exploit their core competencies are, themselves, government-owned or influenced. This suggests that the ability of governments and private firms to work together (for example, with respect to innovatory activities, retraining, environmental protection and the promotion of inter-firm alliances) might be a competitive advantage in its own right. Again, developing countries would do well to take note of this particular aspect of alliance capitalism as they seek to develop and capitalize on their unique strengths in a global economy.

The third implication of globalization and alliance capitalism is that it requires national governments to reappraise their role as overseers of economic activity. To the economist, the only justification for such a role is that the net benefits arising from it can be achieved at a lower real cost than any other form of organization, such as the market, individual hierarchies or networks of firms. It has long been recognized that, as well as being responsible for the defence of the realm, law and order, and the definition and enforcement of property rights, governments are particularly well equipped to supply – or to organize the supply of – some kinds of public and social goods; and especially those whose benefits accrue as much to the community at large as to the producing institution.

Yet, there is nothing fixed or immutable about *which* organizational form is best suited to produce particular products. Yesterday's case for the public ownership of public utilities or transportation systems may no longer hold today. Technological developments, for example, have undermined most of the *raison d'être* for a government monopoly of mail and telephone services. New methods of monitoring and charging for the use of highways have better enabled private firms to supply these products; while the growth of inter-firm networks offer an alternative to government funding of expensive capital projects.

At the same time, it would be wrong to conclude that the renaissance of the market system should reduce the role of government to a minimalist one. It is yet another paradox of globalization and alliance capitalism that, to ensure its efficient functioning, there needs to be a closer cooperation between the public and private sectors. The underlying characteristics of most markets of the 1990s are very different than those of the craft or the scale production eras. There is more uncertainty attached to them. The specificity of assets has enormously increased. There is more information asymmetry between buyers and sellers. There are more opportunities for opportunism. Markets cost more to set up and monitor; and they generate more externalities than they once did. Underlying demand and supply conditions are continually changing, and an increasing number of products are taking on the form of "public" goods. Moreover, globalization brings with it its own governance costs, such as those which arise from the structural integration of different cultures and institutional regimes. At the same time, the market system is *par excellence* an example of a social good, and it is the government's responsibility to see that this system works to the interests of its constituents.

Too often, one could argue, governments, hierarchies and markets are considered as substitutes for each other. This is a false dichotomy. Today's economy requires a pluralism of organizational modes, each working in tandem with the other - each supporting the other. Too often taxation is regarded as a necessary evil, rather than a price which has to be paid for the supply of competitiveness enhancing public or social goods and services. And too often, governments are perceived as regulatory and controlling agencies, rather than as facilitators of markets, and as suppliers or stimulators of the appropriate learning systems and mind sets for the upgrading of human and physical assets.

To some extent the problem is one of re-forming opinions and attitudes towards the role of governments. There is need for a new vocabulary to promote the image of government as a public good rather than as a necessary evil. We need a *perestroika* of government. We need to recognize that, just as "Fordism" is an out-dated method of organizing work, so the kind of government interventionism appropriate to a "Fordist" environment is outdated. And, just like the emerging managerial structure of twenty-first century firms, we need governments to be lean, flexible and anticipatory of change. The new paradigm of government should eschew such negative or emotive sounding words such as "command", "intervention" and "regulation", and replace them by words such as "empower", "steer", "cooperative", "coordination" and

41

"systemic". Moreover, not only must governments recognize the need for a much more integrated and holistic system of organizing their responsibilities, but it is necessary for all those affected by governments, and particularly ordinary tax payers, to take a more positive view of the benefits which only the former can produce.

It is beyond the scope of the present chapter to suggest how the organization of governments should change to accommodate the kind of remoulding that has been articulated. But, this issue is now very much being considered in the literature. Douglas Hague has, in a book with the intriguing title *Transforming the Dinosaurs* (Hague, 1993), identified four ways in which institutions – be they public or private – can reengineer themselves, viz by coercion, contagion, coaching and learning. While the latter three are usually more acceptable agents of change than the first, in practice, such change usually has to wait until some kind of crisis coerces action. While Hague's remarks are primarily addressed to the situation in the United Kingdom, they would strike a chord of sympathy with the business leaders of Japan who made a powerful plea for a radical redesign of the central administrative structure of the Government of Japan. Among other things, they argued for a greater degree of coordination between the different ministries and agencies of the executive; and for a flattening of the pyramidal system of decision-taking. Unless this is done – and done efficiently – then, according to the *Keidaren* - Japan's economic future may be put at risk.

We do not wish to imply that actions taken by national governments to overcome or reduce market failure are costless, or that such actions are necessarily the most cost effective way of achieving that objective.[13/] At the same time, it is possible to identify the kind of situations which favour government intervention of one kind or another. Figure 1, which is derived and adapted from Robert Wade's evaluation of the role played by national administrations in fostering the economic development of Japan, Taiwan Province of China and the Republic of Korea (Wade, 1988), sets out some of these situations, and the ways in which they may help reduce the transaction costs of governance. While the data are fairly self explanatory, and provide a set of guidelines for governmental intervention, they have not yet been subject to rigorous scrutiny by scholars. The globalizing economy may well enhance the need for such a scrutiny, as it increases the costs of misinformed or inappropriate government action.

In many respects, governments of developing countries are in a good position to meet the demands of the global economy. In almost all countries there is a history of strong interventionist governments, and also an ability to change trajectory speedily. In the last decade, there has not only been a marked realignment in macro-economic policies, but, also a movement towards a less confrontational stance between governments and the business community. Some of the actions taken normally take several years to have any real effect. Others involve major institutional and attitudinal changes, which could take a generation or more to accomplish.

International regimes

In conclusion, a brief reference should be made to the role of supranational forms of governance. Because of space limitations, however, one can do little more than acknowledge the role of privately sponsored international associations or consortia of firms.

There are two main reasons why supranational regimes may be necessary in a global economy. The first is that the unilateral behaviour of governments, which is geared to promoting the good of their own citizens, may not be globally welfare maximizing. This is because of the possible adverse affects, that is, negative externalities, of this behaviour on the citizens of another nation. These might arise, for example, from the pursuance of geo-economic and rent seeking strategies by one government, which might lead to retaliatory action by other governments. The "beggar my neighbour" trade sanctions imposed by governments of industrial countries in the inter-war years are a classic example of welfare reducing policies; and it was precisely to deter this kind of behaviour that GATT was established in 1946 to draw up the "rules of the game" for international trade. But, as has been seen, the globalization of the world economy has considerably widened the scope of competition and interdependence among governments. This has, consequently, enlarged the international playing arena, and has made it necessary for more rules to be established if geo-economic conflict is to be avoided and if the game is to be played fairly and to the benefit of all (Luttwack, 1993).

The second reason why supra-national regimes may be needed is that there are some cross-border market failures which cannot be fully compensated for, or surmounted, either by the actions of hierarchies or by national governments. The presence of international politico-market failure is most dramatically seen in the fields of satellite communications, the exploration of the sea bed, the protection of the ozone layer, environmental pollution and military security. In each of these instances, supra or intergovernmental action may be necessary either to reduce the coordinating and transaction costs of such activities, or to capture the extraterritorial benefits of intercountry networking. The twenty-first century seems certain to witness a growing number of these international public and social goods, each of which will require pluralist governance structures if they are to work for the global good.[14/]

It is, perhaps, worth reminding ourselves that intergovernmental cooperation on non-economic matters dates back many years. Agreements on technical standards, weights and measures, and meteorological systems were all first concluded in the last century. However, the idea that supranational regimes may be an appropriate means of governing *economic* activity is relatively new, and is still very controversial. Two things, however, should be considered. The first is that it is becoming increasingly difficult to distinguish between what is and is not an economic activity. For example, each of the examples of politico-market failures just described, affect, in some way or another, the infrastructure of modern economic activity. The second is that the emergence of the global economy, alliance capitalism and the widening competing interface between governments, is forcing a reappraisal of our attitude towards the role of transnational economic regimes.

There are essentially two ways of implementing supranational governance. The first is by the subordination of the sovereignty of nationhood to some kind of supranational authority. One form of such subordination is a merger of nation states – which, carried to its extreme, leads to world government. While all the evidence seems to point to the disintegration, rather than the integration, of nation states, we are also witnessing – and here there are some interesting parallels with what is happening in the corporate world – the growth of intercountry alliances, or networks. These are usually set up to achieve a specific objective, but they all address problems, challenges and opportunities which can only be effectively dealt with at a supranational level.

In the economics arena, however, supranational control is likely to be primarily exercised at a functional or issue level. In spite of the protracted and tortuous GATT negotiations establishing the World Trade

Organization (WTO), there is a lot of room for grafting on other issues to the agenda of the new organization. The indirect ways in which national governments can, for good or bad, affect trade and FDI are growing all the time. Besides the most obvious of below cost competition measures (that is, dumping), price competition, industrial, environmental and social policy can all be used as instruments for tilting the level of the playing fields. Perhaps the World Trade Organization (WTO) (we say newly established, although it was first recommended nearly 50 years ago) will provide the institutional framework for this.[15/]

Alongside the strengthening of global governance systems – particularly at an issue level – regional governance systems are also becoming more important. It is much more likely that national governments will be prepared to surrender parts of their economic jurisdiction to a supranational authority made up of nations with similar institutional, cultural and ideological backgrounds to their own, than to one which comprises nations which are widely different in these respects.

At the same time, there is nothing to prevent representatives of regional schemes from getting together to discuss issues of extraregional interest. This, in fact, is what the G7 is mainly about, and it has had a good deal of success in the past. While it would be anticipated that regional integration - of one form or another – is likely to be an increasingly preferred way of supranational governance – particularly where the harmonization of national policies is desired – one can foresee a whole set of new alliances among nations being established in the next few years; and these could pose new problems for the coordination of governance itself. Again, there are lessons to be learned from the success and failures of inter-firm networking.

The other main (and complementary) avenue to supranational governance is, in many respects, more in the spirit of alliance capitalism, in that its success rests less on mandates and regulations and more on the sharing of ideas, cooperation, trust, reciprocity and forbearance of its participants. The aim of this form of polity is to coordinate the actions of national governments in their response to cross-border market failure. Attempts to achieve this objective usually originate in the debating chambers of the United Nations and its various agencies, OECD, the European Community, ASEAN and similar institutions. But the influence of such bodies should not be taken lightly – particularly as it affects developing countries. These institutions will certainly not play a less important role as globalization proceeds. Indeed, we are reasonably sanguine that, with the ending of the cold war, and with at least some harmonization of economic policies among governments, that, in tackling the remaining, but no less serious, problems facing the nations of the world, a spirit of fusion, rather than fission, in the ideas expressed and decisions reached will prevail.

Conclusions

To sum up, then, globalization is requiring the adoption of a new form of capitalism – which has been called alliance capitalism – if it is to be successful in promoting economic welfare and sustainable development. The distinctive feature of alliance capitalism is that its success depends upon the harmonious interaction between the wealth creating constituents in society and those of governments. Cooperation and competition go side by side; they are opposite sides of the coin of economic progress.

Where it has been permitted and where it has been in response to market forces, it is believed that FDI – like trade – has had a generally positive affect on both economic growth and the international division of labour. As subsequent chapters in the present volume will show, the relationship between trade, FDI and cross-border cooperative ventures is ambivalent. In some cases – for example, in response to barriers to trade – FDI may be a substitute for trade; in others – for example, in most natural resource based and efficiency seeking investment – it is likely to be trade enhancing. For the most part, and until recently, FDI and cooperative arrangements have been regarded as substitutes for each other, with the latter often being regarded as a second best alternative to FDI.

In today's globalizing economy, however, and with the emergence of alliance capitalism, they are becoming more complementary and supportive of each other. This new trend is particularly being demonstrated in the activities of the large TNCs in the industrialized countries; and governments do well to recognize this fact in the formation of their policies towards trade, foreign investment and competition – which, all too often, are conceived and implemented in isolation of each other. FDI is one of the deepest forms of structural integration between countries. Not only are the resources and capabilities of one country transferred to that of another, but their use – as well as that of the complementary assets of the recipient country – is controlled, or influenced, by the transferring firms. Thus, the motives for FDI, and the conditions under which it is undertaken, are, through the "embedded" factor, likely to determine its impact.

It has also been argued that the transition from hierarchical to alliance capitalism has very considerable implications for sustainable development. On balance, it is believed that these implications are welfare-enhancing, although the extent and form of the benefits is likely to differ between sectors and countries. At the same time, it has been argued that it is desirable for developing countries to try to create their own networks of value-added and inter-active learning activities, and to do so in a way which promotes their own comparative dynamic advantage. We are somewhat less optimistic that, in the near future, the most impoverished nations, and particularly those which are most distant from the hubs of economic power, will gain much from globalization *per se,* although the secondary, or spillover, effects of other economic and political events may be more positive.

We have further asserted that, in the formation of their macro-economic and organizational strategies, national governments are being forced to interact more closely with each other. Sometimes, this interaction takes the form of competition, and sometimes of voluntary or involuntary cooperation. At the same time, the globalizing economy is demanding a re-examination of the scope and authority of supranational economic regimes, both to minimize the regional or global welfare reducing actions by national governments, and to encourage the harmonization of these actions whenever they can help reduce the costs of organizing cross-border production and transactions. It has finally been suggested that emerging economies may well have a comparative advantage in the implementation of domestic economic policies in the globalizing economy, *inter alia,* because they are not faced with the same institutional rigidities which face the older industrialized nations.

Notes

1. The respective authors of these books are Henry Wendt (1993), R. J. Barnett and John Cavanagh (1994), and John Naisbitt (1994).
2. McGrew and Lewis, eds. *Global Politics: Globalization and the Nation States* (Cambridge, The Polity Press, 1992), p. 23.
3. Kennedy and Florida, 1993, p. 303.

4. Measured in SDRs, these growth rates would have been rather different; in particular, the FDI growth rates in the 1980s would have been lower, and those since 1990 higher.

5. India's realized annual inward FDI increased from $113 million in 1991 to $959 million in 1994. It is estimated that total inflows for 1995 would amount to $1.7 billion. (UNCTAD 1995).

6. Which is the fourth type of FDI, along with *market seeking, resource seeking* and *efficiency seeking* FDI.

7. The exception is that strategic asset acquiring FDI is still very limited in Japan - not so much by legal restrictions as by less tangible entry barriers, for example, to do with business customs and practices, and <u>keiretsu</u> relations in Japan.

8. UNCTAD (1994).

9. The increasing need for close proximity would appear to run counter to the reduction in transaction and coordinating costs arising from telecommunication advances. Yet, the example of the City of London is instructive. While many of the routine banking, financial and insurance operations have been decentralized, a network of the core and innovating activities remains firmly embedded in the square mile. This is because the perceived gains from face-to-face contact between the constituents of the network are greater than ever. As manufacturing firms - at least in dynamic sectors - upgrade their R&D and skilled labour, they become more closely interdependent in their informational and technological needs; and as trust and forbearance become a more important component of transactions, then, at least at the top end of the value chain and in the early stages of their production cycles, the need for close physical proximity increases rather than diminishes. This need was recognized nearly 30 years ago by Raymond Vernon (1966). The idea of the factory as a research laboratory also suggests closer physical linkages between R&D and production activities (Kennedy and Florida, 1993).

10. For example, in the garment and footwear industries, although the first tier suppliers of flagship TNCs are usually located in the more advanced developing countries, for example, Hong Kong and Singapore, these suppliers may, themselves, "put out" the more labour intensive production processes to small firms and artisans as far afield as Bangladesh, Sri Lanka and Nigeria.

11. Sometimes this funding may help to support outbound FDI by other developing or developed countries to the poorer developing countries (for example, investment by Chinese firms in parts of Indo-China and by Canadian firms in Central Africa).

12. This is particularly the case as between governments of countries of a similar size, economic structure and stage of development.

13. Among the possible failures of direct government intervention to overcome successfully the deficiencies of the market, one might mention the rent seeking activities of powerful pressure groups; the magnification of market failures (for example, with respect to the supply of environmental or social products) by the news media or other politically motivated interests; the inability of governments to attract the best talents (due *inter alia* to ineffective incentive systems); the lack of commercial expertise and bounded rationality of public decision-takers; the pursuance of non-economic (especially ideological) goals by politicians; the inadequacy of market related performance indicators which may lead to the establishment of sub-optimal standards (for example, with respect to budgets, investment and control of information flows); the high-time discount (or short-termism) of political decision-takers; the lack of market pressures to minimize X-inefficiency, especially in the case of public monopolies; uncertainties and ambiguities inherent in the provision of goods

and services, which are in the domain of governments, for example, defence equipment, educational and health services; and the lack of a coordinated system of governance (c.f. with that in case of private hierarchies); and the difficulty of adjusting policies and institutional structures to meet quickly the needs of techno-logical and economic change. For a more detailed examination of these and other factors which might lead to excessive or inappropriate governmental intervention or the sub-optimal provision of public goods and services, see, for example, Grestchmann (1991), Stiglitz (1989) and Hämäläinen (1994).

14. Since the present chapter was written, OECD has announced its intention to conclude a multilateral investment agreement (MIA) which, *inter alia*, will set high standards for governments in their treatment of TNCs, and in their macro-organizational policies which are likely to affect the costs and benefits of FDI. For further details see Witherell (1995).

15. In the present chapter, it is not the intention to deal with the issue of bilateral governance.

References

Barnett, R. J. and J. Cavanagh (1994). *Global Dream*. New York: Simon and Schuster.

Bergsten, C. F. (1990). The world economy after the cold war. *Foreign Affairs*, vol. 69, pp. 96-112.

Brennan, G. and J.M. Buchanan (1985). *The Power to Tax*. Cambridge: Cambridge University Press.

Dunning, J. H. (1993a). *Multinational Enterprises and the Global Economy*. Wokingham, England and Reading, Massachusetts: Addison Wesley.

_____(1993b). *Globalization of Business: The Challenge of the 1990s*. London and New York: Routledge.

Grestchmann, K. (1991). Analyzing the public sector: The received view in economics and its shortcomings. In Franz-Xaver Kaufman (ed.), *The Public Sector: Challenge for Coordination and Learning*. Berlin: Water de Gruyter.

Hagedoorn, J. (1993). Strategic technology alliances and modes of cooperation in high technology industries. In G. Grabher (ed.), *The Embedded Firm*. London: Routledge.

Hague, Douglas C. (1993). *Transforming the Dinosaurs*. London: Demos.

Hämäläinen, T. J. (1994). *The Evolving Role of Government in Economic Organization*. Newark, New Jersey, Rutgers University (mimeo).

Huntington, Samuel (1993). The clash of civilizations. *Foreign Affairs, vol. 72*, (Summer), pp. 22-49.

Kennedy, M. and R. Florida (1993). *Beyond Mass Production*. Oxford and New York: Oxford University Press.

Luttwack, E. N. (1993). The coming global war for economic power. *The International Economy*, September/October, pp. 18-21 and 64-67.

McGrew, Anthony G. (1992). Conceptualizing global politics. In A.G. McGrew and P.G. Lewis (eds.). *Global Politics: Globalization and the Nation State*. Cambridge: The Polity Press.

Naisbitt, John (1994). *Global Paradox: The Bigger the World Economy, the More Political its Smallest Players*. New York: William Morrow.

Osborne, D. and T. Gaebler (1992). *Reinventing Government: How the Entrepreneurial Spirit is Transforming the Public Sector*. Reading, Massachusetts: Addison Wesley.

Quinn, J. B. and F.G. Hilmer (1994). Strategic outsourcing. *Sloan Management Review* vol. 35, Summer, pp. 43-55.

Stiglitz, J. (1989). *The Economic Role of the State*. Oxford: Basil Blackwell.

UNCTAD (1994). *World Investment Report 1994: Transnational Corporations, Employment and the Workplace* (United Nations publication, Sales No. E.94.II.A.14).

UNCTAD (1995). *World Investment Report 1995: Transnational Corporations and Competitiveness* (United Nations publication, Sales No. E.95.II.A.9).

UNCTAD (1996). *World Investment Report 1996: Investment, Trade, and International Policy Arrangements* (United Nations publication, Sales No. E.96.II.A.14).

United States Department of Commerce (1992a). *US Direct Investment Abroad: 1989 Benchmark Survey Final Results*, Washington, D.C.: Department of Commerce Bureau of Economic Analysis.

_____ (1992b). *US Direct Investment Abroad: Operation of US Parent Companies and Their Affiliates, Preliminary 1990 Estimates*. Washington, D.C.: Department of Commerce, Bureau of Economic Analysis.

_____ (1993a). US direct investment abroad 1990-1992. *Survey of Current Business*, July, pp. 97-120.

_____ (1993b). *Survey of Current Business*. August, September and October editions.

Vernon, Raymond (1966). International investment and international trade in the product cycle. *Quarterly Journal of Economics*, vol. 80, pp. 190-207.

Wade, Robert (1988). The role of government in overcoming market failure in Taiwan, Republic of Korea and Japan. In H. Hughes (ed.), *Achieving Industrialization in East Asia*. Cambridge: Cambridge University Press.

Weinberg, D. B. (1993). US international transactions second quarter 1993. *Survey of Current Business*, September, pp. 94-156.

Wendt, H. (1993). *Global Embrace*. New York: Harper Business.

Witherell, W.H. (1995). The OECD Multinational Agreement on Investment. *Transnational Corporations*, 4 August.

World Bank (1993a). *Global Economic Prospects and the Developing Countries*. Washington, D.C. The World Bank.

_____ (1993b). *The East Asian Miracle*. Oxford: Oxford University Press.

_____ (1994). *World Development Report, 1994*. Oxford: Oxford University Press.

World Economic Forum and IMEDE (1993). *World Competitiveness Report 1993*. Geneva and Lausanne: World Economic Forum and Institut pour l'étude des méthodes de direction de l'entreprise (IMEDE).

2

The world trade and investment system and developing countries

Robert Z. Lawrence

Introduction

The world economy is becoming increasingly globalized. Declining transportation and communications costs, the international convergence of technological capabilities among developed economies and the spread of transnational corporations (TNCs) with global reach have made many countries fairly close locational substitutes. In such an environment, relatively small differences in institutional practices and shifts in relative competitiveness can have large effects on international trade and investment flows. Consequently, the regime for trade and investment can have important consequences for the allocation of global resources.

The nature of the international regime for trade and investment is also important for developing countries. The "demonstration" effect of the successful outward orientation of the East Asian economies has persuaded many developing countries that trade can indeed be an engine of growth. Debt problems have made the attraction of direct foreign investment a vital source of new capital while programmes adopted at the behest of organizations such as the World Bank and IMF have made trade liberalization an essential component of adjustment. The success of such policies depends not only on the domestic economic responses but also on a hospitable international environment.

In the present chapter, I will outline briefly four alternative scenarios which the global system for trade and investment could follow. I will then consider their implications for developing countries. Specifically, I will outline (i) a continuation of the system under the World Trade Organization (WTO); (ii) the sustained expansion of regional arrangements; (iii) managed trade and investment; and (iv) a regime with much deeper integration.[1/]

The international environment is important for developing countries, not simply for the market access it provides, but also for the demands it imposes on developing country policies. Indeed, the most important conclusion I have reached is that all four scenarios require increased obligations by developing countries. *The WTO system* is evolving in the direction of increased participation by developing countries as full members. In particular, the Uruguay Round Agreement extends disciplines to all members, although it gives developing countries more time to adjust. *Regional initiatives* may increasingly include developing countries, individually or in groups, but their participation will typically require (i) providing reciprocal access for developed country goods, services and investment; (ii) moving more closely towards developed country regulatory standards; and (iii) reducing structurally distorting industrial and related policies. *Managed trade arrangements* could well be selective and more onerous on countries perceived as relatively closed or different. Again the pressures will be to conform to international norms. Finally, to participate in *deep integration* arrangements, developing countries need not only to remove trade barriers, but to adopt institutional practices more typical of developed economies.

These trends mark a major change in attitudes and philosophies. Over the years, developing countries have claimed and received exemptions from the rules of the General Agreement on Tariffs and Trade (GATT). In regional arrangements and in Generalized System of Preferences (GSP) they were granted access — albeit limited — without having to assume reciprocal obligations. In their negotiations for a Code of Conduct for TNCs, developing countries emphasized their need for national sovereignty and the freedom to follow national development strategies. The major challenge in the future will be reconciling the increased requirements for global conformity of "deeper" integration with demands of national sovereignty and the needs of developing countries to follow independent development strategies which involve government intervention. Let us turn now to the four scenarios and then consider their implications for developing countries.

The World Trade Organization

The GATT has been instrumental in facilitating freer trade. Since the end of the Second World War, tariff rates around the world have plummeted. Among the major industrialized countries, weighted-average tariff levels have been lowered to below 5 per cent. Despite these achievements, there remained considerable dissatisfaction with GATT which the Uruguay Round of trade negotiations tried to address. Its 15 working groups were divided into three broad subject matters: (i) *increased market access*, including more open trade in agriculture, textiles and natural resources and removal or reduction of remaining tariff and non-tariff measures; (ii) *extension of GATT to new areas*, principally trade in services, standards and enforcement of intellectual property rights, and trade-related performance requirements imposed by governments on foreign investment; and (iii) *strengthening of GATT rules*, especially those covering anti-dumping, subsidization, product standards, import licensing, "safeguards" (temporary import protection), and dispute settlement. In short, the Uruguay Round covered a broad, ambitious agenda.

The successful completion of the Round represented an impressive accomplishment.[2/] For developing countries, the prospect of the elimination of the Multi-Fibre Arrangement in particular, was an important accomplishment. Despite these accomplishments, however, WTO as presently structured, could play a diminishing, albeit still important, role in governing economic relationships between countries.

The original conception of GATT was based on the most favoured nation (MFN) removal of tariffs as the principle means of achieving free trade. While its scope has broadened, GATT is still essentially based on the principle of "shallow integration", that is, that international trade can be regulated primarily by dealing with problems as they appear at the border or where they involve explicit measures that discriminate against foreigners. On this view, different national practices that *affect* trade should be tolerated, as long as actors operating within each economy are granted national treatment and not discriminated against, and /or as long as they do not cause injury to other nations.[3/]

As border barriers have been lowered, however, it has become increasingly apparent that many policies and practices can inadvertently discriminate against foreign products and firms. Accordingly, there are pressures to move beyond the shallow integration as embodied in GATT, towards a much deeper form of integration which standardizes, harmonizes and/or reconciles divergent national practices. These goals have emerged quite clearly, for example, in the deliberations over the European Community in 1992 and the Structural Impediments Initiative between Japan and the United States.

These pressures have also emerged in the multilateral arena, as countries discuss the post-Uruguay Round agenda. In particular, items for inclusion which have been suggested include foreign investment, competition policy, environment and labour standards. There is considerable resistance to the introduction of those items, however, in both developed and developing countries. It is doubtful, therefore (with some notable exceptions such as intellectual property rights) whether, at least for some significant period of time, WTO will provide a major forum for negotiating such measures of deep integration. Instead, it is probable that deep integration will be accomplished in regional arrangements before seriously being negotiated, let alone accomplished, at such a broad level as WTO. Even with the success of the Uruguay Round, therefore, international trade and investment policies will continue to be pursued through bilateral, regional and extra-WTO measures and agreements.

Investment. One of the new areas on which GATT has focused is TRIMs (Trade-Related Investment Measures). The aim is to prevent those performance requirements imposed on foreign-owned firms which affect trade flows directly. They include requirements on local content, exports, local manufacturing, trade balance, technology transfer, foreign exchange and domestic production mandates.[4/]

Many countries, both developed and developing, will find subscribing to such an agreement requires changing practices they have long followed. (Indeed, even Mrs. Thatcher's United Kingdom was an avid practitioner of performance requirements.)

The TRIMs Agreement that was concluded at the Uruguay Round was an achievement. The early 1990s offered an opportunity to obtain an agreement which could not have been attained earlier. In the past, the United States, as the most important source country, was the most enthusiastic supporter of such an agreement. TRIMs were seen by its TNCs as a costly constraint on doing business, while labour viewed them as an unwelcome costly source of job loss. In other countries, particularly host countries such as Canada and Australia, however, TRIMs were seen as legitimate policy measures for appropriating the national benefits of foreign direct investment (FDI). Over the 1980s, however, Europe and Japan have become increasingly important sources of FDI. In addition, Canada has liberalized its investment regime and Australia too, has adopted more liberal macroeconomic policies. As a consequence, views among developed countries have become more convergent. Indeed, as noted by Graham and Krugman (1990), the positions of the major industrial economies are quite close.

Similarly, many developing countries now view restrictions on performance requirements as less inhibiting than they might have been in the past. Typically, performance requirements reflect a *quid pro quo* assumed by foreign firms in return for an explicit or implicit subsidy granted by the government. In general, therefore, the greater the subsidy, the more demanding the requirements by governments of TNCs. It is no coincidence that the economies with the most elaborate performance stipulations have also been the most protectionist (for example, India, Mexico (through the mid-1980s), Brazil, Canada, Australia and Spain). As countries have reduced their external barriers, however, the extent of these subsidies are reduced. Hence the need for the requirements (and the ability to impose them) is also diminished. In addition, the environment for attracting FDI is becoming increasingly competitive among developing countries. Countries are more likely to compete to attract FDI using subsidies than they are to seek to impose requirements.

Finally, as the chapters in the present volume show, several developing countries have emerged as source countries for foreign investment. As development has increased labour costs at home, firms from the Republic of Korea, Taiwan Province of China and Singapore have set up production facilities abroad. This has led to some shifts in their positions on the TRIMs issue.

In the early 1990s, it seemed that this confluence of sentiment favourable to prohibiting performance requirements might not last, however, if attitudes changed in the United States. As inbound direct investment increased in the United States, there were growing demands to ensure that foreign firms have "sufficient" local content and contribute to the United States technology base. Such demands were resisted, however, and in the mid-1990s the pace of inflows of investment from Japan into the United States slowed dramatically. In addition, it became clear that, in numerous cases, Japanese investors had overpaid for the acquisitions they had made. In the United States the call for imposing requirements on foreign investors died down.

While the TRIMS agreement in the Uruguay Round was successfully concluded and represented an historic achievement in introducing investment provisions into the multilateral trade rules, it left important investment issues unresolved. Indeed, the agreement reflected the legacy of a bygone era. The agreement confined its concerns to the impact of investment measures that distort trade in goods. In addition, it did not reflect a comprehensive approach to investment issues. Indeed, as Sauve (1994) makes clear, the agreements on services (particularly those liberalizing services delivered through a domestic commercial presence) and intellectual property were probably more significant in liberalizing nvestment than the TRIMS.[5] In particular, the TRIMS Agreement did not deal with the most important prerequisite for free investment: the basic right of establishment. Indeed, even in the United States, there are inhibitions on foreign ownership in sectors such as communications, transportation and national defense industries. Nor did the Uruguay Round agreement really deal with the general rights of foreign firms to "national treatment" as opposed to those relating to trade distorting measures. (Should foreign-owned firms, for example, be allowed to bid for government contracts and participate in government-sponsored R&D consortia?[6])

Finally, there are even deeper concerns which would require moving beyond "national treatment" towards the more ambitious goal of reciprocal treatment. In particular, countries do not all provide similar access and allow similar business behaviour. Thus treatment of foreign firms is not always reciprocated.

One example concerns differences in the ability of foreigners to purchase domestic firms. It is relatively easy for firms from Sweden, Switzerland and Japan to acquire major firms in the United Kingdom and the United States using hostile or friendly methods. It is virtually impossible, however, for any foreigners to buy Swiss, Swedish or

Japanese firms — even under friendly circumstances. In 1988, for example, the bid by Swiss-based Nestle for British Rowntree provoked an outcry because the Swiss, with their division between registered and bearer shares, prevented British firms from buying Swiss firms.[7]

In some instances, the barriers are not necessarily aimed at foreigners specifically. None the less, differences in corporate governance systems may have exclusionary effects. These asymmetries have become increasingly contentious. As discussed below, there are bound to be increased efforts to cope with them either by discriminating against firms based on the nationality of their headquarters or by reforms which grant similar or equivalent access.

In sum, as in the trade area, there are numerous problems related to international investment which the Uruguay Round did not resolve. In response, therefore, a variety of bilateral, regional and plurilateral measures will be pursued, some of which are discussed in the following paragaphs.

Regional blocs

The spectre of global fragmentation is haunting the global trading system. The fear is that progress towards global integration over the past four decades will be reversed as the world economy splits up into three regional trading blocs, each centred on a major currency, each closed to outsiders.[8]

Building Blocks? But, in fact, regional arrangements might actually turn out to be the building blocks of a more integrated global economy rather than stumbling blocks preventing it. Stronger regional integration need not be associated with higher external barriers. Indeed, as has been recognized by GATT, regional integration could have positive effects on the rest of the world provided the emerging regional blocs are "open" to trade from outside.

A key question is whether the regional arrangement remains confined to a few members, or whether it is open to all who seek to join. The European Union has clearly been an open arrangement. It began with 6 nations, has been enlarged to 15 and there are now prospects of additional members from Eastern Europe. As was the case with the European Union, the North American Free Trade Agreement also is not developing as an exclusive process. In Miami, Florida, in late 1994,

President Clinton announced that negotiations would begin on the accession of Chile to NAFTA and 34 nations from the Western Hemisphere agreed that they would conclude an agreement for a Free Trade Area of the Americas (FTAA), in which barriers to trade and investment will be progressively eliminated and for which negotiations are to be concluded no later than the year 2005.

The Asian bloc, allegedly emerging around Japan, is the least likely to develop into a formal protectionist arrangement. This region is particularly dependent on extraregional trade and unlikely to explicitly adopt higher barriers against non-Asian nations. Asia is also particularly heterogeneous politically. To be sure, Japan's influence in the East Asian area is likely to increase, but precisely because other Asian nations are reluctant to submit to an arrangement with a single dominant economy, progress is likely to be slow, towards a single regional arrangement centred solely on Japan. Moreover, the United States will be unwilling to "concede" Asia to Japan. It is likely to use its influence to prevent a formal Pacific arrangement. Indeed, this motive lies behind the United States support for the Asia-Pacific Economic Cooperation Forum (APEC), the members of which have agreed to the long-term goal of achieving free and open trade and investment in the Asia Pacific region no later than the year 2020 (and 2010 for developed countries). Two rather than three major regional arrangements could emerge.[9]

Moreover, the forces driving nations into regional arrangements are dramatically different from those that drove them into preferential trading blocs in the interwar period. The motive for completing the internal market is not to secure the European market for European producers by providing them preferential access, but instead to facilitate the free movement of goods, services, labour and capital throughout the Union.

This deeper integration within Europe will facilitate trade with the rest of the world. A common set of standards, for example, makes it easier for all who wish to sell in Europe — not just insiders. A tough set of rules which prevents governments from subsidizing domestic firms aids all their competitors, not only those located in the European Union. To be sure, some European countries will continue to implement industrial policies, but the restraints on those initiatives will be greater than in the absence of EC92. Once the larger European economies are committed to allow the free flow of resources within Europe, they will no longer be able to ensure that each has a national champion in every industry located within its territories. This undermining of the nationalist sentiments (which drives much of the protectionism in the larger European countries) will benefit outsiders.

Likewise, Mexico did not seek the North American Free Trade Agreement (NAFTA) with Canada and the United States to avoid liberalization with the rest of the world. On the contrary, since the mid-1980s, Mexico has engaged in an extensive unilateral reduction in external restrictions accompanied by internal liberalization. Instead, much of the appeal of a free trade agreement (FTA) is that it provides credibility and permanence to Mexico's liberalization measures. A free trade agreement with the United States has important advertising value for Mexico, raising its profile in the minds of foreign investors. A third rationale is that an export-oriented Mexico requires secure access to its major trading partner. Thus a free trade agreement is an important complement to an outward-oriented policy which is based on attracting foreign investment.

The key point here is that once Mexico accepts obligations *vis-à-vis* the United States to permit foreign investment, to enforce intellectual property rights, and to unwind its elaborate protectionist programmes for automobiles and electronics, these changes will provide benefits for all its trading partners — not just the United States. United States involvement, in particular, would dramatically enhance the credibility of intra-Latin American regional liberalization arrangements by making the costs of violating the agreement for any individual Latin American country particularly high.

Again the context and motivation for those efforts in Latin America must be appreciated. Nations throughout Latin America, in addition to Mexico, have all significantly reduced tariff levels, as well as dispersed tariff levels, while Chilean liberalization has been in place even longer. It is no surprise that the earlier Latin American regional initiatives were failures, since they were implemented in the context of import-substitution policies. The aim of governments with interventionist philosophies was to achieve economies of scale in protected regional markets. But those protectionist motives precluded success. The current policies, however, are different. They are being implemented by governments proclaiming market-oriented philosophies, seeking domestic liberalization and the attraction of foreign capital to service global rather than domestic markets.

Stumbling blocks? This optimistic viewpoint needs to be qualified. While overt protectionist barriers are unlikely, each of the regional arrangements might resort to more subtle protectionist measures. Measures that divert trade and investment could be taken at the regional level when questions such as rules of origin, rights of establishment and national treatment are resolved.

Regional arrangements involve discrimination against products from outside the region. Rules of origin are required, therefore, to define regional production. Regional members are often concerned that products could gain access to the entire regional market by entering the market of the regional member with the lowest barriers. Typically therefore, products must contain a minimum regional content to qualify for entry to other regional members.

In the United States-Canada Free Trade Agreement a 50 per cent regional value-added content requirement was required for eligibility for regional access. In NAFTA, those rules were particularly protectionist in the case of textiles products. They were the major source of the negative effects for outsiders. Everything else being equal, the more restrictive those measures are, the more significant trade diversion is likely to be.

A related question concerns the definition of which products are, or should be, subject to anti-dumping rules. The rules of fair trade differ for foreign and domestic products. In the European Union, there was a fear that foreigners might set up "screwdriver plants" and escape anti-dumping measures by performing a minimal amount of local production. Generally, the European Union uses the test which requires "substantial transformation" domestically as a condition for exemption from anti-dumping rules. For semi-conductors, however, the European Union has required that, for chips to qualify as European, the "diffusion process" must take place in Europe. The widespread adoption of such requirements could turn into the functional equivalent of an extensive local content programme with all of the negative implications for trade such measures might entail. The definition of local products in determining eligibility for European Union-wide government procurement programmes could have similar effects.

Increased local content requirements obviously afford domestic products with increased protection. Their impact on foreign investment is actually ambiguous. In some cases, foreign producers may be induced to shift production to the regional market. Thus both trade and investment could be diverted. In other cases, however, foreign firms could suffer competitive losses and be driven out of the market. For example, firms from the Republic of Korea have set up operations in Canada which produce standardized electronics products and automobiles. These firms' competitive advantages are based not on superior technology, but rather on access to assembly kits produced in the Republic of Korea. Increased local content requirements erode those competitive advantages.

Regional arrangements could, in principle, also lead to greater discrimination against non-regional firms with respect to both rights of establishment and operation. The United States-Canada FTA did not give American firms complete freedom to invest in Canada, but it did grant them greater access than Canada grants to firms from other nations. In particular, United States-based firms could undertake larger investments without submitting these for review than firms from other countries. This form of preferential treatment could induce investment diversion, which is analogous to traditional trade diversion. Particularly in the area of services, however, NAFTA was actually less discriminatory against outside firms granting foreign affiliates based in other North America access that was similar to that for domestic firms.[10/]

In Europe, the rights of establishment to be enjoyed by foreign affiliates have been the subject of considerable discussion, particularly in the area of financial institutions. The second directive has made it clear that reciprocity rather than national treatment will serve as a criterion. Firms from countries which the European Union deems do not provide European firms with equivalent access, could be denied some of the rights enjoyed by European firms and those from preferred areas.

European decisions on the issues relating to the sale of Japanese automobiles in the Union also took an ominous turn with a new form of protectionism which is based on the nationality of firm ownership rather than the location of production. The Union limits (albeit in principle temporarily) total sales of Japanese brand automobiles — both imports and those produced within the Union — to a particular market share until the end of the decade. Measures of this type will eliminate or severely limit the inducements which trade barriers provide for foreign investment. They would reduce rather than increase the investment diversion towards the Community represented by the European Community 1992.

In the case of the Asian economies, foreign concerns relate not only to formal rules, but to informal government and private practices. In some areas, Japanese practices are now formally more liberal than those in the United States or the European Union. For example the Japanese have increased the access provided to foreign-owned firms in nationally-sponsored technology projects. Serious problems remain, however, relating to the feasibility of foreign acquisitions (discussed above) and to the links between investment and trade. In certain industries, particularly electronics and machinery, it is extremely difficult for outsiders to sell in Japan. Indeed, an extremely high percentage of Japanese imports take the form of purchases from foreign affiliates (see Takeuchi 1990 and Lawrence 1990). In addition, there is some evidence that Japanese firms are usually unwilling to purchase inputs from non-Japanese suppliers (Kreinen 1988). These concerns suggest the danger of a strong, relatively closed Asian network under the control of Japanese-owned companies, implicitly sanctioned by the Government of Japan. In 1994, the APEC countries concluded an agreement on investment principles, but the provisions were very weak. The agreement was not binding on members and, as noted by Bora and Graham (1994), countries pledged only to avoid policies that were not contentious (such as avoiding double taxation), but issues such as performance requirements were either ignored or dealt with in weak language.

Finally, it is important to distinguish the trade and investment diversions which result from protectionist regional actions and from the effects on trade and investment, which result from the improvements which those arrangements may make in the region as a productive location. Indeed, it was no coincidence that the major influx of United States investment into Europe corresponded to the initial formation of the European Union. Countries with small domestic markets, such as Belgium, became important hosts for foreign direct investment not because those firms were fearful of higher trade barriers, but rather because they discovered that these nations were competitive production locations with close and secure access to thriving markets. More recently Mexico, by changing its foreign investment regime and offering access to the United States, has improved its competitiveness as a location for production. These are changes which increase the competitive pressures facing other countries in Latin America and elsewhere.

Managed trade and investment

The third scenario for the future development of the world trading system — more "managed trade" — is favoured by some academics and politicians in the United States who have grown increasingly frustrated with the apparent stubbornness of the bilateral United States trade balances with a number of trading partners, most importantly Japan. Managed trade proponents are, of course, not confined to the United States, however. Proposals come in various forms, but all share the common feature of attempting to specify outcomes rather than rules.

The broadest managed trade proposal, or "macro trade management", would have countries set bilateral trade balances (ideally after negotiation, but, if that fails, then unilaterally).[11] Less sweeping would be overall bilateral export targets (and their counterpart, import targets) for other countries.

Alternatively, trade could be "micro-managed", with targets set for individual products or industry sectors, such as the quantitative import restrictions (quotas or Voluntary Export Restrictions) that now govern trade in automobiles, semiconductors, steel and textiles. Finally, the activities of foreign-owned firms could be managed to ensure that they meet certain performance requirements.

The motives for managed trade and investment are changing. In the past, they were simply designed to protect domestic markets. Many quota arrangements were the response to the adjustment problems of declining industries. Increasingly, however, they reflect concerns about industries of the future, about alleged differences in economic structure that generate an "unlevel playing field", and about access to foreign markets. A particularly noteworthy innovation, for example, was the setting of goals for the sales of foreign computer chips in Japan — for import expansion rather than export restriction.[12] Global competition, according to some advocates of managed trade, is a zero sum game, in which nations which fail to adopt strategic trade policies lose out to those that do. Since agreements over international rules for the conduct of such policies are unlikely, or since countries interpret the rules differently, numerical targets should be set for trade and production in key sectors.

The world trading system in the future is likely to see more efforts at sectoral management — largely because this is the way many trade disputes have been resolved in the past. The outcome of the Uruguay Round may not have as much effect on the prospects for managed trade at the "macro" level—targets for bilateral trade balances and/or import/export levels. The key factor will be whether current trade frictions between Japan and its trading partners subside or intensify.

Over the years, managed trade arrangements have tended to originate in responses to rapid influxes of Japanese products. As Japan has moved up the technological spectrum, it has been forced to restrain its export growth in products such as textiles, steel, televisions, automobiles, machine tools and semi-conductors. These measures may begin bilaterally – typically between the United States and Japan – but then expand to include other exporting and importing nations. Many of the instruments and measures originally devised to deal with Japan have subsequently been applied to other nations.

In the 1990s, trade and investment frictions between Japan and its major trading partners seem likely to continue. Japanese firms are increasingly leaders in world markets. Foreign firms and products, however, have a comparatively small share of the Japanese market as the volume of Japanese imports of manufactured goods, the share of intra-industry trade and the share of sales by foreign firms are unusually low. Instead of transforming its domestic economy to absorb more imports, Japan has generally preferred to restrict exports and increase its production offshore. The increase in Japanese FDI, however, is generating new policy responses.

In the early 1980s, a so-called voluntary restraint was placed on Japanese car exports to the United States. In response, Japanese automobile producers and their suppliers set up large assembly operations in the United States. While those operations may have enhanced the United States industrial base in a general sense, they did not alleviate the long-term pressures on the big-three American-owned producers of automobiles. Indeed, by creating a situation of excess capacity in the United States auto assembly and supply industries, they may have exacerbated them. In the early 1980s, United States autoproducers could seek relief by obtaining a voluntary restraint arrangement. Today, such are meaningless. The Bush and Clinton administrations have both pressured Japanese automakers to meet numerical targets for their purchases of auto-parts from "traditional" United States-owned parts suppliers. The emphasis thus shifted from not only managing trade, but also towards managing investment. In Europe, protection in autos has also expanded to limit not simply the sales of Japanese automobile exports, but also those Japanese brands produced in the European Union.

In the 1990s, managed investment of this sort could spread. Initially Japanese firms abroad would serve as the major targets. Over time, however, discriminatory measures could spread. The nationality of the headquarters of a TNC rather than the location of its activities could serve as the basis for discrimination. The widespread adoption of protectionist measures of this kind would seriously impede the flows of foreign investment. Investment wars could replace trade wars as the major threat to a liberal economic order.

One reason why the costs of trade protection have not been as high as they might have been has been the ability of firms to skip over barriers with foreign investment. If firms are denied this response, however, protection could become much more costly. Alternatively, if foreign-owned firms are denied market access unless they purchase parts from domestically-owned firms, this would put foreign-based suppliers at a competitive disadvantage. Increased protectionism in investment could undermine the relaxation of restrictions on trade.

Deep integration

It was argued earlier that globalization has induced major pressures towards deep integration that have been seen in efforts to broaden the scope of WTO and to increase harmonization of practices at the regional level. The final scenario, therefore, involves liberalization among participating countries, which would be more revolutionary than any of the trade-policy measures that have thus far been debated in the political arena. The principal argument for such an arrangement among like-minded countries, whether developed or developing, is that only limited progress towards liberalization can be expected multilaterally because WTO contains over 100 highly diverse economies. In addition, the internal and external barriers that remain will be even more difficult to negotiate away in the future. Only those countries truly interested in further liberalization and harmonization of their economies will be able to participate.

Arrangements for deep integration require more extensive political commitments than conventional GATT-type rules. Accordingly those arrangements can only be concluded on a selective basis. One approach might be sectoral. It may be easier to obtain agreement for common standards for capital requirements for banks than to obtain agreement on common safety standards for drugs. Another approach would begin with a small group of countries. Some industrialized countries, in particular, might join together with any like-minded advanced developing countries to begin negotiations for achieving a single unified market for goods, services and capital by the year 2000.

Some years ago, Gary Hufbauer called for an OECD Free Trade and Investment Area (FTIA). In addition to free trade, such an arrangement would guarantee rights of establishment and operation throughout the area for foreign owned firms. "It should (also) achieve goals such as the harmonization of technical standards, uniform protection of intellectual property, open access to government procurement, parallel corporate takeover legislation, similar competition policies and comparable corporate tax systems."[13]

While such an arrangement would be open to developing countries, they would not be granted access on a preferential basis. According to Hufbauer:[14]

> "An OECD FTIA would be open to countries that adhere to democratic traditions, pursue market-oriented economic policies and approach OECD levels of social welfare legislation...Such entry conditions are necessary to ensure that existing OECD members have a high political and economic comfort level with their new partners and *vice versa* and to provide strong impetus for the developing countries to measure up across a spectrum of social indicators."

It should be emphasized, however, that this type of arrangement need not produce identical economic and regulatory systems in all participating countries. Indeed, some competition among regulatory regimes could be beneficial. The difficult task would be to determine those issues on which harmonization would be essential and those in which differences must be tolerated (while guaranteeing national treatment and mutual recognition of technical standards). Ideally, participating countries would agree to common procedures for handling unfair trade allegations and safeguards measures, to rules encouraging innovation, to provisions for non-discriminatory government procurement, and to a supra-national entity to supplement national antitrust policies.

Implications for developing countries

WTO system. What would a continuation of the GATT regime imply for developing countries? If it operated according to the principles enshrined in its original articles and the pious statements contained in more recent declarations, the WTO system would provide a favourable environment for trade with developed countries, both for developing countries that followed liberal trade policies and for developing countries that did not.

The essence of GATT is non-discrimination achieved through most favoured nation (MFN) treatment. The strategy is to leverage the bargaining power of the strong into an open system for all. Overall, the developing countries have been beneficiaries of the liberalization of global markets in which GATT has played a major role. In particular, the MFN provisions have lowered barriers to their goods in major markets, making possible several spectacular success stories based on export-led growth.

Moreover, over the years, developing countries have claimed and received exemptions from GATT rules (Whalley 1990). By invoking article XII to safeguard their balance of payments or article XVIII, which allows promotion of infant industries, developing countries can, for the most part, permanently escape GATT disciplines. Thus the typical developing country is able to follow whatever trade policies it chooses at home while benefiting from liberalization in developed countries. In principle, developing countries are given a free ride.

Over the years developing countries have in some cases, actually obtained better than MFN treatment through GSP arrangements and from both the European Union and the United States, through regional schemes such as the Lome Convention and the Caribbean Basin Initiative. But these arrangements have been limited in scope. Indeed in several cases, developing countries have not received preferential treatment:

(i) GATT itself explicitly enshrined negative discrimination against developing countries in the Multi-Fibre Arrangement;

(ii) Article 24 of GATT, which allows customs unions and free trade areas, has been used mainly by developed countries — among OECD countries only Japan is not part of a free trade area;

(iii) In the codes of the Tokyo Round, GATT shifted towards conditional MFN. Only signatories to the Government Procurement Code, for example, rather than all GATT members, benefit from its rights;

(iv) The full array of GATT liberalization has not been extended to the same extent to sectors such as agriculture, which are vital to many developing countries;

(v) Tariff reductions have tended to be much lower in specific categories that are important to developing countries (hence the inclusion of tropical products as a distinct area in the Uruguay Round); and

(vi) The special treatment of developing countries has also meant much less progress in reducing developing country tariffs. The result has been less expansion in South-South trade, particularly in regions in which many developing countries are to be found.

The completion of the Uruguay Round offers important opportunities for developing country exports, particularly in vital areas such as agriculture, tropical products and textiles. There was a noteworthy shift in developing country negotiating strategy away from the earlier North-South schism aimed at achieving special and differential treatment. In numerous cases developing countries took positions reflecting their commodity interests rather than their developing country status.

At the same time, the round did not increase the preferential treatment of developing countries. While it gave those countries more time to make adjustments (particularly the least developed nations), eventually developing countries have to adhere to the same rules as their developed country counterparts. Moreover, developing countries agreed to increased inhibitions on national sovereignty in intellectual property, services and trade related investment measures. They could also face stricter anti-circumvention measures and national rules of origin in the dumping area.

Developing countries which are members of WTO will, as a result of the TRIMs Agreement, be more constrained in their ability to impose performance requirements on foreign investors. Countries adhering to the obligations of such an agreement foreswear the use of policies which even many developed countries continued to use in the late 1980s.

Regionalism. Developing countries are not all affected in the same way by either the open or the closed versions of these regional scenarios.

One important distinction is between those that join these groups and those that do not. For countries in Latin America and those with European associations, participation entails trading off reductions in national economic sovereignty in return for increased and more secure access to foreign markets. Inevitably, particularly for developing countries, participation in a regional arrangement will require increased conformity to the rules and norms of developed country partners. Some are skeptical whether this trade-off will be worth it. They argue, for example, that products from Mexico are still likely to be harassed by United States fair trade rules, while on the other hand, Americans are likely to dominate the Mexican economy. None the less, in principle, this is a trade-off which will be attractive for countries with the capacity to attract foreign investment, particularly in manufacturing. To be sure, a country such as Mexico can provide export processing zones for foreign investors — such as the *Maquilladoras*— without signing a free trade agreement with the United States. The free trade arrangement, however, offers greater visibility, credibility and permanence, and is therefore more likely to succeed.[15/]

As the regions broaden their scope, however, the value of access is likely to erode. Spain and Portugal, for example, will find increased competition from Eastern Europe as the European Union is extended. Similarly Mexico will experience increased competition from the rest of Central and Latin America in the North American market if NAFTA is extended. For countries which currently enjoy special access to regions under schemes such as the GSP, the Caribbean Basin Initiative and the Lome Convention, the value of these privileges are likely to erode as the regions broaden participation. If the regions become protectionist and already include some developing countries, the trade diversion could be significant.

A key issue for members of regional programmes concerns regional rules of origin. Developing country negotiators face some difficult choices. In particular, if the rules of origin are set too high, developing countries may not be able to succeed in attracting investment from third countries. If they are set too low, the benefits from investing within the region could be reduced.

In sum, therefore, considerable adjustment will be required for developing countries which become members of regional blocks. In particular, industries which have been protected will be forced to compete with those from developed country partners. And countries will be required to assume increased obligations in sectors such as services and in practices relating to industrial policies and intellectual property rights.

On the other hand, for those excluded, closed regional arrangements with restrictive rules-of-origin could lead to trade and investment diversion to developing country competitors who produce substitute products and are regional members. The open scenario in which GATT-type constraints are imposed on the regions, however, could increase trade opportunities for outsiders. If the regional arrangements such as those for Latin American countries are successful in making the current shifts towards multilateral liberalization permanent, they will open up increased opportunities for South-South trade. If they succeed in stimulating overall growth for their members, again those outside these regions will find increased export opportunities.

A final issue of concern to developing countries which are becoming sources of FDI relates to the national treatment of firms owned by nationals outside the region. If regions such as the European Union insist on reciprocity, firms from developing countries could face discriminatory barriers to their European investment.

Managed trade and investment. If managed trade is systemic and comprehensive, smaller participants without political clout will be adversely affected. If it is selective and partial, however, opportunities for unconstrained smaller newcomers could actually improve. Comprehensive managed trade arrangements subject trade and investment to political influences and are inherently discriminatory against newcomers, since quotas are generally distributed on the basis of historical market share. Some more powerful and more developed countries may manage to secure their trade, but many small developing countries would undoubtedly be hurt. Where managed trade has been selective, however, it has provided opportunities to newcomers either directly to penetrate markets in which one country has been constrained, or to attract investment from the constrained country with a view to providing an export platform. Thus, for example, in the late 1950s, United States imports from Hong Kong surged once Japanese textiles had been subject to a voluntary restraint arrangement. Similarly United States imports of televisions from Taiwan and the Republic of Korea — typically by Japanese-affiliated companies — surged when televisions from Japan were subject to an orderly marketing agreement in the late 1970s. None the less, restraints were later placed on televisions from those countries as well. Constraints on Japanese products could afford opportunities for developing countries which produce similar substitutes.

This does not mean, of course, that managed trade is not harmful to developing countries that are affected by it. The experience in textiles and footwear is illustrative.

If managed trade were to be applied at an aggregate level, it would probably also be applied selectively — that is, against countries such as Japan and perhaps other Asians that are perceived to be too different to play by normal trading rules. Frequently proponents of these approaches argue that there is no reason to apply managed trade to economies with similar institutional practices. To avoid being subjected to such arrangements, those countries will be subject to increased pressure to conform more closely to international norms. Even under a managed trade system, therefore, Asian countries will experience considerable pressure to harmonize or reconcile their institutional practices to avoid such treatment.

The selective application of local content requirements could damage countries which have become important sources for components. A more restrictive investment regime could therefore severely inhibit the use of direct-investment export led growth.

Deep integration. If the movement towards deep integration were confined to a rich man's club, it could prove detrimental to developing countries that were excluded. In particular, if such an arrangement made transactions within the club much easier than outside it, trade diversion could outweigh trade creation.

Much would depend, however, on the precise form of deep integration. Harmonization of regulatory and environmental standards — the "social dimension" could well raise production costs in some developed countries and thereby create new opportunities for countries where such regulations are more lenient. On the other hand, efficiency promoting harmonization might create new forms of competition.

If it were operated as an open arrangement, however, a deep integration arrangement would be unlikely to provide access on a preferential basis, that is, developing countries seeking to join would be obligated to meet the same conditions as other participants. Indeed, the essence of deep integration is precisely that major differences in institutional practices be reconciled. Thus movement towards this type of regime initiates strong pressures in developing countries to meet international norms.

As NAFTA has indicated, demands could well be raised on developing countries to raise safety, occupational and environmental standards. In addition, developing countries could find themselves subject to increasing constraints on the use of infant industry protection, subsidies, and other forms of industrial policy. In both the regulatory and industrial policy areas, there are dangers that the legitimate need for differentiated treatment could be undermined.

Conclusions

The United States, the major source country for FDI, has promoted a TRIMs Agreement at GATT. Those United States proposals have gained increasing acceptance as other industrial countries have become significant sources of FDI, and many developing countries have shifted to more open trade and investment regimes. Developing countries which are members of WTO are now more constrained in their ability to regulate foreign investment behaviour.

The Uruguay Round, however, reflected the agenda of the past, in which developing countries constrained rather than competed to attract foreign investment. The TRIMs Agreement did not resolve important issues relating to rights of establishment and common rules regarding competition policies, government procurement and corporate governance. In addition, liberalization of services was seriously incomplete.

The spread of regional arrangements will present both opportunities and threats to a liberal trade and investment order. If they entrench market-oriented institutions within their members, these arrangements could become building blocks for a more integrated global economy. On the other hand, extraregional trade and investment flows will be sensitive not only to any new trade barriers these arrangements may erect, but also to their rules of origin and rights of establishment. If formulated in a protectionist manner, these measures could divert trade and investment and damage outsiders.

Developing countries which join major regional arrangements will become more attractive locations for foreign investors. Their attraction will reflect assured access to export markets and more visible and credible hospitable policies towards foreign firms. As regions increase their membership, however, the value of preferences accorded by regional arrangements will decline. Developing countries excluded from such arrangements could face investment and trade diversion, particularly if regions move in a protectionist direction (see Katseli (1992)).

Over the past two decades, some of the negative effects of trade protection have been offset by the positive effects of FDI. There is now a danger, however, that investment conflicts could replace trade conflicts as a major threat to a liberal economic order. In particular, managed investment through local content and other performance requirements could be increased, if trade and investment friction continue between Japan and other major industrial countries. Proposals for new restraints on Japanese automobile companies could mark the start of a major shift towards a new form of protectionism which is based on firm ownership rather than location. Once discriminatory rules are enacted against Japanese firms these could be extended to firms from other nations. Moreover a rise in domestic local content requirements could restrict the opportunities of developing countries seeking to specialize in exporting parts and components.

An alternative response to globalization is to move towards harmonizing the treatment accorded foreign firms through agreements to achieve deeper economic integration. Firms from participating countries would enjoy rights of establishment and the ability to compete for government R&D and procurement programmes. In addition, there would be common rules relating to takeovers, competition policy and taxes. In some respects these arrangements could help realize long-standing calls by developing countries for enforcement of international rules relating to restrictive trade practices by multinational companies. On the other hand, they would also represent a direct challenge to another long-standing demand made by developing countries, increasing the scope of national sovereignty.

In sum, much uncertainty surrounds the development of the trading system during the 1990s. Nevertheless, it appears clear the major challenge facing the system will be dealing with the pressures induced by globalization which has made shallow integration arrangements inadequate. The response could take place through regional arrangements or in extensions of the WTO rules.[16/]

It is striking, however, that under each of the likely scenarios, the freedom of developing countries to enjoy special and differential treatment is likely to be eroded. To participate in new arrangements in WTO, regional integration schemes or deep integration arrangements, developing countries will inevitably have to conform increasingly to practices prevalent in developed countries. In some cases, meeting these requirements could aid their development and assist in attracting foreign investment and technology. In other cases, for example, the imposition of social and regulatory standards and constraints on infant industry policies, these requirements will be particularly controversial.

Notes

1. Obviously these scenarios are not mutually exclusive. In addition they are not comprehensive. In particular, bilateral and unilateral approaches have not been considered.
2. For a more complete analysis see Collins and Bosworth (1994).
3. To be sure, article III of GATT recognizes that "internal taxes ... laws, regulations, and requirements" can afford protection to domestic production. It allows members to bring disputes on the grounds that internal measures nullify or impair negotiated trade concessions. However, the effectiveness of dispute settlements is questionable and no effort is made to remove such barriers prior to their being challenged.
4. For a more complete discussion, see Graham and Krugman (1990) and Mutti (1991).
5. None the less, the services agreement itself was limited, excluding important sectors for future negotiation and providing market access and national treatment not as general obligations, but only to scheduled sectors and modes of supply. See Sauve (1994) for a more complete discussion.
6. There are also other areas of relevance to the global competition for investment that GATT will be considering outside of the TRIMs negotiations. These include (i) so-called anti-circumvention provisions, which involve the definitions of "domestic" products and firms when it comes to the application of anti-dumping provisions and eligibility for government procurement, and (ii) disciplines on subsidies.
7. See Montagnon (1990), p. 85.
8. For an historical account, see Kindleberger (1986), p. 280.
9. See Lawrence Krause (1991).
10. For a more complete discussion, see Gestrin and Rugman (1994).
11. See Henry Kissinger and Cyrus Vance (1988).
12. See, for example, Laura Tyson (1990).
13. Gary C. Hufbauer (1989), p. 152.
14. Ibid., p. 150.
15. Some have pointed to Mexico's financial crisis in late 1994 as indicating a failure of NAFTA. In fact, the opposite is true. As a result of NAFTA, there was a spectacular success in attracting foreign investment to Mexico. The problem was that Mexico unwisely used the opportunity provided by such inflows to maintain an

overvalued currency. The ability to attract foreign investment may be a necessary condition for growth, but it is not sufficient. Prudent macroeconomic policy management is also required.

16. For a discussion of the challenge of deeper integration, see Krueger (1995).

References

Anderson, Thomas (1990). Direct foreign investment and local content rules in the European Community. IUI Working Paper No. 288, Stockholm, Sweden.

Bale, Harvey E. Jr. (1984). Trade policy aspects on international direct investment policies. In Robert E. Baldwin (ed.), *Recent Issues and Initiatives in U.S. Trade Policy*, National Bureau of Economic Research Conference Report. Cambridge, Massachusetts: NBER, 1984, pp. 67-100.

Bora, Bijit and Edward M. Graham (1994). *Non-binding Investment Principles in APEC*. Asia Foundation, Center for Pacific Affairs, Report No. 17, December.

Bhagwati, Jagdish (1991). *The World Trading System at Risk*, Princeton, New Jeresy: Princeton University, pp. 58-80.

Belous, Richard S. and Rebecca S. Hartley (eds.) (1990). *The Growth of Regional Trading Blocs in the Global Economy*. Washington, D.C.: National Planning Association, 1990.

Collins, Susan M. and Barry P. Bosworth (1994). *The New GATT*. Washington, D.C.: Brookings Institution.

Dell, Sidney (1990). *The United Nations and International Business*. Durham, North Carolina and London: Duke University Press.

Dornbusch, Rudiger (1991). Policy options for freer trade: The case for bilateralism. In Robert Z. Lawrence and Charles L. Schultze (eds.), *An American Trade Strategy: Options for the 1990s*. Washington, D.C.: Brookings Institution.

Gee San (1991). Technology investment and trade under economic globalization: The case of Taiwan. In OECD, *Trade, Investment and Technology in the 1990s*. Paris: OECD.

Gestrin, Michael R. and Alan M. Rugman (1994). The NAFTA and foreign direct investment, *Transnational Corporations*, vol. 3, No. 1, February.

Gilchrist, Joseph and David Deacon (1990). Curbing subsidies. In Peter Montagnon (ed.), *European Competition Policy*. New York: Council on Foreign Relations Press, pp. 31-51.

Graham, Edward M. (1990). Multilateral discipline on foreign direct investment: Beyond the TRIMs exercise in the Uruguay Round. In Robert E. Baldwin and J. David Richardson (eds.), *The Uruguay Round and Beyond: Problems and Prospects*. Cambridge, National Bureau of Economic Research, 1991.

_____ and Paul R. Krugman (1990). TRIMs in the Uruguay Round. In Schott (1990a).

Greenaway, David (1990). Trade related investment measures: Political economy aspects and issues for GATT. *World Economy* (December), no. 12, pp. 367 - 385.

Guisinger, Stephen (1987). Investment related to trade. In J. Michael Finger and Andrezej Olechowski (eds.). *The Uruguay Round: A Handbook on the Multilateral Trade Negotiations*. Washington, D.C.: World Bank, pp. 217-226.

Hufbauer, Gary C. (1989). Background Paper. In *The Free Trade Debate: Reports of the Twentieth Century Fund Task Force on the Future of American Trade Policy*, New York: Priority Press Publications.

Katseli, L. T. (1992). *Foreign Direct Investment and Trade Interlinkages in Developing Countries*. United Nations publication, Sales No. E.93.II.A.12).

Kindleberger, Charles (1986). *The World in Depression 1929-1939*. University of California Press.

Kissinger, Henry and Cyrus Vance (1988). Bipartisan objectives for american foreign policy. *Foreign Affairs*, vol. 66 (Summer 1988), No. 5, pp. 899-921.

Krause, Lawrence (1991). Can the Pacific save U.S.- Japanese economic relations?. San Diego, California: University of California. (mimeo).

Kreinen, Mordechai, E. (1988). How closed is Japan's market? Additional evidence. *World Economy*, no. 11, pp. 529-542.

_____ and Michael G. Plummer (1991). Effects of economic integration in industrial countries on ASEAN and the Asian NIEs. Hawaii: East-West Center. (mimeo).

Krueger, Anne O. (1995). *Trade Policies and Developing Nations*. Washington, D.C.: Brookings Institution.

Lawrence, Robert Z. (1990). An analysis of Japanese trade with developing countries. UNCTAD Review, No. 3, UNCTAD/SGO/6 (United Nations publication, Sales No. E.91.II.D.21), pp. 31-52.

_____ (1991a). Scenarios for the World Trading System and their Implications for Developing Countries. *OECD Development Centre*, Technical Papers No. 47. Paper prepared for the Research Programme on Globalization and Regionalization. November.

_____ (1991b). Futures for the World Trading System and Their Implications for Developing Countries. Paper prepared for UNCTAD to be published in *Pensamiento IberAmericano* (forthcoming).

McCulloch, Rachel (1990). Investment policies in the GATT. *World Economy*, December, pp. 541-553.

Maskus Keith E. and Denise R. Eby (1990). Developing new rules and disciplines on trade-related investment measures. *World Economy* (December), pp 523 - 540.

Mutti, John. TRIMs, policy change, and the role of GATT. Paper presented to the Conference on Analytical and Negotiating Issues in the International Trading System, University of Michigan, 31 October 1991.

Sauve, Pierre (1994). A first look at investment in the Final Act of the Uruguay Round. *Journal of World Trade*, vol. 28, No. 5, p. 5.

Schott, Jeffrey (ed.) (1989). *Free Trade Areas and U.S. Trade Policy*. Washington, D.C.: Institute for International Economics.

_____ (1990a) *Completing the Uruguay Round: A Results-Oriented Approach to the GATT Trade Negotiations*. Washington, D.C.: Institute for International Economics.

_____ (1990b). *The Global Trade Negotiations: What Can Be Achieved?*. Washington, D.C.: Institute for International Economics.

Stoeckel, Andrew, David Pearce and Gary Banks (1990). *Western Trade Blocs: Game Set or Match for Asia-Pacific and the World Economy*. Canberra, Australia: Centre for International Economics.

Takeuchi, Kenji (1990). Japanese foreign direct investment: A promoter of Japanese imports from developing economies? Washington, D.C.: The World Bank (May).

Tyson, Laura (1990). Managed trade: Making the best of second best. In Robert Z. Lawrence and Charles L. Schultze (eds.), *An American Trade Strategy: Options for the 1990s*. Washington, D.C.: Brookings Institution, pp. 142-194.

United Nations Centre on Transnational Corporations (1988). *The United Nations Code of Conduct on Transnational Corporations*. London:Dordrecht and Boston, Massachusetts: Graham and Trotman.

Whalley, John (1990). Non-discriminatory discrimination: Special and differential treatment under the GATT for developing countries. *Economic Journal*, 100 (December), pp. 1318-1328.

Part II
Regional perspectives

3

Investment dynamism in Asian developing countries

Linda Y.C. Lim and Nathaniel S. Siddall

Introduction

The surge of interest by developing countries serving as host to foreign direct investment (FDI) is partly sparked by the successful experience of Asian developing countries, which have increased their absolute and relative share of FDI since the 1980s. The member countries of the Association of South-East Asian Nations (ASEAN) have attracted a large share of FDI, and are propelling themselves into the ranks of newly-industrialized economies. Following in their footsteps now are the newly emerging former socialist economies of South-East Asia, and China and India, which have until recently remained more isolated from international investment linkages.

Among the member countries of ASEAN, tiny Singapore and Malaysia rank with the much larger Mexico and Brazil as the largest cumulative FDI recipients among developing countries. Thailand and Indonesia have attracted unprecedentedly large flows, which have led both to experience the fastest economic growth in their history. Even the Philippines, the regional grouping's weakest economy, has received respectable amounts of new FDI.

Elsewhere in South-East Asia, Viet Nam has received a surge in FDI in recent years and is perceived by Japanese transnational corporations to be the second most attractive host economy after China. Viet Nam may well provide a test of how fast a foreign-investment-led development strategy can turn a very poor economy around.

Since the beginning of its "open door" policy in the late 1970s, China has experienced average annual growth of GDP of nearly 10 per cent, has emerged as a major exporting nation, and has received substantial foreign investment in selected sectors. Indeed, since 1990, China has attracted more inbound direct investment than any other developing country (UNCTAD 1994). The other sleeping giant of Asia has also substantially liberalized a decades-old policy of severe restrictions and controls on FDI, and the portents for India to join the ranks of rapidly growing Asian FDI hosts in the second half of the 1990s are promising.

The present chapter assesses the recent and likely future FDI experiences of those countries and draws broad implications for other countries. In particular, the ASEAN experience may be suggestive of possible future developments in China, India, Indochina, and, perhaps, other developing countries as well.

Regional trends[1]

ASEAN

Collectively, the six ASEAN countries — Singapore, oil-rich Brunei, and the second-tier newly-industrializing economies (NIEs) of Malaysia, Indonesia, the Philippines and Thailand (ASEAN-4) — comprise the world's fastest-growing regional economy, with a total population of over 330 million. Their relative political and macroeconomic stability and long period of healthy economic growth (5 per cent to 10 per cent per annum since 1965), the Philippines being a partial exception, have long put them ahead of most other developing countries as favoured host locations for FDI. Add to this their large potential market size, rich natural resources, established export base and relatively liberal FDI policies, and it is not surprising that they have received a disproportionate share of FDI going to developing countries. What is of interest here is the sudden voluminous increase in inward FDI flows to the region since the late 1980s, at the very time when other developing countries have been competing more intensely, but less successfully, for such investment.

Like many other developing countries, the ASEAN countries were adversely affected by the world-wide commodity price slump of the early to-mid-1980s, which created balance of payments and external debt repayment problems for some of them and precipitated a region-wide recession or growth slow-down in 1985-1986. Domestic policy adjustments to this externally-induced problem were swiftly and effectively undertaken (IMF and BNM, 1990; Timberman, 1992; MacIntyre and Jayasuriya, 1992). They included the depreciation or devaluation of exchange rates, trade and investment liberalization to attract new domestic as well as foreign investment and to promote non-traditional (mainly manufactured) exports, privatization of state enterprises to reduce government budget deficits and promote efficiency, and deregulation and the encouragement of private enterprise (Ng and Wagner, 1993).

Such conventional domestic economic reforms no doubt made these countries more attractive locations for FDI. But they had not been unattractive locations before, and it is doubtful that the widely-described "surge" of FDI which followed immediately from late 1986 on was entirely or even primarily due to the domestic reforms. Rather, the reforms — particularly the liberalization of investment rules to allow more 100-per-cent-foreign-owned investments — facilitated an influx of FDI.

The main reason for the sharp increase in inward FDI directed to the ASEAN countries in the second half of the 1980s and the early 1990s was the change in international competitiveness in their favour, which resulted from the world-wide currency realignment of 1985. The sharp appreciation (up to 40 per cent) of first, the Japanese yen, and then the New Taiwan dollar, the won of the Republic of Korea and the Singapore dollar against the United States dollar, reduced the international competitiveness of export-oriented manufacturing industry in the North-East Asian countries. This, together with sharply rising labour costs and growing domestic labour shortages in North-East Asia and Singapore, forced a massive relocation, especially of labour-intensive production, to lower-cost neighbouring countries whose currencies had depreciated with or against the United States dollar. This relocation was reinforced by other coincident factors such as anticipated or actual increased protectionism against North-East Asian exporters in world markets, the

United States withdrawal of the East Asian NIEs' (Republic of Korea, Taiwan Province of China, Hong Kong and Singapore) eligibility for GSP trade privileges, and Hong Kong's fears — especially after the 1989 Tienanmen Square unrest in China — for its political and economic future following the scheduled reunification with China in 1997.

The ASEAN countries were favoured as host locations over other developing countries which had experienced similar currency depreciations and liberal domestic reforms because of their stronger underlying economies, greater political stability, successful hosting of previous FDI, and their geographical proximity and cultural similarity to North-East Asian source countries. The strong complementarities between high-wage, labour-scarce, resource-poor, technology-rich, capital-surplus developed countries (Japan and the NIEs) with neighbouring low-wage, labour-abundant, resource-rich and technology-poor developing countries (the ASEAN-4) generated the massive intraregional FDI flows observed. Between 1986 and 1990, other Asian countries accounted more than twice the value of inward FDI received by the ASEAN-4, with inflows from the four NIEs, and from the Overseas Chinese NIEs (Taiwan Province of China, Hong Kong and Singapore) alone exceeding the inflows from Japan. Much of the new investment was in 100 per cent foreign-owned ventures in labour-intensive export manufacturing industries, but there were also investments in high-tech and capital-intensive projects, as well as in the services sector.

The pattern of FDI of the late 1980s thus involved several new features:

(a) The new foreign investments were dominated by neighbouring Asian source countries, especially NIEs, rather than by distant Western developed countries;

(b) They were mostly in manufacturing for export to world markets, rather than in import-substituting industry or raw material extraction and processing;

(c) Many of the new investors were small and medium-size companies, and supplier industries, investing abroad for the first time, as compared with the giant final-product transnationals which had previously dominated FDI in the region;

(d) More of the investments were 100 per cent foreign-owned rather than foreign-local joint ventures;

(e) The annual volume of the new foreign investments was much larger than in the past, both in absolute terms and in relation to local investments and to the domestic economy, especially in the manufacturing sector.

FDI has played a major, if not dominant, role in the high GDP and export growth rates experienced by the ASEAN countries during this period.

Notwithstanding a continued increase in FDI to the ASEAN-4 countries in the 1990s, rapid internal economic growth has led to serious infrastructural bottlenecks in transportation and communications, rising inflation, and to extreme shortages of skilled and even unskilled labour. Urban congestion and widespread industrial pollution have added to the actual and perceived costs of growth fuelled by high rates of industrial FDI. As these countries' ability to absorb continued, large amounts of new FDI has diminished, and so has some of their enthusiasm, especially for low-technology, labour-intensive projects. Malaysia has stated that it will no longer entertain investment in labour-intensive sectors that do not contribute to technology development, and even Indonesia has made similar pronouncements for its Riau industrial free trade zone near Singapore. Some recent foreign investors, especially smaller investors from the NIEs, may feel threatened by the prospect of less liberal investment incentives. Now beset by rising local costs and labour shortages, as well as the normal difficulties of operating in a new environment, they have lost some of their enthusiasm for Malaysia and Thailand as host locations.

In addition, Asian NIE source countries may be reaching the end of a structural transition period that prompted their large investment outflows of the late 1980s in search of lower-cost overseas production locations. The first (easy and obvious) stage of this major relocation may have largely been completed, though as wage rates continue to increase in the NIEs, and labour quality continues to improve in the ASEAN host countries, the latter's cost advantages are likely to continue and to affect additional industries. But ASEAN now has to contend with strong competition from China for the relocation of further labour-intensive manufacturing from the NIEs, particularly from Hong Kong and Taiwan Province of China.

Despite the above (country) factors, we expect the rest of the present decade to see a continued substantial flow of FDI to the ASEAN region.

Those countries will continue to receive manufacturing production relocated from Japan and the East Asian NIEs. Except in a few sectors, only a small fraction (less than 12 per cent) of Japanese corporations' manufacturing production has been relocated abroad thus far — much less than is typical for more mature United States and European transnationals. With the continuing globalization of Japanese corporations, trade and investment liberalization in host countries, and shifts in comparative advantage between nations, more Japanese manufacturing production is likely to move out of high-cost, congested and extremely labour-short Japan — especially in simpler technology, labour-intensive lines, and especially to South-East Asia. And as the manufacturing sectors of increasingly high-wage, labour-scarce Republic of Korea, Taiwan Province of China, Hong Kong and Singapore continue to upgrade into more capital- and technology-intensive lines, more of their labour-intensive production will also move to South-East Asia and China. Over time, this offshore move from North-East Asia to South-East Asia will be accelerated by enhanced technological capacity, increased manufacturing experience, and improved infrastructure in the potential host countries, and will include increasingly capital-intensive and technologically sophisticated products and processes.

In the latter 1990s, more of this offshore production will be directed to serving the South-East Asian regional host markets, the markets of their neighbouring developing economies, and Japanese and NIE home markets, as compared with the third country Western markets served by much of the FDI flows of the 1980s. This is because the ASEAN countries are likely to continue being the world's most rapidly-growing regional economy throughout the 1990s, while the Chinese and eventually Indian consumer markets will become more accessible. Already inward FDI in the South-East Asia region, especially by Japanese corporations, is increasingly motivated by the large and rapidly-growing regional market — which is the fastest-growing in the world in such industries as automobiles, electronics, telecommunications and construction.

Other South-East Asian countries

Relatively new host countries are the emerging socialist economies of Indochina, most notably Viet Nam and Myanmar. Observing the fortunes of other South-East Asian countries, Viet Nam has wholeheartedly embraced the concept of development-through-foreign-investment. It has consequently enacted a liberal legal framework for FDI. By the end of 1994 it had licensed a total of over $10 billion in FDI. Firms from Taiwan Province of China and Hong Kong are the largest investors so far. As relations with the United States have been largely normalized, however, Japanese and United States' investment are likely to pick up.

Intraregional trade and investment have so far been relatively low among South-East Asian countries, largely because they tend to have similar comparative advantages and therefore there are relatively few gains from trade (Lim, 1993a). The increased integration of non-ASEAN members into the regional economy, however, have initiated a change. For example, Viet Nam's biggest trade partner is Singapore, with combined imports and exports of $868 million in 1991 (a 780 per cent increase over 1989). Singapore is also likely to be Viet Nam's major provider of commercial and financial services. Meanwhile, Malaysia has already become the fourth largest investor in Viet Nam, as rapid wage and land price increases at home have caused its three largest plantation groups to invest in edible oil and rubber growing and processing there (Lim, 1993b). Further, Thailand is the major foreign investor in Cambodia, Laos and Myanmar.

China

When China began to experiment with carefully selected liberalization and market incentives in the late 1970s, it opened the door to a flow of foreign investment that has transformed some parts of its economy. A large part of the investment has been in labour-intensive export industries, particularly the very successful (though quota-restrained) textile industry. This export industry is concentrated along the southern coast, and much of the foreign investment is located in Special Economic Zones (SEZs). Roughly $90 billion of FDI accumulated in China between 1981 and 1994 (UNCTAD 1995). During that time, the Pearl River Delta area, where FDI is most heavily concentrated, has experienced annual GDP growth rates averaging more than 15 per cent, and China's exports have increased fourfold. In many respects the sub-economy of Guandong Province (with a population of 65 million) has become like one of the ASEAN-4 countries.

In China, as in ASEAN, the largest share of investment comes from other Asian countries. More than half the foreign investment in China is made by Hong Kong firms, many of which have simply crossed a border into a SEZ. It is estimated that upwards of 18,000 Hong Kong firms have relocated in Guandong Province, where they employ between 2 million and 3 million workers. Hong Kong has played an important role as a gateway to China, similar to the role played by Singapore in ASEAN. Many of the Hong Kong-based investors have links themselves with foreign investors from other countries. In particular, many Hong Kong investments in China (an estimated $2 to 3 billion worth) originate in Taiwan Province, although this is not officially recorded. Japanese investment is perhaps 5 to 10 per cent of the total, and has increased during the 1980s, as has investment from the Republic of Korea. Though still a small fraction of total investment in China, FDI from Overseas Chinese firms in Singapore and elsewhere in ASEAN has increased rapidly.

In 1993, China became the second largest FDI recipient in the world following the United States, and in the period from 1991 to 1994 drew in $76.8 billion of new investment, equivalent to over five times the investment in the preceding five years. In 1994, China accounted for 41.2 per cent of the FDI flowing to developing countries (UNCTAD 1995).

Most of the new investment in China continues to be in labour-intensive export industries, fuelling a continuing export boom in Guandong Province and other south-eastern coastal provinces that resembles the 1980s ASEAN experience. In 1993, foreign affiliates in China were estimated to have accounted for 28 per cent of all national exports, compared to 13 per cent in 1990 (UNCTAD 1994). But as in ASEAN, new foreign investments increasingly targeted to the growing Chinese domestic market. These are more complicated undertakings. The Government of China is also facilitating market-oriented FDI by easing restrictions on foreign retail activities. Other regions of China are eager to share in the success of the southern SEZs, and investment is being solicited in Beijing, along the Yangzi River and elsewhere. The central Government is also granting more autonomy to local provincial administrations, allowing them to develop some investment incentives on their own.

Meanwhile, Taiwan Province is liberalizing its trade and investment policy towards the mainland, and increased regional links are inevitable in the long run. The Taiwan legislature has approved measures to improve trade relations, and securities industry reforms are expected which will facilitate financial linkages. In a near future it is likely that Taiwan Province banks will operate branches in the mainland, joint ventures will be listed on mainland stock exchanges, and Taiwan Province investment firms will trade Chinese stocks for Taiwanese clients. These changes are likely to reduce the role of Hong Kong as a gateway to China. In any event, Hong Kong's identity as an independent economy is destined to diminish in 1997. The merger may benefit both economies, given the strength of investment from and in China. China is also affected by its links with Overseas Chinese business throughout South-East Asia. As firms in this region mature and internationalize, they too are likely to seek opportunities in the China-Hong Kong conglomeration.

At the same time, large *chaebol* (conglomerates) in the Republic of Korea in the process of restructuring are interested in combining their technological and administrative strengths with China's resources and labour, and economic linkages between the two countries are being facilitated by new political developments as well. Diplomatic relations were established in 1992. Of 129 overseas investment projects of the Republic of Korea registered in 1992, the great majority were directed to China. This is a natural corollary to the rapid increase in trade between the two nations that occurred after they established direct shipping links in 1988.

Increased levels of foreign investment stock would seem ultimately inevitable in China's huge, rapidly-growing, increasingly open economy with its vast labour supply and a GDP already estimated by the World Bank as the third largest in the world, and projected to surpass the United States as the world's largest by the year 2010. Currently, FDI in China is affected largely by domestic macroeconomic and political variables. China has already gone through several cycles of inflation and external imbalances, which may be a feature of its transition from a planned economy, and further integration into the world economy may well be punctuated by periodic credit and currency crises. There is also some uncertainty about the process of political succession as China's aging leaders are replaced.

Unlike the ASEAN countries, China is a communist country and is considered a significant, even leading, actor in the international community. Its relations with the West, especially the United States, are often adversarial (for example, over such matters as intellectual property rights, human rights, labour practices, domestic market access and overseas arms sales). Bilateral trade relations, international loans and investment, and China's future WTO membership may be affected. Loss of access to United States markets for any reason would seriously undermine China's export-led development and reduce its attractiveness to FDI.

India

FDI flows into India throughout the 1980s were relatively insignificant, totalling perhaps not much over $1 billion. India has always required an extensive review and approval process for all investments, and foreign investors were restricted to minority ownership, barred entirely from many industries, and subject to a labyrinth of regulations on currency transactions, distribution practices, and details such as the use of foreign brand names. During the late 1980s under Rajiv Gandhi, a push was made to import new technology, but restraints on transnational corporations did not significantly ease.

In 1991, Prime Minister Narasimha Rao initiated a series of sweeping reforms which may ultimately bring India into the global economy, facilitate large amounts of new international commerce, and open opportunities for foreign investment. The results can already be seen in a dramatic increase in both approved and actual direct investment flows into India. In 1988, the FDI stock in India was $1,179 million, by 1994 it had risen to $2,531 million, and inflows rose from $91 million in 1988 to $300 million in 1994 (UNCTAD 1995).

The hope is that new foreign investment in India will boost exports and speed technological advances, as it has in ASEAN and China. In some ways the Indian economy is well positioned to attract and benefit from FDI. It has a large pool of well-educated and English-speaking labour, including the world's third largest population of technically-trained college graduates. But India is lacking in important infrastructure and institutions. External transportation costs, poor port facilities, and distance from potential markets reduce its attractiveness as an export platform, despite low labour costs. High start-up costs make it difficult for small firms to relocate in India, as they have done in the ASEAN-4 and China's SEZs. India has developed seven export processing zones, where foreign investors receive tax incentives and are allowed duty-free imports, and there is a proposal to develop Bombay and Goa into free ports. When adequate infrastructure is established, these locations could serve as host to a labour-intensive, export-oriented sub-economy, like that of China's southern coast.

The sources of FDI are quite different in the Indian subcontinent. India, like Pakistan, has experienced much less of the small-enterprise, labour-intensive, Asian-source FDI that has been characteristic in other Asian developing countries, although it has gained a number of transplant textile operations from Hong Kong. Its investment is mostly from the West — including a substantial, and apparently increasing amount from the United States (perhaps 20 to 40 per cent of the total). This reflects a traditional North-South economic pattern resulting from a number of historical circumstances, and also is a direct heritage of colonialism in the case of many large British firms. It is an "older" style of FDI, one that was common in South-East Asia barely a generation ago.

In the near term, FDI in India — unlike in ASEAN and China — may be dominated by large Western firms, experienced transnationals which can assume risk and deal with political problems, and have the administrative capability to manage joint ventures and penetrate the Indian bureaucracy.

Transnationals are investing in India today largely for access to its long-protected, but large and growing domestic consumer market. There is a middle-class population of perhaps 100 million earning incomes equal or above those earned in Southern Europe, who can make substantial purchases of modern consumer products. Firms such as Procter and Gamble or Nestlé, Coca-Cola and Colgate Palmolive may have great success servicing India's middle-class consumers, since they will be competing with domestic firms that have become inefficient and backward behind protectionist barriers. The adjustment may be difficult for local business, but this will be the first step in the process of developing a competitive manufacturing sector, with linkages to domestic distributors and suppliers, and eventual export capabilities.

Intraregional

Throughout developing Asia, several factors are operating to increase the importance of intraregional trade and investment. In addition to the rapidly growing consumer markets in ASEAN and southern China, there are potential new markets in Viet Nam, India and the rest of China. This has created new intraregional trade flows, such as the rapidly growing exports from ASEAN countries to China (some of which are products manufactured by Japanese and other foreign affiliates). This sets the stage for later intraregional investment. Furthermore, the possibility of planning investment strategies for the region as a whole also increases the interest of extra-regional investors. This is especially true when single country markets are relatively small, and sophisticated and capital-intensive consumer products are involved.

An ASEAN Free Trade Area will increase inward FDI as it accelerates ongoing market-led integration (Lim, 1992), given that the global strategy of multinational firms increasingly dictates a corporate presence as "insiders" in all major regional markets. Within ASEAN, an intraregional relocation of industry in line with individual nations' comparative advantages is already being promoted through the development of subregional "growth triangles" pioneered by Singapore in partnership with the contiguous States of neighbouring Indonesia and Malaysia (Lim, 1993a). Further north, "triangular" trade and investment linkages already exist among Taiwan Province, Hong Kong and south-eastern China. Throughout the East Asian region outside of Japan and the Republic of Korea, the burgeoning cross-regional investments of Overseas Chinese businesses are creating an increasingly complex and interlocking web of intraregional FDI. Many non-Asian transnationals are also making multiple linked investments in different ASEAN countries, generating trade and capital flows between them.

Underlying factors

International factors. Most foreign direct investment takes place between industrialized economies, and FDI in developing countries is heavily concentrated in the most industrialized of these countries. In the 1980s, a "Triad" pattern emerged, in which Japan, the European Union and the United States were major sources and recipients of FDI to and from each other. At the same time, there emerged a clear regional pattern, in which a single Triad member was the major source of FDI for a number of developing countries in a distinct geographical area (its economic "cluster"). In most of Asia, Japan is the dominant Triad investor, having increased both the proportion of its total overseas investment directed towards developing Asian host countries, and its share of their inward FDI.

Japan's regional dominance, however, is not complete or unchallenged. Traditional Western source countries remain well-represented in the region (especially taken as a group, and in cumulative FDI totals) and, since the late 1980s, the East Asian NIEs have emerged as major sources of FDI as well — in some years and some host countries, both singly and as a group actually overtaking Japan as the largest foreign investor. In the longer term, China may be poised to challenge Japan's economic as well as political influence in the rest of East and South-East Asia. In part, because of the distaste of all these countries for Japanese hegemony, and some lingering suspicions of each other, they continue vigorously to encourage Western economic participation, as well as to compete with Japan itself. Thus Western economic and political influence in Asian developing countries remains strong, and has the capacity to affect significantly intra-Asian trade and investment linkages, as the tensions in the United States-China relationship suggest. For although the United States is overshadowed as a foreign investor in the region, it is still the largest trade partner of most of the countries.

Still, diversification of trade and investment sources away from Japan and the West served Asian developing countries well as these "Triad" nations plunged into recession in the early 1990s. Most Asian countries outside Japan managed to maintain economic growth at only slightly below the high rates they enjoyed since the late 1980s, expanding trade and investment with each other. Faced with stagnant or declining markets at home, some companies from Triad nations even increased their investments in the rapidly-growing markets of Asian developing countries.

If Asian developing host countries are now less affected by macroeconomic conditions in the traditional Triad source countries of FDI than they have been in the past, they may become more affected by two other international developments — the growing regionalization of the world economy, and the emergence of new developing-country markets and competitors for FDI. These emerging market economies may offer the prospect of new export markets for Asian-based manufacturing industry, thereby attracting new FDI to Asian developing countries. But they are also potentially competitive new host locations for FDI that might otherwise go to the Asian countries, including FDI from Asian companies themselves. Pioneering investors from non-Japanese Asian countries have already ventured to these new investment locations, primarily for access to resources and anticipated markets, rather than for labour, which is still most abundant, cheap and efficient within East Asia itself. Examples include mining and consumer electronics investments from the Republic of Korea in Russia, Kazakhstan and Uzbekistan, Taiwanese consumer electronics ventures in the former Eastern Germany (to serve the European Union market); and manufacturing investments from the Republic of Korea and Taiwan in Mexico (NAFTA-inspired).

Growing economic regionalization, particularly the deepening of European Union integration and the emergence of a North American Free Trade Area, has similar potentially opposing effects on FDI in Asian developing countries. On the one hand, regional economic blocs in Europe and North America may divert some FDI from Asian developing countries into these bloc markets. On the other hand, their emergence may stimulate further regional integration of the much larger and more dynamic potential Asian bloc, thereby encouraging more "defensive" FDI there, not only from Japan and NIEs, but also from Western firms fearful of being shut out of the world's largest and most rapidly-growing regional market.

The potential for investment diversion away from Asian developing countries, if it exists, is unlikely seriously to diminish anticipated expanded FDI flows to those countries. Japanese companies are likely to continue their strategic investments in Europe and North America, especially where necessary to forestall protectionism. But the very large 1980s flows of Japanese FDI to other Triad locations have already tapered off, and may have been in part a temporary phenomenon. Japanese investment in non-Asian developing countries is likely to be relatively limited and to take place only in fairly special circumstances; in general, Asian locations are still the most attractive in terms of both costs and markets.

Asian exporters may even gain from European Union integration and from NAFTA if these regionalization efforts stimulate growth in their member economies and make it easier to serve previously segmented multiple markets, thereby increasing export-oriented FDI in Asia. If trade barriers to non-members increase and Asian exporters respond by replacing exports with FDI in the new regional bloc markets, this would divert some FDI and exports away from Asian countries. In particular, labour-intensive Asian exporters are concerned that NAFTA will make low-wage Mexico a more competitive source of imports for the United States, their major export market, and thus for export-oriented FDI. At the same time, however, proposed high local-content requirements for free trade within NAFTA in industries like textiles, electronics and automobiles, reduces the likelihood that Asian manufacturers of those products will relocate production there. Even if they do, much if not most of this relocated production is likely to be from the home rather than competitive Asian host countries of Asian FDI. Another alternative is that Asian manufacturers facing restrictions in the North American market will concentrate their investments and activities even more in developing Asian countries instead, thus leading to an increase in intra-Asian FDI. In any event, both trade and investment diversion as a consequence of economic regionalization elsewhere will be outweighed by the effects of Asia's own rapid market growth, which will lead to increased intraregional trade and investment flows that more than compensate for reductions in extra-regional flows.

The international factors leading to an expectation of increased FDI flows to Asian developing countries in the 1990s include a shift in the structure of the world economy towards service industries; differentiated, specialized and high value-added products; and other sectors in which direct trade is not the most efficient way to serve foreign markets. International economic integration therefore (as shown in chapter 1) increasingly takes the form of direct investment and strategic alliances. As the industries and markets of Asia continue to grow and develop, they will attract and initiate more TNC activities.

Regional factors. In addition to those international factors, a number of regional factors add to the expectation that FDI in Asian developing countries will increase in the coming years. Patterns of FDI in Asia have long had a regional component, with investment following a kind of cascade pattern in which "Triad" (first Western, then Japanese) firms have poured investment into welcoming small pools such as Hong Kong and Singapore, which have then overflowed and spilled out into the surrounding regions. Brand names, distribution channels and corporate structures reflect those linkages that have developed over the years, such that multinational FDI takes place in the context of a regional network (often first established in colonial times), rather than a simple home country-host country transaction. Overseas Chinese business networks further transcend national borders throughout East and South-East Asia.

Over the next years, comparative advantage will most certainly propel more regional FDI in Asia. Extreme labour shortages, rapidly rising wages, growing affluence, increased local market demand, and trade and investment liberalization in the primary Asian source countries (Japan and NIEs) will continue to stimulate industrial relocation to their developing Asian neighbours. In the ASEAN region, moves towards subregional economic integration ("growth triangles") and an ASEAN free trade area (AFTA) will also encourage more inward and intraregional FDI, including intra-ASEAN flows. Regional integration attempts beyond AFTA include Malaysia's proposal for an East Asia Economic Caucus (EAEC) that would link ASEAN with Japan, China and NIEs, and the trans-Pacific Asia-Pacific Economic Cooperation forum, which adds Australia, New Zealand, Canada and the United States to the group. Neither of these initiatives, which are defensive reactions to NAFTA and European Union integration respectively, is currently projected to take hold seriously in the 1990s, though APEC has established a small secretariat in Singapore. Malaysia has also called for accelerated ASEAN membership for the socialist South-East Asian countries, whose post-Cold War emergence into the regional and world economies will add to inward and intraregional FDI flows.

The existence throughout East and South-East Asia of an active, entrepreneurial Overseas Chinese capitalist class which has traditionally invested across national boundaries will also serve to drive intraregional FDI flows and linkages. Overseas Chinese businesses are now the single largest source of (domestic and foreign) private enterprise capital investment within South-East Asia. They are also the dominant investors in the emerging "South China Economic Community" comprising Taiwan Province, Hong Kong, and the coastal areas of South-Eastern China, among which trade and investment links are growing rapidly on the basis of both comparative advantage and common ethnic heritage.

As yet, it is not clear where India will fit into this pattern of growing economic regionalization. Unlike the other Asian developing economies, India has received most of its investment and credit from the West. Although Japan-India trade flows have tripled since 1979, Japanese investors have so far invested relatively scarce amounts. It is possible that India may develop new export markets for its low-cost manufactures in Central and Eastern Europe.

National factors. Continued political stability, economic prosperity and government policies conducive to FDI in individual Asian developing countries will help maintain their attractiveness as host locations for FDI in the 1990s. Recent economic growth has already created rapidly-expanding markets that are attracting new market-oriented FDI. The existence of a competent and experienced local private sector (often ethnic Chinese) able to provide business partners, suppliers and customers for foreign investors is an added attraction of the ASEAN countries. National economic growth and development there will lead to shifts in comparative advantage which will affect patterns of FDI throughout the region. As some of the ASEAN countries advance to NIE status and make the transition from labour abundance to labour scarcity, they will cease to attract new labour-intensive industry, which may relocate to lesser-developed neighbours while being replaced by higher-value, more capital-intensive FDI projects. Malaysia, in particular, has already embarked on programmes to develop its local technological capacity in conjunction with foreign investors (Lim, 1993). Throughout the entire Asian region the trend is towards regulatory policies that are increasingly liberal and friendly to FDI and multinational firms. This is a consequence, as well as a cause, of economic forces. National economic policy alone will not create new FDI, but can attract and facilitate it in cases where underlying incentives exist.

Firm-level factors. In the 1980s, an integrated production and marketing strategy became an increasingly favoured modality of internationalization by large developed country TNCs which have traditionally accounted for the bulk of world-wide FDI, including that in developing countries. This involves establishing a corporate presence, usually with local production, "inside" all major world markets to compete directly with rival firms in multiple arenas. It also includes strategic cooperative ventures with other large firms, often transnationals of different nationalities, in order to expand individual firms' access to

95

increasingly shared resources, markets and technological advantages. Because of the focus on major national or regional markets and corporate partners of close to equal standing, globalization, and the regionalization taking place or anticipated in the West, has had the effect of concentrating global FDI flows in intra-developed country investments within the "Triad" of Japan, North America and Western Europe.

As intra-Triad investments mature in the 1990s, ASEAN as the world's most stable, fast-growing and established emerging regional market will attract more strategic FDI stimulated by the continued globalization of Triad-based companies and their competition with each other on a global scale. Already Japanese companies have turned to the ASEAN region as their priority FDI host location for the 1990s, and there is a renewed level of United States investor interest and activity in East Asia due to rapid market growth there and stagnation in North America and Europe.

The glass industry, a major supplier to the automobile and construction industries, provides an example of how globalization affects FDI in the ASEAN countries. The world market is dominated by Guardian Industries of the United States and Asahi Glass of Japan, which compete with each other in several markets world wide, including ASEAN. Guardian has recently broken Asahi's long monopoly of the glass market in Thailand by opening a capital-intensive plant there, and is negotiating for another one in Indonesia, as well as attacking the domestic glass cartel in Japan, of which Asahi is a prominent member. If it did not do so, Asahi could use its monopoly profits from the booming ASEAN or "cartelized" Japanese markets to subsidize price competition with Guardian in other world markets such as Europe, Latin America and the United States itself. As such corporate strategic responses to globalization spread, Japanese domination of FDI flows into the ASEAN countries may actually induce competitive flows from its global competitors of other nationalities.

Still, Japanese firms which have dominated the large FDI flows to Asian developing countries in the late 1980s are likely to continue dominating throughout the 1990s, largely because of their international competitiveness and global technological and market leadership in important industries such as automobiles and electronics. Japanese corporations have the firm-specific advantages which have always propelled companies of any nationality overseas, and these advantages combine especially well with the ASEAN countries' location-specific advantages. This "marriage" of the world's most competitive large industrial corporations with the world's most competitive newly industrializing host region is thus no surprise.

At the same time, many smaller Japanese companies (as well as firms from the Asian NIEs, which are typically small to medium-size on a world scale) have begun venturing abroad for the first time. Given their smaller size, lower capitalization, weaker firm-specific advantages, and lesser international experience, it is again not surprising that these "second- and third-tier" Asian firms would choose geographically closer and culturally more familiar host locations in neighbouring Asian developing countries. For many of the smaller and medium-size Japanese supplier firms, their offshore move to the ASEAN countries is both motivated and facilitated by tight long-term linkages with their giant corporate customers which are moving production here — what some see as a transplantation overseas of the Japanese *keiretsu* system. An example is the automobile industry, where large new investments in the ASEAN countries by established companies like Toyota, Nissan and Mitsubishi are drawing first-time investments by their home-country supplier firms as well.

For most firms from the Asian NIEs, South-East Asia is the "natural" first overseas host location for their international investments, as it was for Japanese transnationals at an earlier stage of their development. For investing firms from the three Overseas Chinese NIEs — Taiwan Province of China, Hong Kong and Singapore — the area offers another location-specific advantage, which is the dominance of the local private enterprise sector by Overseas Chinese domiciled in these countries, who can act as partners, facilitators, managers and employees. The same advantage is enjoyed by ASEAN-domiciled ethnic Chinese businesses, which account for most of the foreign investment flows from one ASEAN country to another. Like the NIE firms, these local Chinese firms invest abroad to maximize their firm-specific advantages, while exploiting new location-specific advantages offered by neighbouring countries, although their ethnic origin may be a political liability in host locations long sensitive to minority Chinese dominance of the local private business sector (Lim, 1991). For those firms, investing abroad may also help to diversify their political risk at home. Overseas Chinese firms from both NIEs and the ASEAN countries are likely to continue investing heavily in China, where in addition to economic gains they are also attracted by ethnic-based sentiments and enjoy certain ethnic advantages (for example, in language, culture and official favour).

In the 1980s, firms in the Republic of Korea were much slower than Overseas Chinese firms to invest in the ASEAN countries. This is primarily because their larger size and world market presence (for example, in consumer electronics, steel and automobiles) enabled and required them to concentrate initial market-protecting overseas investments in developed countries, particularly the United States and then Europe. Secondarily, they face a greater cultural (including linguistic) gap in South-East Asia than arguably either Western (English-speaking) or Overseas Chinese foreign investors, while lacking the international experience, organizational capacity and group support of Japanese investors. In the 1990s, however, investment from the Republic of Korea into South-East Asia — including Viet Nam and Myanmar, as well as the ASEAN-4 — is accelerating, especially in electronics and autos, two industries in which firms from the Republic of Korea are internationally competitive.

Several factors are driving outward FDI by both ethnic Chinese and indigenous ASEAN-domiciled firms. First, the foreign investment liberalizations of the 1980s now permit outward as well as inward investments on a more liberal basis. Second, many ASEAN-based companies have developed firm-specific competitive advantages and cash hordes through operating in their own (often protected) home markets that they are now eager to exploit abroad. Examples include Singapore Government-linked companies in infrastructure construction and management; Singapore service sectors companies in restaurants, drugstores, book stores and hotels; Thai agribusiness corporations in chicken and shrimp farming; Malaysian rubber and palm oil plantation companies; the Philippines in beer and packaged foods; and various Malaysian, Singapore and Indonesian companies in property development (hotels, shopping complexes, condominiums, etc.). Third, many local Singapore and Malaysian companies are labour-intensive, low-tech businesses which can no longer produce competitively in their own now higher-cost home countries, and so are interested in venturing to Viet Nam and Indonesia, in particular, for access to cheaper land and labour (Lim, 1993b).

Fourth, investing abroad by ASEAN companies may be part of a corporate strategy of geographical diversification in order to reduce dependence on home markets, which are either saturated in terms of market share, or newly-liberalized, increasing the threat of foreign competition.

Though it may be based on recognizable globalization strategies, most ASEAN outward investment is and will continue to be concentrated in the immediate Asia-Pacific region, thereby fostering further regional economic integration. Some ASEAN companies, however, have already ventured outside the region, like NIE firms, and this process should continue. The business associations and Governments of Singapore and Malaysia are also encouraging local companies in those countries to venture beyond the Asia-Pacific, specifically to Africa and Latin America, for trade and investment opportunities.

Policy implications

Government policies influencing FDI have varied and continue to vary greatly among different Asian-Pacific host countries, and at different times within individual countries. This makes it difficult to generalize about what constitutes a successful policy in terms of both attracting more FDI and of maximizing returns to the host country from that FDI. None the less, an attempt will be made in the section below to make such a generalization, outlining government policies which appear to have had a positive effect on the flows and developmental impact of inward FDI.

Political stability is not necessarily a policy variable, but it is always at or near the top of the list of crucial host country factors for foreign investors. This is because national politics conditions the entire domestic policy and economic environment in which investors operate, thus affecting not only attitudes and policies towards FDI itself, but also factors which affect operational efficiency and profitability — everything from price and currency stability to risk premiums on borrowed capital and the reliability of public services and employee attendance and work performance.

Except for the Philippines, the ASEAN countries have a record of national and regional political stability which extends back over 20 years in most cases. Malaysia and Singapore, which are among the top developing country recipients of cumulative FDI, have had the same elected Governments in power since the late 1950s, while Indonesia has had the same ruling party and the same President since 1965. In Thailand, despite frequent military coups, the basic stability of economic and social life and business operations have generally not been disrupted by politics. In contrast, the Philippines has been the least politically stable of the ASEAN-4 and it has correspondingly received the smallest amount of FDI of the ASEAN countries.

Still, it is difficult to tie political stability *per se*, in isolation of other factors, to flows of FDI. Policies towards FDI — often tied to specific circumstances in the domestic political economy (see for example, Lim and Pang, 1991) — are also important, as are the resources and potential market that a country can offer foreign investors. For example, political instability in Myanmar has not stopped foreign investors from responding to the present Government's open door policy, mainly because they are offered opportunities for fast profits in resource extraction ventures. Viet Nam lacks even the most basic infrastructure and skills, and suffers from periodic high inflation and an unstable currency. But both countries have rich natural resources and potentially large domestic markets, as well as geographical locations close to the already successful ASEAN countries and China. They also have some shared cultural legacies that may be favourable to FDI — including recent histories of active indigenous and ethnic Chinese entrepreneurialism. These factors apparently outweigh the liability of political instability in the minds of some prospective investors.

These country experiences suggest that, while political stability is clearly a plus in attracting FDI and, everything else being equal, the most politically stable countries attract the most FDI, it is neither necessary nor sufficient for attracting FDI. Attractive resources and market possibilities in the host country can overcome the disadvantages of political and even economic instability. Politically unstable countries may still be able to attract FDI if they have other attractive assets to offer, but they will probably have to grant more favourable terms to the foreign investor. A politically stable environment, however, is more likely to attract long-term value-added investment from foreigners than a politically unstable environment, which tends to attract mainly short-run resource- and labour-exploiting ventures.

Macroeconomic stability is another important variable in creating a policy environment attractive to foreign investors. In most cases for over 20 years, the ASEAN countries have managed to maintain low-inflation, growth-oriented macroeconomic policies. Like other developing countries in the late 1970s and early 1980s, the ASEAN-4 borrowed heavily abroad for domestic development programmes and accumulated large external debts, which they found hard to service when faced with the commodity price recession of the mid-1980s. But all adjusted quickly by cutting their government budgets, restricting monetary expansion, floating and depreciating their currencies, and liberalizing trade and investment rules to promote exports, domestic savings and private capital inflows. All of the ASEAN countries, even the Philippines, maintained or accelerated their (sometimes rescheduled) external debt repayments. The ability to attract large amounts of new export-oriented FDI and to generate new domestic private investment, was key to this success. This is an important example for India, which is going through a similar structural adjustment, and for socialist South-East Asia.

By the early 1990s, the ASEAN-4 were facing the different challenge of overheating economies, with years of rapid growth leading to accelerating inflation and deteriorating balance of payments. Belatedly in some cases, Governments reined in monetary expansion to slow growth, reduce trade deficits and stabilize the economy, and they have become somewhat more selective about new FDI. Financial markets are being liberalized to mobilize more domestic savings for investment.

China suffered from inflation rates up to 80 per cent in the 1980s, which led to an austerity policy in 1988-1990. Recent increases in price levels may foreshadow another episode in this cycle. Transnationals in China, however, seem to take either a very short-term or very long-term perspective, and may not be greatly affected by macroeconomic uncertainties. Investors in China have always faced currency restrictions and problems with currency valuation, accounting and remittances, which may, if anything, increase in the near future, as the official currency rate is increasingly subject to pressures of the market. In the long run, the Government of China seems committed to developing a modern foreign exchange trading system.

In India, as in China, macroeconomic policy is largely a question of domestic and international politics. The current Indian administration seems committed to working with IMF and international commercial regimes in a way that will be conducive to investment and the conduct of international business, although there are at present few macroeconomic policy certainties. Free trade zones may be a way to shield smaller and more vulnerable export-oriented investors from domestic economic problems, as they have done in China.

Good and reliable macroeconomic management has contributed to the ASEAN countries' ability to attract FDI, but it is unlikely if they would have attracted as much FDI as they have if they did not have other favourable underlying domestic, international and regional economic variables. The policy implication here is probably that macroeconomic stabilization and structural adjustment policies have been necessary, but not sufficient conditions for attracting FDI and maintaining growth.

Trade liberalization has been an important policy change in the ASEAN countries since the mid-1980s. Earlier, import substitution dominated industrial development and foreign companies invested in individual countries in order to avoid import barriers which restricted direct exports from the investors' home countries. But such FDI was limited both by the small size of the ASEAN markets, and by restrictions on foreign ownership. Singapore was the first country in the region to do away with import protection for domestic industries in the late 1960s, when it actively sought FDI to develop export-oriented manufacturing industries.

By the early 1970s, Malaysia and the Philippines had set up free trade or export processing zones (FTZs/EPZs) allowing the duty-free import of inputs and duty-free export of manufactures locally produced by 100 per cent export-oriented foreign subsidiaries. The FTZ/EPZ policy was modelled on similar zones in the Republic of Korea (for example, Masan) and Taiwan Province of China (for example, Kaohsiung). Part of the attraction of those zones to host countries was that they allowed the maintenance of import barriers on the domestic market while promoting pockets of export manufacturing based on free trade as practised by the free port cities of Hong Kong and Singapore. Malaysia, whose import barriers for domestic market industries were the lowest of the ASEAN-4, made the greatest use of FTZs not only to attract FDI and develop manufactured exports, but also geographically to disperse industry to less-developed areas of the country and to create large-scale industrial employment especially for ethnic Malaysians under its New Economic Policy focused on ethnic economic redistribution. In the Philippines, EPZs were developed as part of the new economic policies of the Marcos martial-law regime and with the encouragement of the regime's external creditors, such as the World Bank and the International Monetary Fund.

Thailand and Indonesia, which until the mid-1980s concentrated their industrial development on import substitution for the domestic market and their export development on the agricultural and mineral (oil) sectors, respectively, did not similarly promote export manufacturing through EPZs or their low-cost alternative, bonded manufacturing warehouses (individual export factories granted special customs status for duty-free imports and exports). Not surprisingly, they did not attract as much export-oriented manufacturing FDI as did Singapore, Malaysia and even the Philippines in the 1970s and early 1980s.

The commodity price recession and related debt crisis of the early to mid 1980s finally persuaded Thailand, Indonesia and the Philippines to promote more vigorously both export manufacturing and FDI, and trade liberalization was a tool to that end. Import tariffs, quotas and other barriers fell gradually in all of these countries, and more new foreign (and domestic) industrial projects were allowed to trade imports and exports freely through a variety of institutional arrangements, including the eventual establishment of FTZs in Thailand and Indonesia. In Malaysia, already established FTZs have proliferated and have been expanded to accommodate the new wave of export-oriented FDI. India has also been spurred by balance-of-payments pressures to reform its trade regime, and has established several EPZs. But general tariffs remain relatively high, though substantially reduced, and the impact of these limited reforms on trade patterns is yet to be seen. Elsewhere in the Asian region, the export and FDI success of China's coastal "open economic zones" is well-established, and Viet Nam and the Democratic People's Republic of Korea have recently established FTZs to attract export-oriented FDI.

The policy lesson here is clear: trade liberalization promotes FDI. This is true especially in export-oriented projects, and FTZs/EPZs are a particularly effective policy instrument in this achievement. It is less clear, however, that FTZs are the most effective way to promote technology transfer to domestic industry, since they may have the effect of isolating foreign industry. More complete liberalization of previously protected domestic market segments (as has taken place recently, especially in Thailand and the Philippines) could in a few cases actually discourage some market-oriented FDI and, in the extreme, result in some disinvestment. For example, especially where sales volumes are small, foreign auto makers with excess capacity in world-wide production may decide to export directly to those markets rather than set up local production facilities. Mitigating against this effect are the rapid growth and large long-term potential of the Asian national and regional markets, and their cost-competitiveness as a production location, which is enhanced rather than impaired by import liberalization. In the ASEAN countries, national-level trade liberalization also promotes integration of the regional ASEAN market, even in advance of a formal regional free trade area. This attracts more inward FDI to serve the larger regional market and intraregional FDI by both ASEAN and non-ASEAN investors now able to trade more freely among different production locations within the area.

Liberalization of investment rules is another key policy which has been responsible for increased FDI to Asian developing countries since the late 1980s. Among the ASEAN countries, Indonesia has progressively reduced to a very few the sectors of its economy closed to foreign investment, Malaysia has suspended the ethnic ownership quotas required by its New Economic Policy since 1986, and Thailand and Indonesia have become much more liberal in allowing 100 per cent or close to 100 per cent foreign ownership of enterprises, especially in export industries. In Indonesia, where joint ventures with local partners are required in virtually every sector, export-oriented manufacturing projects now must show only a 5 per cent local ownership share within five years of their establishment (even though this requirement can be waived in many cases). Allowing foreign investors to invest more freely has had the desired effect of increasing investment. Together, trade and investment liberalization are probably the most effective policy means of attracting FDI, especially export-oriented FDI, to developing countries. Within the ASEAN region, the countries with the most open trade and investment policies — Malaysia and Singapore — have also attracted the most cumulative FDI, despite being the smallest in size.

In China, published rules on foreign investment may be relatively less important, and the somewhat intangible matter of official attitude more critical, and increasingly liberal. On the other hand, India's rules have been distinctly liberalized (for example, in 1993 the Foreign Exchange Regulation Act was amended to remove restrictions on foreign-owned enterprises and accord them national treatment), but its official attitude remains in question. The Indian bureaucracy may not be entirely responsive to new policy direction by the Ministry of Finance. India's state and local administrations may take a more or less liberal approach in various regulatory matters, aside from the question of foreign ownership shares. Nevertheless, policy in both of these Asian giants is clearly moving in the right direction with respect to attracting FDI.

Investment promotion and incentive policies can also be effective in attracting FDI. Promotion involves disseminating information about the host country in potential source countries, through advertising in business publications, organization of investment missions to and from potential source countries, and establishment of national investment promotion agencies with overseas offices to court directly potential foreign investors and provide them with assistance in the host country itself. At the national level this is done by investment promotion agencies (IPAs). Most of those agencies, however, do not have full control of the foreign investment process in their countries. They instead share the task with many other central and provincial state agencies and ministries. This presents a problem of bureaucratic and political coordination, which can be quite daunting for especially the inexperienced smaller foreign investor without a powerful local partner. Thus the minimization of bureaucratic red-tape and "one-stop" coordination of the investment process itself is a powerful incentive to foreign investors.

Besides promoting and coordinating FDI, which includes assistance in finding local or foreign joint-venture partners, the ASEAN Governments also offer investors various financially-based incentives to locate in their countries. These include: profit tax exemptions, tax deductions and credits for various investment expenses, provision of or assistance in locating factory space and infrastructural facilities, subsidies on the cost of public services and on loans from state-owned banks, etc. These incentives may be selectively tailored to encourage investments and activities particularly favoured by the Government — for example, they may be more generous for companies investing larger amounts of capital, employing more labour, bringing in higher technology, promising to train workers, locating in less-developed regions, developing new exports, etc.

Properly designed and administered financial incentives for FDI can be fine-tuned to achieve development goals of the Government of the host country. But they require technical competence, administrative honesty, bureaucratic efficiency and insulation from political pressures to be fully effective and to avoid competitive "beggar-my-neighbour" effects, which reduce the net gains to all host countries of the FDI received. Incentives may also render the host country vulnerable to "unfair trade practice" charges by competing industries in other countries.

Industrial policy has been important in harnessing foreign investment and technology to the development of some import-substituting industries in the ASEAN countries, as it has in NIEs. The automobile industry is the prime example in all the ASEAN-4 countries, with policies including national ownership, import protection, local content requirements and eventual "rationalization" (see Doner, 1991). Lesser examples are provided by the steel, cement, textile and other industries in individual countries. But, unlike the situation in NIEs, industrial policy in most ASEAN countries has been limited and has tended to consist of ad hoc responses to short-run domestic political pressures rather than part of an overall state-led strategy for long-run industrial development. Overall, it may have had a discouraging effect on FDI, as well as on industrial efficiency and exports, though policies in specific industries and countries are constantly evolving and some may yet succeed in achieving their goals (for example, automobiles in Thailand).

The exception here is Singapore, which has long targeted individual industrial sectors as priorities for development and has used various selective investment incentives to attract specific foreign investors to help develop those sectors. Beginning in 1967, Singapore promoted labour-intensive export manufacturing; in 1979, it launched a "Second Industrial Revolution" emphasizing capital-intensive and high-tech industry; and in the 1980s, it promoted high-value manufacturing, research, design, training and other industrial, financial and business services for the regional and world markets. FDI, which accounts for three-quarters of all manufacturing investment in Singapore, was harnessed by "finely-tuned" government policies to play a critical role in all these stages and transitions. In the country's largest industry, electronics, for example, Singapore has moved from being one of many developing country offshore assembly locations for Western and Japanese transnationals in a relatively narrow line of simple products (televisions, cassette-recorders, semiconductors) in the late 1960s and 1970s, to becoming in the 1980s a major world high-tech manufacturing, research and development, engineering and marketing centre in industry segments like computer systems, telecommunications, aerospace and robotics. For the 1990s and beyond, the Government is moving away from single product-based planning and is targeting particular "clusters" of activity — from information technology and precision engineering to shipping and tourism — for focused developmental attention (Singapore Ministry of Trade and Technology, 1991).

Unlike the Republic of Korea and Taiwan Province of China, which made their leap into NIE status largely through the endeavours of locally-owned firms which, for the most part, are still second-tier players in the world market, Singapore achieved its current industrial status by becoming indispensable to leading global corporations and by forming strategic international partnerships with some of them, usually through large state-linked enterprises. Unlike laissez faire Hong Kong, whose technological attainment in manufacturing is thought to be lower, Singapore has used active state intervention to shape its industrial progress and constantly to reinvent its world economic role in line with changing circumstances (Lim, 1993c).

In China and India, industrial policy has been based on efforts to develop capacity in large basic industrial sectors. This often involves complex negotiation and contracts with individual multinational firms, such as in the joint venture of the state-owned Beijing Automotive Works' with Chrysler Corporation. This is the only way a United States auto maker could gain access to China's market and, in return, Chrysler is expected to provide the necessary technology and expertise to make China's auto manufacturing efficient. India has developed a similar relationship with Suzuki, and, since the late 1980s, has also been trying to develop a high-tech sector. Policy inconsistency and lack of resources, however, have limited the effectiveness of industrial policies in both countries.

Technology policy and labour policy have been and remain important elements of the Singapore strategy not only to attract FDI, but also to use it to acquire the latest in world-class technology and to maximize learning from such technology (Lim, 1993c). In addition to the selective use of investment incentives, the Government has long invested heavily in human capital, from basic pre-school education and vocational and technical training to the latest post-graduate scientific and engineering research, and in industry-related scientific and technical institutions and public-private sector collaborative projects. Protection for intellectual property rights, once weak, has improved dramatically and is close to accepted international standards, and there is heavy public investment in constantly upgrading the physical infrastructure necessary to support high-tech industry and services and international linkages.

Unlike the Republic of Korea and Taiwan Province, Singapore has not sacrificed labour incomes and living standards to the needs of protected local capital, but has tried to maximize them by providing workers with full employment in some of the world's leading international corporations. In the quid pro quo relationship between Singapore workers, managers and bureaucrats, on the one hand, and transnational corporations on the other, the former provide excellent skills, high productivity, efficient infrastructure, political stability and labour peace in exchange for sophisticated technology, training and learning opportunities, high incomes, economic security and a guaranteed place in world markets.

Only Malaysia among the other ASEAN countries has adopted anything like a similar long-term strategic technology policy in its dealings with FDI, or to support industrial development generally (Lim, 1993c). Malaysia's policies are limited compared with Singapore's, but they are evolving very rapidly and include selective investment incentives, improved protection for intellectual property rights, extensive public investment in human capital, infrastructure and public-private sector scientific and technical institutions, state intervention in the industrial relations system and, most recently, an emphasis on capital-intensive and high-tech investments.

By contrast, Thailand, Indonesia and the Philippines are not yet investing or planning to invest adequately in expanding and upgrading the physical infrastructure and, especially, the human capital needed for eventually moving up the technology ladder in the manner of the East Asian NIEs. Instead, these three countries appear to expect to rely for some time to come on the exploitation of abundant labour and natural resources and of their own large potential domestic markets, to attract FDI and develop their economies. But infrastructure and skilled labour bottlenecks are already constraining economic growth and the ability to attract and absorb more new FDI. Sometime in the 1990s this will eventually require massive state intervention or concerted action by private sector institutions themselves (for example, in education and infrastructure companies) if economic and industrial growth are not to founder. Thailand, however, has recognized the importance of technology development through commercial relations with foreign transnationals, and the Thai Board of Investment has established a Unit for Industrial Linkage Development (BUILD) to develop backward linkages between transnationals and local supplier industries.

Since the late 1980s, India has been trying to develop a high-tech industrial sector. Those efforts include tax incentives for R&D activities, various promotions and industrial awards, consultancy services, and attempts to work with foreign transnationals in high-tech industries. But India's main asset is the substantial human capital resources it has available to support technological development. It has an excellent university system providing Western-oriented technical and engineering training, though this has not yet translated into upgrading of the country's industrial technology. But in some cases, industrial linkages have developed and the area around Bangalore, for example, has become an Indian version of Silicon Valley as a result of scientific and technical institutes in the area. Several foreign firms have followed and have established R&D facilities there.

China has similarly promoted academic exchanges and technological training, but there has been a tendency for technologically capable Chinese to emigrate, rather than to aid in the technological development of the country. Substandard intellectual property protection—until early 1992 — inhibited the transfer of foreign computer and chemical engineering technology. China has also begun a campaign of technology acquisition through acquisition of overseas firms. This strategy of technology transfer through outward, as opposed to inward, FDI has also been pursued by Singapore. These campaigns as yet do not appear very effective, although it is difficult to evaluate all the potential externalities involved.

Compared with China, India and even the Republic of Korea and Taiwan Province, the ASEAN countries have relied much more heavily on FDI for their industrial development and economic growth, and have conducted economic policy accordingly. They have generally had more open trade and investment policies, but (except for Singapore) weaker industrial policy, and much weaker to non-existent technology and labour policies. In particular, public and private investments in education were much higher in the Republic of Korea and Taiwan Province even at a comparably early stage of their industrial development, though public investments in infrastructure also lagged. Among the ASEAN countries, Singapore and Malaysia rely the most heavily on and attract the most FDI, and also have the most open policies towards. They are also much smaller than Thailand, Indonesia and the Philippines and can thus rely less on cheap labour, natural resources and a sizeable domestic market, to attract FDI and sustain economic growth. This may partly explain their greater attention to technological upgrading and to dynamic comparative advantage than is the case in the larger Asian countries.

Implications for trade and technology

FDI-generated trade patterns

FDI flows in the ASEAN and wider Asia-Pacific regions are trade-creating. Since the late 1980s, FDI from Japan and the NIEs into the ASEAN-4 and China has generated imports of machinery, equipment and industrial raw materials from the source into the host countries, and produced exports from the host countries to third countries and to the source countries themselves. Thus by 1990, Japan's trade with the rest of Pacific Asia (NIEs, China and ASEAN) had exceeded its trade with the United States, while United States trade with the rest of Pacific Asia was already much greater than its trade with Japan, and about equivalent to its trade with the European Union. Part of these expanded trade flows are the direct result of FDI in the Asian LDCs — for example, exports to the United States and Japan of products manufactured in Thailand by Japanese and Taiwanese corporations, and imports into Thailand of capital goods, material and equipment from Japan and Taiwan Province, to manufacture those exports. In terms of trade balances, the immediate impact has been widening current account deficits for the ASEAN host countries in their trade with Japan and NIEs owing to immediate imports of machinery and equipment following FDI. But as exports increase from recent FDI projects, the trade balance for the host countries should improve. In China, FDI has led to export surpluses, while in Indochina it is mainly targeted at export sectors, but most new FDI in India to date has been oriented to its domestic market.

Foreign investment in service industries, which makes up a large and rapidly increasing share of Asian FDI, is likely to enhance trade as well. Not only is it not a direct substitute for imports, but in many cases it facilitates exports. The same is true of many physical infrastructure-related FDI projects, such as the development of the Hainan Island free trade zone in China by a foreign-led consortium, the proposed development of free trade zones in Viet Nam by Singaporean state and private enterprises, and the bids by Singaporean and Taiwanese State-led consortia to develop the former United States base at Subic Bay in the Philippines into an industrial estate and export processing zone.

Intraregional FDI will also increase intraregional trade flows as home and host countries buy and sell more from and to each other as a consequence of these new investments. For example, when a Japanese corporation simultaneously invests in Thailand, Malaysia and Singapore, trade arises between its subsidiaries in each ASEAN location, as well as between each ASEAN subsidiary and the parent company in Japan and between each ASEAN subsidiary and the Japanese parent company's markets in other, mostly Western, countries. Trade liberalization policies undertaken in part to attract new export-oriented FDI will also result in ancillary trade creation.

At the same time, the increasing shift of FDI in the 1990s towards market-oriented investments in the ASEAN countries is not likely to diminish imports, since FDI will be serving new market growth, will at least initially rely on imports of machinery and equipment from the source countries, and will likely be targeted at serving more than one country from a single host location, for example, as Japanese companies produce elevators and washing machines in Thailand for sale in Thailand, Malaysia, Indonesia and China. These intraregional, FDI generated, trade flows will be enhanced as regional integration progresses and the ASEAN countries move towards a free trade area. Already, the ASEAN auto parts complementation scheme is generating new intraregional trade flows in this industry. In addition, the rising incomes generated by export-oriented FDI-led economic and industrial growth will create trade by increasing demand for all types of imports from, as well as by expanding exports to, countries both within and outside the Asia-Pacific region. In

China and India, production of consumer goods by foreign affiliates is theoretically import-substituting. In practice, however, this is more likely to increase consumption than to displace trade which, given the prevailing tariff and currency situations, probably would not take place in any case.

Further trade creation is likely to result from other anticipated FDI trends in the region: increased inward FDI from non-Asian sources as global corporations seek to establish "insider" positions within the dynamic Asian regional economy; increased outward FDI from NIEs and ASEAN countries to developed countries and to emerging developing country regional markets in South Asia, Latin America and Eastern Europe; increased FDI into the ASEAN countries, China and India to serve these newly emerging regional markets; and increased FDI from both Asian and non-Asian sources into the emerging economies of socialist South-East Asia.

Technology transfer

Industry relocating from Japan and NIEs to ASEAN and China will bring with it not only standardized mature technologies that may be new to the host countries concerned, but also separate and complementary higher technologies, especially in industries like electronics, the largest foreign-invested manufacturing industry in the ASEAN region, where only state-of-the-art technologies can compete in world markets. The degree of technology transfer will depend to a large extent on the technological absorptive capacity of the host location, which in turn may constrain FDI flows dependent on the transfer of new technology, that is, foreign investments may not take place in particular host locations if they are unable to handle the specific technological demands of those investments.

Most of the new FDI that Thailand, Indonesia, the Philippines, China and, later, Viet Nam, India and Myanmar, may expect to receive in the 1990s will still involve relatively unsophisticated and standardized technology. But the rate of technological progress in any industry or host location will continue to accelerate as it has in the past decade. For example, a radio, a children's toy or an athletic shoe manufactured in Indonesia in the 1990s is likely to be technologically more sophisticated, if not already an entirely different product, than its predecessor manufactured in Malaysia in the 1980s or in Taiwan Province in the

1970s. It will also likely require higher levels of technical production, worker skill and quality control than have been present in earlier-established industries in Indonesia itself. In other words, FDI even in relatively simple labour-intensive industries will transfer higher technology to developing host countries. The burden is thus on the host country, as well as on the investing company, to increase the former's capacity to absorb new technology brought by the latter. This capacity can be enhanced by improved education and training provided by the Government of the host country, the community and by the foreign investor (see chapter 8).

From the host country perspective, FDI is a quick way to obtain new technology and manufacturing experience without investing scarce resources in developing new technology itself or in acquiring proprietary technology at arm's length on the world market. The danger is that this very ease in obtaining new technology may cause the host country to underinvest in developing its own technological capacity, which in turn will constrain the amount of new technology that it can acquire even through FDI. Eventually as wages rise as a result of economic growth, the country will lose its international competitiveness in serving as host to new FDI, especially in export-oriented industries, if local productivity and skills do not improve sufficiently to permit the hosting of higher-value-added activities. It is necessary for an economy, if it is to continue to receive FDI, continuously to enhance domestic technological capacities. The desire to host FDI can thus be a catalyst promoting domestic technological development activities in host countries.

The lesson of the East Asian NIEs is that FDI is desirable primarily because it provides opportunities for learning new technologies and developing skills and knowledge that may eventually be used to develop indigenous technologies or to move more rapidly up the ladder of imported technologies, thereby raising local productivity and incomes. Governments, families and individuals in NIEs spent decades investing heavily in human capital, especially engineering skills, even in advance of the technological requirements of locally-based industry at the time. They were thus in a good position to attract ever higher levels of technology through FDI, to absorb and learn from the foreign technology, and eventually in many cases to develop their own technology and even to supplant their former foreign investors in international competition. This was the road taken by the Republic of Korea in steel and consumer electronics, and increasingly by Taiwan Province in computers. While the Republic of Korea now manufactures products for the world market under its own brand names, Taiwanese firms are still largely OEM manufacturers subcontracting to foreign companies under their brand names. Singapore, on the other hand, manufactures products for global corporations in wholly-owned subsidiaries which use the latest technology. In all three cases, despite the different paths taken, the ability to learn new technology has been the key. The opportunity to learn new technology is provided by FDI, but the capacity to learn from it must be locally developed.

Conclusions

Trends

To sum up, the likely FDI trends in Asia over the 1990s include the following:

(1) Flows of FDI to Asian developing countries are likely to remain substantial throughout the 1990s, motivated by a host of international, regional, national and firm-level factors.

(2) While new FDI will continue to include export-oriented industry, investment to serve the local national or regional market will become increasingly important as the decade progresses.

(3) Asian source countries will continue to dominate FDI flows within the region, with ASEAN companies gradually joining Japanese and NIE firms as important foreign investors.

(4) Many of the new investors will be small or medium-size companies from developed countries and NIEs which are venturing abroad for the first time. They may require more assistance from governments of host countries or partnership with local private or public sector enterprises, and the host country's bargaining position may be stronger *vis-à-vis* such smaller transnationals.

(5) The ASEAN countries and China will be joined by the emerging socialist economies of South-East Asia and India as popular host locations for FDI.

(6) In the region FDI will be mostly trade-creating, with intraregional investment flows generating subsequent intraregional

trade flows and serving to integrate further the Asian regional economy.

(7) FDI will transfer technology from home to host countries, subject to the latter's capacity to absorb the technology.

(8) FDI will contribute to the region's continued economic growth and rising incomes, and to the advance of some of the ASEAN countries to NIE status by the end of the decade.

For Asian developing countries, then, both the trend towards globalization of corporate strategies and the trend towards regionalization will increase FDI inflows. In large part this is due to the fact that Asia is both the fastest-growing and will eventually be the largest regional market in the world, and the most competitive production location for world markets for industries and products ranging from the resource- and labour-intensive to the capital-intensive and high-tech (in different countries). The inflows of capital and technology that FDI brings, the competition between industrial-country transnationals, and the emergence of new regional FDI actors, resulting from the forces of globalization as expressed within the Asian region, will enhance growth and development here subject to progressive responses from Governments of host countries and local companies.

Theory

The experience of Asian developing host countries with FDI suggests the following theoretical implications.

First, developing countries today can expect to go through various stages in hosting FDI which parallel stages in their economic development, moving from resource-based to labour-based and then to skill- and technology-based exports, with local market-oriented production becoming increasingly attractive as rising incomes are achieved through both labour- and technology-based export production. In the process the developing country shifts from resource-intensive to labour-intensive and finally to capital- and skill-intensive production. It moves up the technology ladder to become an NIE, and shifts from being primarily a host country to becoming also an outward investor. This does not, however, necessarily mean a reduction in inward FDI flows as a country's economy matures. On the contrary, like most developed countries which are simultaneously source and host countries for FDI, many NIEs may receive more inward FDI as they increase their outward investments, due both to their greater attractiveness as affluent markets and to technological upgrading into more capital-intensive production, which requires more capital investment.

Second, the above described investment development path takes place as TNCs and other firms adjust to market shifts in comparative advantage, that is, upgrading their product lines and technology as labour surpluses are exhausted, wage costs and labour incomes rise, and host markets grow in size and affluence. Firms which are unable or unwilling to upgrade are forced to relocate to new host locations where the old comparative costs they have been used to still exist.

The choice between upgrading and relocation is influenced by many factors. One factor is the global market position and technological competitiveness of the investing firm, which determines its access to the capital and technology necessary for upgrading, and its ability to sell the output of the usually expanded production (since capital-intensive production produces scale economies). Weakness on both counts tends to force NIE-based firms to relocate out of their home or host countries. Large developed country transnationals, however, particularly those from Japan, are more likely to upgrade. There have been exceptions. In the 1980s, the international uncompetitiveness of American electronic firms caused some to exit segments of the electronic industry (for example, consumer electronics and semiconductors) altogether, and thus to close their Asian offshore plants rather than to upgrade them.

Conditions in the original host location also influence the choice between upgrading and relocation. Because of the much larger capital commitment required by capital-intensive higher technology, the longer pay-back period and often larger market share involved, political and macroeconomic stability are more important than at the labour-intensive stage. Adequate infrastructure is also more important, because of greater reliance on machinery and equipment, and the need to transport greater volumes of inputs and outputs. The accumulated skills of local managers, technical personnel and production workers, and the availability of more technically-trained manpower and well-educated workers able to operate a more sophisticated technology will also encourage upgrading rather than relocation. All these factors require some anticipatory policy action by the Government of the host country before the change in comparative costs occurs, if the country is to retain and to attract new FDI.

In short, a combination of ownership and location-specific advantages is required for stage progression to take place under FDI, and this depends on both the investing firm's competitive world market position and international management and on the evolution of the host country's competitive advantages which are affected by government policy. This is where strategic industrial policy by the Government of the host country focused on dynamic comparative advantage has an important role to play. Different forms of such a policy have been undertaken in the Republic of Korea, Taiwan Province, Singapore, belatedly and to a lesser extent in Hong Kong, and more recently in Malaysia. Significantly, all these economies are smaller and started out with higher labour costs than Thailand, Indonesia and the Philippines, and of course China and India — which have not embarked on similar strategic industrial policies. For the latter, larger and poorer countries, like many other developing countries, static comparative advantage based on abundant natural resources and cheap labour will last much longer than it did for NIEs as an attraction for FDI, thus discouraging the quick adoption of suitable policies to anticipate and cope with eventual shifts in comparative advantage. But, as international competition and globalization force more rapid technological change, FDI itself could prove to be the agent nudging reluctant host countries along the path of more public involvement in building enhanced indigenous technology capacity.

Third, FDI theory and policy should take greater account of regional factors. For example, the large amounts of FDI historically received by Singapore and Hong Kong have been and still are partly related to their special *entrepôt* or "middleman" functions with respect to South-East Asia and China respectively. The large amounts of FDI that China and the ASEAN countries receive are partly due to their geographical proximity to the major source countries of Japan and the Asian NIEs, which are also expected to become important investors in the Far Eastern territories of the Russian Federation for the same reason.

Much of the FDI going into the ASEAN countries is influenced by regional factors, such as region-wide political stability, economic prosperity and good infrastructure; the availability of Singapore as a regional trading and services centre introducing outside transnationals to the region, as well as a source of FDI itself; the ability to locate linked multiple plants in different locations in the region with relatively easy access among them; the widespread existence of FTZs, which create a *de facto* partial free trade area among the neighbouring countries; the development of subregional "growth triangles"; unilateral trade liberalization by neighbouring countries; and an anticipated regional free trade area.

Regionalization reduces firms' overhead, transport, communications, inventory, information, coordination and training costs, and more efficiently utilizes scarce management time. For example, many transnationals operate regional training and/or engineering centres in Singapore and Taiwan Province, which provide technical support for assembly plants in neighbouring countries, creating an integrated regional production complex that is more efficient than duplicative parallel national complexes and allows for utilization of scale economies. This regional division of labour is a subset of the international division of labour increasingly practised by transnationals in their globalization strategies.

Regional factors influencing FDI are also linked to cultural factors such as linguistic compatibility and ethnic trading networks. The importance of Overseas Chinese FDI in China and South-East Asia has already been mentioned. Along these lines, Overseas Vietnamese (especially Vietnamese-Americans) and Overseas Cambodians are expected to be prominent investors in Viet Nam and Cambodia, respectively. There are also other cultural similarities among host locations that can help them attract and facilitate FDI. For example, Sony Corporation has made a policy of employing experienced line-workers from its Malaysian subsidiaries to train production workers in new assembly plants in Indonesia, because they have the same language, religion and culture. Ethnic links can thus help reduce some of the cultural gaps that remain a barrier to FDI flows between culturally different source and host countries. But they can also make it difficult for developing countries to attract FDI from source countries with which they have no ethnic, cultural or other emotionally-defined links.

Policy

The conventional wisdom in the development policy arena today regards FDI as desirable and even necessary for economic growth in developing countries. This proposition is supported by the experience of the ASEAN countries and China, which have been among the most successful developing countries both in attracting FDI and in achieving rapid economic growth and industrialization with its assistance. In terms of attracting FDI, the conventional wisdom is that the establishment of macroeconomic stability and liberal trade and investment regimes are sufficient policies. Here the Asian experience suggests more complex policy implications.

First, a developing country's ability to attract FDI is highly contingent on international, regional, national and firm-level factors — including international trade policy variables, major currency alignments, and shifts in global corporate strategies — that lie largely beyond the control of the individual Government of the host country. This implies that FDI policy needs to take into account external environmental or market constraints and not assume that FDI can be attracted simply on the basis of "correct" domestic policies. The trends towards both globalization and regionalization may provide many new opportunities for countries to attract investments on different bases than in the past, for example, to produce for world or regional rather than merely domestic markets, to produce in specialized segments rather than integrated wholes of global industries, and to source from global and regional networks. But they may also divert and concentrate investment away from some developing regions of the world.

Second, within these "external" constraints, FDI is attracted to individual developing countries largely by their intrinsic competitive advantages, such as natural and human resources, and potential market size. Thus even economically and politically unstable countries can attract some FDI if their intrinsic advantages are strong, and if they follow relatively open FDI policies (the recent examples of Myanmar and Viet Nam). Countries without strong intrinsic advantages need to develop and enhance their resources and market potential, through such means as investing in labour skills and infrastructure, and economic cooperation with regional neighbours.

Third, macroeconomic stability facilitates domestic as well as foreign investment and makes a country more attractive to investors, but is not necessary to attract FDI if a country has strong intrinsic advantages (for example, China), while it is not sufficient to attract FDI if the country lacks such advantages.

Fourth, even countries with substantial intrinsic advantages usually need to liberalize trade and investment in order to attract FDI. Liberalization encourages FDI by removing restrictions which increase the costs and difficulties of doing business in a country, and by increasing the availability of necessary imported inputs and improving the competitiveness and exportability of locally-produced goods. But the experiences of ASEAN and the East Asian NIEs still raise policy questions of the extent to which liberalization is necessary to attract FDI for all countries, especially large countries with strong intrinsic advantages like China and Indonesia, and of whether an open-door policy towards FDI is desirable if a country wishes to develop indigenous industries, such as the Republic of Korea did with the aid of restrictive trade and investment policies.

Fifth, to attract FDI in manufacturing, a host country should have abundant and efficient labour resources and/or a sizeable potential domestic market. Much more FDI can be attracted for export-oriented manufacturing than for the domestic market, but the two are increasingly linked, for example, in projects which produce both for the domestic and export markets, especially in the context of the evolving globalization and regionalization strategies of transnationals. Export manufacturing itself can quickly generate incomes which enlarge the domestic market, while domestic industries can supply inputs for export industries. The policy implication here is that old dichotomies between export- and domestic-market-oriented industries may no longer apply, making separate policies targeted to each obsolete.

For example, FDI in export-oriented manufacturing is usually more sensitive to political and macroeconomic stability, open trade and investment policies, infrastructure and investment incentives than FDI in natural resources or for the domestic market, and a country with fewer intrinsic locational advantages may feel the need to offer more generous financial incentives to attract such FDI. But changing the policy environment to be more favourable to export-oriented industry may reduce the need for special financial incentives, as well as benefit domestic-market-oriented industry and encourage it to export.

Sixth, the experience of Asian host countries shows by both positive and negative example that host countries need to develop their indigenous capacity to absorb and learn from new technology in order to maximize FDI and FDI-related technology and domestic value-added. This requires investment in human capital and infrastructure (which also builds "intrinsic advantages"), and also raises the policy question of the need for the host country to consider FDI as part of a strategic national industrial policy involving state intervention beyond a simple open-door policy and reliance on "market forces".

Seventh, a final broad policy question relates to a regional strategy for attracting FDI, since a country's attractiveness to FDI is often enhanced when it is viewed in a broader regional rather than merely a limited national context. In the ASEAN countries, for example, the proposed regional free trade area, already active subregional growth triangles, and national-level trade liberalization are already attracting FDI which can locate production simultaneously in more than one country of the region according to differential national comparative advantages, and also produce in one or more countries to serve the entire regional market. Thus Singapore promotes itself as a regional production and services centre for all of South-East Asia, while Thailand is promoting itself as the capitalist gateway to the emerging socialist markets of mainland South-East Asia, in much the same way as Hong Kong has been for China. In policy terms, however, it is not clear if regional cooperation on FDI requires a bureaucratically-coordinated regional strategy, or if private enterprise and FDI itself may do a more efficient job of regional integration than public policy. A regional strategy must also be accommodated to different national strategic industrial and investment policies.

To conclude, a developing country's ability to attract FDI depends on a complex of international, regional, firm-level and even national factors, most of which it cannot control. For developing countries in the Asia-Pacific region, these factors are largely favourable for the 1990s — that is they can expect to continue receiving large amounts of new FDI. A similarly positive configuration may not exist for other developing countries. What a developing country can do to increase its ability to attract and benefit from FDI is: liberalize its trade and investment policies; improve domestic political and economic stability; aggressively promote itself to potential investors, especially in NIEs; enhance its own capacity to absorb new investment and technology by making strategic investments in infrastructure and human capital; and explore regional linkages with neighbouring countries. Most of those policies will also encourage domestic private investment and stimulate economic growth, and are thus worth undertaking even if the prospects for attracting FDI are not particularly good.

Finally, both globalization and regionalization can provide new opportunities for developing countries to attract and benefit from FDI. Globalization pushes companies to become involved in global rather than only national markets, thereby increasing the strategic significance of individually small developing country markets and attracting more investment to them. Regionalization pushes companies to be represented in all major world regions, which also increases the attractiveness of individually small markets and production locations which can form part of an integrated larger regional whole. Both trends can enable individual countries to attract foreign capital and technology that they otherwise would not attract on the basis of national advantages alone. But policy to attract this capital and technology, and the ability to maximize the developmental benefits from such flows, is still largely nationally-based, though regional policy cooperation is becoming more common, especially among the ASEAN countries. It is at this national level that government policy primarily needs to operate. Without such strategic national policy, developing countries cannot fully benefit from the opportunities presented by globalization and regionalization.

Note

1. The statistics cited in the present paper are derived from a variety of sources. The *World Investment Report* and the *World Investment Directory* produced by United Nations Conference for Trade and Development (UNCTAD) are the main references.

References

Bollard, Alan and David Mayes (1992). Regionalism and the Pacific Rim, *Journal of Common Market Studies*, vol. 30, no. 2, June, pp. 195-209.

Do Duc Dinh (1992a). Marketization and economic cooperation between Viet Nam and ASEAN countries. Paper prepared for the Social Science Research Council Conference on Marketization in South-East Asia, Chiengmai, Thailand, January.

_____ (1992b). Viet Nam's foreign economic policies before and after 1986. Paper prepared for the Conference on the Political Economy of South-East Asia's Foreign Policy in the New World Order, Department of Political Science, University of Windsor, Canada, October.

Doner, Richard F. (1991). *Driving a Bargain: Automobile Industrialization and Japanese Firms in South-East Asia.* Berkeley, California: University of California Press.

International Monetary Fund and Bank Negara Malaysia (1990). *Strategies for Structural Adjustment, The Experience of South-East Asia*, Washington, D.C.: IMF and BNM.

Institute of Management Development (1991). *World Competitiveness Report*, Lausanne, Switzerland.

Kamath, Shyam J. (1990). Foreign direct investment in a centrally planned developing economy: The Chinese case. *Economic Development and Cultural Change,* October, pp. 107-130.

Krause, Lawrence B. (1992). The North American Free Trade Agreement and the Asia-Pacific Economic Community. Paper presented at the Conference on Issues in the Formation of a Western Hemipshere Economic Bloc, Institute of Public Policy Studies, University of Michigan, Ann Arbor, Michigan, November.

Lall, Sanjaya (1991). Direct investment in S.E. Asia by the NIEs: Trends and prospects. *Banco Nazionale Del Lavoro Quarterly Review*, No. 179, December, pp. 463-480.

Lim, Linda Y.C. (1991). The New Ascendancy of Chinese Business in Southeast Asia: Political, Cultural, Economic and Business Implications. Paper presented at the annual meeting of the Association for Asian Studies in New Orleans, Louisiana, March.

_____ (1993a). The role of the private sector in ASEAN regional economic cooperation. In *New Forms of South-South Cooperation in Developing Countries*, Lynn Mytelka, ed., Paris, France: OECD Development Centre.

_____ (1993b). Models and partners: The economic development of Singapore and Malaysia and their implications for socialist economic reform in South-East Asia. Paper prepared for the Social Science Research Council Conference on Marketization in South-East Asia, Chiang Mai, Thailand, 15-17 January.

_____ (1993c). Technology policy and export development: the case of the electronics industry in Singapore and Malaysia. Paper prepared for the first conference of the United Nations University Institute for New Technologies, Maastricht, the Netherlands, 21-23 June (mimeo).

_____and Eng Fong Pang (1991). *Foreign Direct Investment and Industrialisation in Malaysia, Singapore, Taiwan and Thailand.* Paris, France: OECD Development Centre.

MacIntyre, Andrew J. and Kanishka Jayasuriya, eds. (1992). *The Dynamics of Economic Policy Reform in South-East Asia and the South-West Pacific.* Singapore: Oxford University Press.

123

Ng Chee Yuen and Norbert Wagner, eds. (1993). *Marketization in ASEAN*. Singapore: Institute of South-East Asian Studies.

Ramstetter, Eric D., ed. (1991). *Direct Foreign Investment in Asia's Developing Economies and Structural Change in the Asia Pacific*. Boulder, Colorado: Westview Press.

Singapore Ministry of Trade and Industry (1991). *Strategic Economic Plan: Toward a Developed Nation*, Singapore.

Soon Lee Ying, ed. (1990). *Foreign Direct Investment in ASEAN*. Kuala Lumpur, Malaysia: Malaysian Economic Association.

Srinivasan, T.N. (1990). External sector in development: China and India, 1950-1989. *American Economic Review* (May), Papers and Proceedings, pp. 113-117.

Stewart, Sally, Michael Tow Cheung and David W. K. Yeung (1992). The latest Asian newly industrialized economy emerges: The South China Economic Community. *Columbia Journal of World Business*, vol. 27, no. 2 (Summer), pp. 31-37.

Than, Mya (1991). ASEAN, Indo-China and Myanmar: Toward economic cooperation? *ASEAN Economic Bulletin*, vol. 8, No. 2 (November), pp. 173-193.

Timberman, David G., ed. (1992). *The Politics of Economic Reform in Southeast Asia: The Experiences of Thailand, Indonesia and the Philippines*. Manila, Philippines: Asian Institute of Management.

Tokunaga, Shojiro, ed. (1992). *Japan's Foreign Investment and Asian Economic Interdependence*. Tokyo, Japan: University of Tokyo.

United Nations Centre on Transnational Corporations (1991). *World Investment Report 1991: The Triad in Foreign Direct Investment*, (United Nations publication, Sales No. E.91.II.A.12).

_____ (1992). *World Investment Directory 1992, Asia and the Pacific* (United Nations publication, Sales No. E.92.II.A.13).

_____ (1994). *World Investment Report 1994: Transnational Corporations, Employment and the Workplace*, (United Nations publication, Sales No. E.94.II.A.14).

_____ (1995). *World Investment Report, 1995. Transnational Corporatrions and Competitiveness*, (United Nations publication, Sales No. E.95.II.A.9).

Yamashita, Shoichi, ed. (1991). *Transfer of Japanese Technology and Management to the ASEAN Countries*. Tokyo, Japan: University of Tokyo Press.

4

Beyond macroeconomic stability in Latin America

Daniel Chudnovsky

Introduction

Following early attempts in Chile and Mexico, other Latin American economies entered the 1990s in the middle of stabilization-cum-structural adjustment programmes. The aim, *inter alia*, was to transform the traditional import substitution industrialization process into an outward oriented growth process, through privatization and the opening of their economies to international trade, foreign direct investment (FDI) and technology. Partly as a result of those programmes, inflation has been sharply reduced, external debt renegotiated, growth resumed (though in per capita terms still at a low level) and external financial flows (including capital repatriation) and imports have boomed in most countries. Domestic investment is also showing signs of some recovery, and FDI has increased sharply in the early 1990s.

These achievements are noteworthy, but can stabilization and liberalization improve Latin America's international competitiveness[1/] and revert the recent marginalization of the region from the dynamic centres of the world economy? Although the opening of Latin American economies is too recent to be properly assessed, there is reason to believe that additional policies are needed to foster the dynamic competitive advantages that can sustain growth in today's global economy. In particular, the experiences of OECD and some Asian developing countries suggest the need for combining macroeconomic stabilization and trade and FDI liberalization with a new set of policies that may be labelled "innovation policies".

Innovation policies in developed countries focus on activities that push forward the technological frontier (although the diffusion of new technologies is a priority issue as well). The focus is different for many developing countries that operate inside the technological frontier. In Latin America, an increase in enterprise productivity (by reducing the technological gap between actual and the best available practices at the international level) and the efficient entry into production of higher quality goods and services (for both domestic and external markets) is a necessary first step for enhancing competitiveness. Hence, the focus of innovation policies should be on activities that facilitate the restructuring of existing industries and encourage the adoption of more modern technologies and organizational techniques.[2]

Transnational corporations (TNCs) play a crucial role in innovatory processes. Notwithstanding the significant role played by universities and research centres, innovation activities in OECD countries are basically located in private firms, many of which are TNCs.[3] With the recent revival of FDI in Latin America, can TNCs play a similar role in innovation processes in the region's economies? Even though the R&D activities of TNCs still remain mainly concentrated in the home country (Patel and Pavitt, 1989), there is increasing evidence to suggest that it is being gradually dispersed to other locations (Casson 1991, Granstrand, Håkanson and Sjölander 1992, Dunning 1993). If some innovatory activities or even proper R&D take place within subsidiaries, it is likely that spillover effects via suppliers and customers and/or competitive pressures on indigenous firms may become significant (Blomström, 1991). As discussed by Lall in chapter 8, however, to benefit from the opportunities provided by such spillovers, an absorptive capacity (that often includes R&D) is required in the receiving firms and industries. Hence, innovation policies that aim to expand this absorptive capacity are crucial if imported knowledge is to be properly identified and assimilated and, eventually, help to upgrade indigenous technological capacity.

The main purpose of the present chapter is to develop further this line of argument and to suggest types of integrated trade and innovation policies that can better enable developing countries to capture the externalities to be obtained from FDI and other means of actively participating in the globalization process. The chapter begins by noting the decline in international competitiveness in Latin America in the 1980s. Next, the limitations of stabilization programmes and the case for incorporating innovation policies are considered. The advantages and likely problems in implementing innovation policies are also discussed, followed by some concluding remarks.

International competitiveness of Latin America

Main features

For many decades Latin America led the developing regions in increasing her share in world GDP, trade and FDI inflows, but her declining role in the world economy has been clearly visible in the past decade. The performance of Latin American exports in the 1980s was one of the few relatively positive economic indicators in what has been referred to as a "lost decade" to illustrate the magnitude of the setback suffered in terms of development (ECLAC, 1990). The growth in manufactured exports, however, was largely a result of the continuous devaluation of domestic currencies and extremely low wages, which gave international competitiveness to a number of branches that were built in the import substitution era and had substantial idle capacity (due to depressed conditions in domestic markets). Export growth was thus not based on capital accumulation, improved technologies and corresponding productivity gains. This sort of competitiveness has been labelled as "spurious" (ECLAC, 1990) and is considered as hardly sustainable (Kell and Marchese, 1991).

In contrast with the crisis faced by Latin American countries, a number of countries in Asia managed to achieve good economic performances in the 1980s. As was seen in the previous chapter, in the Asian NIEs and some ASEAN countries, a process of manufactured export-led growth continued in the 1980s, especially after the recovery in world demand. In countries like Indonesia, Malaysia, Pakistan, Republic of Korea, Sri Lanka and Taiwan Province of China, strong growth in manufactured exports (and increasing shares in world manufactured exports in the 1980s) was generally accompanied by high rates of growth in investment, manufacturing output and/or GDP in the 1980s. Furthermore, in the Republic of Korea, Thailand and Malaysia, real wages in manufacturing rose near 50 per cent (and in Indonesia 20 per cent) between 1980 and 1987 (UNCTAD, 1989). Thus in a number of Asian countries, exports of manufactures were clearly accompanied by significant structural changes in the economy and by better living conditions. This has not happened in Latin America.

The fiscal crisis and a slow-down in economic growth and productive investment in Latin America has also impacted on the resources available for education and for R&D. In this connection, the contrast between Latin America and the East Asian NIEs regarding science and technology indicators is sharp. Resources allocated to R&D as a percentage of GDP (0.5 per cent) in Latin America in the late 1980s were only a third of what the Asian NIEs devoted to this activity. Although the stock of engineers and scientists was similar in both Latin America and East Asian NIEs (11.5 per thousand of economically active inhabitants), the corresponding flow of college graduates was much lower (15.6 *vis à vis* 47.8) per thousand inhabitants (Peres Nuñez, 1992).

The overall impact of the 1980s development crisis in Latin America on enterprise competitiveness is hard to gauge in the absence of detailed studies. It would appear that those most adversely affected were the smaller and medium-sized domestic firms. Foreign affiliates, with access to financing and restructuring support from parent TNCs, were able to switch production from domestic to export markets. The participation of foreign affiliates has been very significant in the production of some key branches and in exports, as clearly indicated by the high share of foreign firms in the manufactured exports of Mexico and Brazil (Fritsch and Franco, 1991; Peres Nuñez, 1990). Some domestic firms, particularly those belonging to large private groups, were also able to weather the crisis. Although these groups have very diversified activities, in some cases they have well equipped factories with qualified personnel making high value added goods not only for the internal market, but also for export. At the same time, these groups have formed joint ventures or technological agreements with partners from industrialized countries to strengthen their productive and marketing skills and to obtain relatively modern product and process technologies (Basualdo and Fuchs, 1989).

Foreign direct investment

Foreign direct investment flows to Latin America more than doubled during 1988-1994 (as shown in table 1). A recovery in FDI flows (as compared with the early- and mid-1980s) is visible in most large and medium-size countries. Countries like Mexico, Argentina and Colombia were already attracting increased FDI flows by the late 1980s, and in Chile and Venezuela this happened in the early 1990s. Inflows to the largest host country, Brazil, began to recover in 1992.

Table 1. Inflows of foreign direct investment

(Annual average inflows, in millions of dollars)

Countries	1982-1984	1985-1987	1988-1990	1991-1992	1993-1994
All countries	54 620	92 820	190 180	164 769	218 494
Developing countries	20 310	18 081	30 780	47 757	77 387
Asia	4 891	7 655	16 804	26 125	53 298
Latin America	6 417	7 606	8 896	16 464	19 077
Argentina	227	492	1 337	3 309	3 753
Bolivia	15	19	-2	73	63
Brazil	2 023	964	1 379	1 276	1 151
Chile	205	464	969	667	1 712
Colombia	523	672	426	682	642
Costa Rica	49	70	129	225	265
Dominican Republic	39	58	116	163	176
Ecuador	47	69	81	90	107
El Salvador	13	18	11	20	35
Grenada	3	8	13	19	18
Guatemala	53	94	151	93	130
Guyana	5	-1	3	7	7
Haiti	7	5	9	11	9
Honduras	19	32	48	50	40
Jamaica	-8	13	61	38	98
Mexico	1 878	2 339	2 849	4 578	4 667
Paraguay	16	2	32	111	111
Peru	-1	18	42	60	1 522
Trinidad and Tobago	145	6	107	174	311
Uruguay	6	29	42	23	58
Venezuela	120	35	251	1 304	683

Source: *World Investment Report 1995* (United Nations publication, Sales No. E.95.II.A.9).

A significant part of the inflows were due to debt-equity swaps that gained momentum mostly in the late 1980s. In the case of Argentina, Brazil, Chile and Mexico, 40.7 per cent of FDI flows in 1988-1990 were made through debt-equity conversions (UNCTAD, 1994). This method of attracting FDI is inclined to be very expensive because it involves a subsidy to investments that might have been made any way. It may also create macroeconomic problems (for example, inflation) and redistribute assets rather than bring in new funds (for a more favourable view, see Bergsman and Edisis, 1988).

In countries like Argentina, Venezuela and Mexico, FDI inflows have largely been channelled to the privatization of State firms, often through debt-equity swaps. In 1991 alone, over one-third of FDI into these countries was due to privatization schemes (UNCTAD, 1994). Foreign partners usually bring new managerial and technological inputs to modernize the privatized firms (although the net financial and economic benefits of these operations is hard to assess).

Can FDI be an important channel for acquiring modern technologies in services and manufacturing? At the macro level, it would appear that relatively few domestic activities are affected by FDI. On average, FDI as a proportion of gross fixed capital formation in Latin American and Caribbean countries was only 3.6 per cent in 1986 to 1990, but it rose sharply in 1991 and 1992 to 7.5 per cent and 11.6 per cent, respectively (UNCTAD, 1994). If stocks, instead of flows of FDI, are taken into account, the picture looks quite different. Transnational corporations are an extremely important actor in many activities in Latin American countries. They have a significant participation in production and trade and have shown, in many cases, a high degree of flexibility towards certain government policies, such as export promotion schemes (Fritsch and Franco, 1991).

A study of 63 TNC affiliates operating in Mexico indicates that the firms had made efficiency investments to modify the product mix, reduce costs and improve quality during the period of crisis after 1982 (UNCTC, 1992; Peres Nuñez, 1990). Most exports derived from such measures, however, are concentrated in the automotive sector and were made in the context of the international restructuring of the parent (United States) companies. Similarly, a study of 55 TNC affiliates operating in Brazil found that the companies have taken many rationalization measures to deal with the new conditions in 1990 and 1991 (Bielschowsky, 1992).

Jointly with the introduction of total quality control techniques and better managerial and administrative schemes, the employment of technical and production personnel has been sharply reduced. Furthermore, a clear trend towards lower vertical integration, a specialization of the product mix and a reduction of the manufacturing of high-tech goods was detected. Hence, the technological implications and the spillover effects of these strategies for the host economy and domestic enterprises are unclear.

Policy reforms

Most Latin American countries entered the 1990s needing structural changes, to narrow external and fiscal gaps, and to foster long-term and productive investments. One of the most important and influential responses to this challenge is the policy package based on what Williamson (1990) termed the "Washington consensus" approach to stabilization-with-growth.[4/] The package included measures such as strict fiscal policy, tax reforms, positive interest rates, competitive foreign exchange rates, trade liberalization, encouragement of FDI, privatization, deregulation and securing property rights. Where implemented, the policy changes have yielded results: Argentina, Bolivia, Brazil, Chile, Ecuador, El Salvador, Mexico, Nicaragua, Paraguay, Peru, Trinidad and Tobago, and Uruguay have all achieved notable progress in stabilization (UNCTAD, 1995a). Though more significant long-term effects are still pending, these policy reforms set the framework to discuss innovation policies in the 1990s.

Macroeconomic stability

Although the timing, sequence, internal consistency, scope and likely effects of policy reforms are at issue (see Williamson, 1990; Fanelli *et al.*, 1990 and The World Bank, 1991 for different views on the matter), it is important to bear in mind that little attention has been paid to the sustainability issues in implementing policy reforms (Rodrik, 1990). Maintaining realistic real exchange rates — which should facilitate exports, avoid undue expansion in imports after trade liberalization measures and, at the same time, face the external debt service and the stop-go cycles experienced by many countries — is one of the key variables where sustainability is quite difficult to achieve. Furthermore, taking into account that most external financial flows entering into the region are short-term in orientation, it is crucial to get long-term external resources to help finance productive investments that enhance supply capabilities.

While, in principle, stabilization is supposed to precede structural reforms, in practice stabilization has proved to be an ongoing process. Under these conditions, waiting until stabilization with growth is achieved can mean an indefinite delay in the implementation of structural reforms to improve international competitiveness.

As macroeconomic stability starts to be achieved, it can be expected that domestic and foreign resources will tend to flow to exploit natural resources and cheap labour. This has happened in Chile (French-Davis *et al,* 1991) and also in several other Latin American countries with unstable macroeconomic environments. International specialization in industrial commodities and labour intensive goods may have significant benefits. It may lead to economies of scale in capital intensive industries and may facilitate the upgrading of marketing and some technological capabilities (that is, manufacturing standards and quality control). It may also lead, however, to problems regarding price fluctuations for these goods, the reduced long-term consumption of raw materials in industrialized countries due to technological progress, and the growing automation of production. Chile, for example, has not avoided many of these costs (Ominami and Madrid, 1989).[5/]

Consequently, if developing countries aspire to go further to be able to produce high value added goods and services to avoid falling further behind the innovatory advances now occurring in the industrialized world, an efficient macroeconomic policy is a necessary but not a sufficient condition. Trade liberalization and fostering innovatory activities are also needed to develop dynamic competitive advantages.

Trade liberalization

At the end of the 1980s, most Latin American countries had adopted or were heading towards more liberal trade policies. Within this general trend, a variety of approaches regarding tariff levels by type of goods, the dispersion and sequence of tariff reduction have been implemented. Non-tariff measures have also been reduced in most countries. However, significant differences among them remain. At the same time, exchange rate policies, macroeconomic conditions and specific policies for export promotion have not been applied in a similar manner throughout Latin America.

The recent revival of integration schemes, mostly taking the form of free trade agreements among Latin American countries and eventually with the United States, as proposed by the Enterprise of the Americas Initiative, is an important development that should be taken into account (Porta, 1991; Saborio *et al.*, 1992). These new arrangements may offer preferential access to specific markets with some tariff protection against third countries. The eventual tensions, however, between unilateral and bilateral trade openings, the trade and FDI creation and diversion and, more generally, the difficulties of these trade negotiations in the current macroeconomic situation cannot be underestimated.

Whereas most Latin American countries have been already applying trade liberalization measures, very few countries have attempted to combine trade liberalization with industrial and technological policies. So far the major exception is Brazil that, in 1990, launched, jointly with a gradual programme of trade liberalization [6] and new instruments for domestic competition policy, the Programme on Industrial Competitiveness and the Brazilian Programme on Quality and Productivity.

The industrial competitiveness programme has been conceived to develop high-tech branches and restructure existing sectors so as to achieve international standards on prices and quality. The main objective of the quality and productivity programme, launched in November 1990, is to encourage the Brazilian modernization effort by promoting quality and productivity of goods and services made in the country.

On paper, the trade and industrial policy regulations that the Government of Brazil has formulated is a significant departure from its traditional protectionist policies. At the same time, in so far as trade liberalization is conceived as a gradual process in which explicit industrial and technological policies are supposed to operate, the Brazilian approach differs from the neo-liberal approach adopted by other Latin American countries.

A number of microeconomic issues related to trade liberalization, that are almost completely ignored in current trade policies, should be taken into account. From the point of view of the present chapter, a key issue is the relationship between trade liberalization and technological innovation.

It is conventional wisdom that growing competition in product markets will spur technological efforts. As mentioned in a World Bank paper:[1]

> "A growing body of case studies from developed and industrializing countries indicates that competition is the prime motivation for managers to cut waste, improve technical parameters of production and allocate resources efficiently. Subsector evidence shows in addition that competition is a compelling force for firms to restructure outdated operations, introduce new product lines, and search for new markets."

Although there is certainly room to implement policy measures to foster competition among local producers (for example, reducing barriers to entry and exit), the small size of the domestic market in most developing countries makes oligopolistic supply structures in many industrial branches unavoidable. It is possible, however, that competition via imports may become a significant factor if two key conditions are present. First, changes in the import regime should be perceived by the private sector as credible and sustainable. Otherwise a "wait and see" attitude will prevail. Second, the impact of import competition should not be reduced by organizational arrangements that link foreign sellers and domestic buyers, or by the fact that the wholesale importer is the dominant local producer (Frischtak *et al.*, 1990).

As competing imports enter the country, the reduced protection in the domestic market may make available key inputs at prices near the international ones. Provided other measures are taken (see below), it may also favour technological efforts (basic and detailed engineering and design capacity) at product and process levels (increase product quality, upgrade product mix, reduce costs through more efficient production processes, etc.) to face the new competitive conditions. Existing enterprises, however, may also abandon their production activities and become importers, or move production to simpler phases (that is, assembling imported inputs), or concentrate their production in goods with little value added, or diversify their business into non-tradable areas.

The positive effects of trade liberalization are likely to be enhanced if private firms perceive that the domestic market is going to expand and/or if measures are taken to promote exports. In this connection, export rivalry may have positive effects on technological developments, especially regarding quality control and delivery times. Since, however, the effects of import liberalization on export performance are doubtful or at best delayed because of transitional costs and lags in supply response, policy ought to concentrate on enhancing supply capabilities and financial incentives for facilitating exports.

Unilateral trade liberalization policies should be implemented in a gradual manner with an adequate foreign exchange policy and with well designed anti-dumping devices to protect domestic producers against unfair competition (and not against any competition). At the same time, a clear system of incentives should be designed to foster export activities. If trade policies are not applied in this manner, as appears to be the case in some Latin American countries, the possibilities of reallocating the human and physical resources in existing firms are greatly reduced and the social costs of the adjustment process will certainly be high. Even if trade policies are relatively well designed, however, other measures are needed to induce firms to allocate resources for improving their structural competitiveness (Lall, 1990).

Before considering this question, the likely reaction of technology suppliers to trade policy reform should be noted. Instead of using FDI or licensing agreements to exploit foreign markets, foreign suppliers may directly export intermediate products, including technology, to those markets; and they may be particularly encouraged to do so whenever intellectual property legislation can assure an adequate protection for the product embodying the technology. It seems that one of the main reasons behind the offensive of the United States to enforce intellectual property legislation at the world level is to use international trade as a means to exploit technological assets (Correa, 1989).

If, despite trade liberalization, the country in question is implementing sectoral policies or has specific locational advantages that may justify exporting the technology rather than the good embodying it, it is likely that fully or majority controlled ventures will be preferred by technology suppliers, especially when they are allowed by the current policy changes in this respect.

Daniel Chudnovsky

Foreign direct investment and technology transfer deregulation

By the mid-1980s (and even before), many Latin American countries had modified their previously restrictive policies towards inward FDI and technology transfer and had shifted towards encouraging such investment in almost all domestic sectors (see UNCTC, 1988; UNCTAD, 1988; Calderón, 1992). The increase in FDI to Latin America is, however, probably more due to changes in trade policies (including subregional agreements) and sectoral regulations. These measures are far more important factors in influencing the behaviour of TNCs than the modifications in FDI and technology transfer policies.

In this connection, it is important to bear in mind that, in the case of Mexico, following its initial opening, the improved efficiency and the growing exports by TNC affiliates were not only consequences of the real devaluation of the exchange rate and access to imported parts and components in view of the trade liberalization measures. Sectoral programmes in the automotive and computer industries by which protection from foreign competition in the domestic market was granted in return for certain performance requirements, have also been crucial incentives for such moves. None the less, in other sectors like pharmaceuticals, neither the macroeconomic situation nor the sectoral programme led to similar results in terms of export expansion (UNCTC, 1992).

In the Argentine case, rationalized investments in the automotive sector were encouraged by negotiations initiated in 1987 that led to a sectoral trade agreement with Brazil, which came into force in 1991. In view of this possibility, Ford and Volkswagen created Autolatina in 1987, a joint venture whose goal is to rationalize and integrate its Argentine and Brazilian operations. A wholly-owned subsidiary was set up in Argentina (under a debt-equity conversion scheme) to manufacture gear boxes to export to Brazil. The local associate of Fiat in Argentina has also specialized part of its engine production for exports to Brazil.

Rationalized investments in the automotive and other sectors[8/] have been further encouraged with the implementation of the Southern Cone Common Market (Mercosur) by Argentina, Brazil, Uruguay and Paraguay.

Similarly to Mexico, within the current trade liberalization programme, the companies operating in the automotive sector in

136

Argentina have gained import protection through quotas and high custom duties. Furthermore, in exchange of an export commitment to Brazil and other destinations and an efficiency investment plan, they are allowed to import finished vehicles from their parent companies at very low customs duty.

The need for innovation policies

Although an increasing number of companies have improved the competitiveness of their products through some technological effort, many productive firms have shown little dynamism in their manufacturing and technological activities. Overall, rent-seeking and financial manoeuvring activities have received far more priority than technological efforts in the strategies of many domestic and foreign firms operating in Latin America.

To increase their competitiveness, firms urgently need to invest in new physical and technological capacities (including R&D) to modify their product mix, find new internal and external sources for product and process technologies, review their relationship with suppliers and customers and to improve their management practices (in marketing, procurement, financing, production and R&D). In this internal restructuring process, available information technologies can be extremely useful for improving productivity, if applied in the right organizational environment and with adequate manpower.

Transnational corporations can play a catalytic role in the diffusion of technical and managerial innovations in the host country. A number of TNCs have already been active in launching new products both for the domestic and foreign markets, in improving the quality of existing products, in increasing and modernizing the production capacity of affiliates, and in engaging in cooperative agreements with domestic firms (UNCTC, 1992; Basualdo and Fuchs, 1989). As TNCs increasingly perform R&D in host countries, it can be expected that they will play an increasingly important role in capacity-building in Latin America.

In a context of greater global competition, as TNCs upgrade the products and services offered by their affiliates, domestic firms too are induced to adopt similar practices. As dometic firms rise to the competitive challenge in local markets, and train labour and management, significant intra-industry spillovers occur. At the same time, inter-industry spillovers also take place when the innovatory activities of the affiliates enhance the competitiveness of their domestic suppliers (Blomström, 1991).

While acknowledging the catalytic role that TNCs play in stimulating innovatory activities, local technological capabilities cannot be advanced without deliberate efforts by competitive indigenous firms. At the same time, the existence of such capabilities and a growing market are powerful incentives to induce resource enhancing FDI into manufacturing and services.

Transnational corporations need dynamic firms to subcontract the manufacturing of parts and components and of products that need no longer be made in industrialized countries. They also need, in some more advanced host countries, local partners (firms or research institutions) to subcontract development work to adapt their products to user specifications and/or to undertake specific applied R&D activities. Some of these developments have gained momentum in Asian developing countries (as described in the Asian flock of "flying geese" Ozawa, 1991), but, as yet are seldom found in Latin America.

There is no doubt that the threat of international competition (both at product and at firm levels) can be a powerful stimulant for the restructuring of domestic companies. But it is also true that, in many of the sectors in which these companies are operating, international trade is often managed trade in terms of intrafirm trade. Furthermore, oligopolistic competition prevails in most countries.

Although the recent modifications in the trade regimes of most Latin American countries should greatly facilitate the task, governments should be able to use incentives to further encourage the restructuring of these companies.[9/] In certain difficult situations, the threat of allowing the entry of a new comer and coercion should not be excluded.

Besides modifying the rules of the game through macroeconomic stability and trade liberalization, private companies, especially small and medium-size enterprises, should be induced to undertake physical and technological investments and be assisted by governments (or by institutions initiated and supported by governments and the private sector) in such tasks.

Private firms, which are the key actors in any process of achieving structural competitiveness, need appropriate stimuli for reorganizing their production and marketing strategies and for creating an absorptive innovatory capacity. Although mutual stimuli for undertaking innovatory activities may appear once the process of technological accumulation is resumed, powerful incentives are needed to mobilize the potentialities of the private sector.

A predictable framework with macroeconomic stability and greater competition, especially international competition through trade and FDI liberalization, may become significant incentives to restructure companies and undertake innovatory activities if, at the same time, other stimuli are provided to create an appropriate business environment which fosters technology absorption and development with adequate spillovers.

Financial and fiscal schemes and time-bound trade protection for an eventual entry into new activities should be used. While in the past these incentives were generally given without any *quid pro quo*, the new context of greater competition may ensure a better spillover out of this resource allocation. In any case, incentives should only be given in exchange of specific performance requirements (for example, regarding exports, prices in domestic and foreign markets, quality achievements, productivity targets).

Before suggesting some specific policy lines, it is important to bear in mind that the process of achieving structural competitiveness through inducing innovatory activities in the private sector is riddled with all kinds of market failures. In addition to typical cases of policy failures, markets in many developing countries operate under quite imperfect conditions. Although it is true that, in certain cases, the lack of competition is aggravated by institutional barriers to entry and exit and some government regulations (Frischtak *et al.*, 1990), other key aspects of the market structure should be explicitly taken into account.

The small size of the domestic market, the existence of scale economies in several manufacturing activities and the presence of powerful private domestic and foreign interests are key conditions limiting the extent to which price and non-price competition takes place. In addition, the existence of strong externalities and imperfections in factor and product markets creates a clear case for government intervention.

Once it is accepted that the significant externalities, as well as the market failures involved in the process of creating structural competitiveness, justify government intervention, the challenge is how to design and implement such intervention. This is an extremely difficult task given the record of government failures and the fact that the ongoing

139

process of reforming the State is constrained not only by the fiscal crisis and the tremendous deterioration of the Latin American public administration, but also by the prevailing "hands off" philosophy.

In these conditions, while relying, as much as possible, on the competitive stimuli of market forces to mobilize private sector capabilities, governments should have the technical capacity to propose and implement selective and well defined pro-active policies like those suggested below. For this new policy set in the making, the name of innovation policies is particularly appropriate not only because the aim is to promote technological and organizational innovations at firm and at industry levels. The name is also appropriate because innovative approaches in the way private companies restructure and governments intervene to foster structural competitiveness should receive priority attention.

Although in some critical branches it is crucial to design and implement specific sectoral policies, it is important to recognize that the boundaries between sectors and technologies are becoming difficult to define. For this reason the concept of industrial complexes (in which the linkages between branches are taken into account) instead of sectors should be used (as has been attempted in Brazil). Besides sectoral policies, horizontal or cross-sectoral policy efforts should be initiated and supported by firms, governments and non-profit institutions, to promote the crucial inter-industry and inter-firm linkages. In this area, some selectivity criteria regarding types of firms or regions should also be used.

At a more general level, the enlargement and improvement of the physical and social infrastructure, the educational and the R&D systems, in which almost no investments have been made in recent years, should receive the highest priority. At a more specific level and depending on particular country considerations, the areas in which the private sector capabilities could be mobilized with some government assistance are set forth below.

First, adequate financial and fiscal schemes are often necessary to favour productive investment, not only in physical assets (that is, facilities, machinery and equipment), but also in intangible assets (for example, training, quality control, consultancy services and R&D).[10] Given the serious problems in the functioning of capital markets in Latin America and the short-term orientation of the financial system, the cost and availability of finance in the pursuit of industrial restructuring and technological modernization needs urgent attention. At the same time, specific attention to design appropriate incentives should be given in the tax reform in progress in most Latin American countries.

Second, it is also often necessary to promote the use of consulting and engineering services that can assist firms in devising industrial restructuring schemes and adoption of new product, process and organizational technologies. In these services, the information and eventual advice on how to obtain and better negotiate technology transfer agreements with foreign and domestic suppliers should receive attention.

Within the relatively little experience in these matters in Latin America, the Chile Foundation, a private non-profit organization created in 1976 as a joint venture between the ITT Corporation and the Government of Chile to transfer technologies for improving natural resources and productive capacity and to stimulate the creation of new enterprises based on these technologies is an outstanding example (Huss, 1991).

Third, the retraining of managers, technicians and workers and the special training of new skills should be encouraged by the provision of specialized services and by specific subsidies at the firm level. Retraining of top and medium-level management should receive high priority to be able to initiate a different production culture in most enterprises.

Fourth, availability of additional support services in the area of design, quality assurance, standards and testing are crucial. These activities can normally be provided by industry associations with some support or supervision by governments.

Fifth, given the prevailing trend towards enforcing industrial and intellectual property rights, it is important to assist companies in applying for and obtaining access to use such rights. At the same time, advice should be given to domestic companies (especially small and medium-size ones) on how to defend themselves *vis-à-vis* abuses of the market power by patent and other industrial property holders.

Sixth, training schemes, physical and financial facilities for start up companies may need improvement. Fresh graduates from universities and technical schools should receive encouragement to create new companies. Large private and state companies should also encourage the formation of subcontractors (to provide parts and components, pre- and after-sales services, etc.) by providing long-term contracts (and technical and, eventually, financial assistance) on the basis of performance requirements. Furthermore, institutions or programmes providing training and services needed for launching new business, such as EMPRETEC, should be utilized.[11/]

Seventh, greater support to basic and applied research at the universities and research institutes while attempting to link them to the productive sector needs attention, on the basis of secondment of scientific and technical personnel and other schemes (for some examples, see ECLAC, 1990).

Finally, considerable imagination is required to give new objectives to existing institutions in order to facilitate the linkages between firms for joint technology projects, between users and suppliers, and between firms and research institutes and universities, which are crucial in developing structural competitiveness. Many of these linkages can be better developed in specific sites or regions within the country, taking account of particular locational advantages that may facilitate the creation of clusters.

In allocating financial and technical resources, some selectivity criteria may be unavoidable. Whereas priority is normally given to those branches in which most firms have serious competitive problems and where employment is more significant, a complementary course of action should also be explored in order to be able to obtain quick results and learn how to intervene in an efficient manner. It may make sense to allocate a portion of the available resources to firms (without necessarily entering into the difficult process of picking winners) which have already shown capacity to compete on the basis of technology, but need some additional focused assistance.

By choosing a number of firms with relatively small competitiveness problems, effects would hopefully show tangible results and appear relatively quickly. Successes would also serve as a demonstration effect for other more problematic firms and branches. By putting in motion a restructuring process with strong emphasis on the diffusion of innovations, it is to be expected that, in addition to the increased use of imported technologies, the restructuring process at firm and at industry levels will also create a demand for adapting technologies to user needs, providing, first, after sales (repairs and maintenance) and, then, before sales services (that may lead to customizing designs and accessories). In this way, a growing market for promoting the indigenous production of these technologies will hopefully arise.

Given the importance of certain new technologies, however, it may be desirable that domestic production should be encouraged without waiting for the normal diffusion pattern of imported technologies. To encourage such entry and facilitate the learning process, trade protection has normally been used and, in some Latin American countries like Brazil, a market reserve against foreign firms has also been applied in the case of "informatics".

Fostering regional cooperation

While innovation policies have primarily a national and even a local dimension, there is a clear scope for regional cooperation in this new field.

To reduce the social costs of entry into high-tech goods and services and facilitate a quicker learning process, serious consideration should be given to regional cooperation. The costs of protection that should be granted to the production of this type of goods would be lower in an expanded subregional market than if the action is taken by each country individually. The size of the expanded market provides a wider basis for absorbing R&D resources and financing the costly investments in fixed assets and the manpower training required by the technologically most advanced industries.

Notwithstanding the obvious advantages of joint efforts in high-tech areas (as the recent experiences in Europe suggests), the difficulties cannot be overlooked. The high tariff protection that some of these activities received in the past made local producers (for example, in Brazil) reluctant to open their market to partners from neighbouring countries (that were considered being basically importers of goods made in industrialized countries).

While exploring the possibilities of joint Latin American projects in this crucial field is obviously very important, other issues have also regional implications or call for cooperation efforts. Regarding TNCs, wider markets may encourage not only new FDI, but also rationalized FDI with the aim of restructuring existing operations and developing new product lines. In this way, more technologically advanced goods and services at reduced prices may be produced in the countries in question and intra- and inter-industry spillovers may be created.

In the Mexican case there is no doubt that the negotiation of a free trade agreement with the United States and Canada has been a significant factor in encouraging FDI flows in recent years. It seems that the better access to the North American market from Mexico has been an important attraction to FDI both for existing companies and new-comers. Furthermore, with the completion of NAFTA, not only is Mexico undergoing significant structural adjustment measures (for example, with respect to privatization and trade and FDI), but it has accepted a long-term commitment as these measures may not be reversed in the future.

The subsequential effects of NAFTA on other Latin American countries have begun to be discussed, and trade and FDI creation and deviation effects have been pointed out in the emerging literature on the subject (Saborio *et al.*, 1992). Since most studies do not take into account dynamic effects, however, it is difficult to gauge the likely impact of this development with any precision.

Although the growth of subregional trade has been significant among Mercosur member countries, given the macroeconomic problems that they are facing - and hence the great difficulties in policy coordination - it is likely that, despite the political will, integration will not proceed to the extent originally envisaged. Depending on the macroeconomic evolution and the way trade and industrial policies are applied, trade expansion would mostly follow the lines of either inter- or intra-industrial specialization, except in some branches in which intrafirm or managed trade may certainly prevail (Chudnovsky, 1992).

It is important to bear in mind that the participation of United States investors (relative to European ones) in both Argentina and Brazil though significant, is lower than in other Latin American countries. It is likely that an enlarged subregional market and a free trade agreement with the United States may provide a strong incentive for attracting fresh United States direct investment, and for rationalizing the activities of existing United States and European affiliates in these countries (Chudnovsky, 1992).

The wholesale restructuring of existing activities in domestic companies can be better managed if a subregional approach is taken. The possibilities of reconverting existing firms are enhanced by the access to greater markets and the eventual contribution by partners from the other member countries (or third countries) in the companies to be restructured. In this way not only trade, but also intraregional FDI and technology transfer may be generated.

In the revival of subregional integration efforts that is taking place in Latin America, the existing bias towards negotiating almost exclusively trade matters should be redressed. As a growing number of Latin American countries seek to put in motion some innovation policy measures that have been successfully applied in the OECD countries and some Asian developing countries, the room for regional cooperation in this field should be greatly expanded.

For effective regional cooperation in trade and innovation policies, it is crucial to exchange views and experiences on how to implement such new approaches, and on the actions which might be taken by governments and non-market institutions. This process should contribute to enriching collective experiences in this novel area of policy-making, and facilitate the conclusion of joint projects.

Concluding remarks

In spite of the fact that the performance of most Latin American economies in the 1980s has been poor by any development indicator, the prevailing neo-liberal view is that, with orthodox stabilization and the introduction of structural reforms in progress in the 1990s, the region will achieve price stability, and a resumption of economic expansion.

On the fact that stabilization is a crucial collective good, and that some of the structural reforms in progress are working, a wide consensus can be acknowledged. No similar consensus exists on how best to design structural adjustment programmes to encourage and finance the kind of physical and intangible investment needed to develop the dynamic comparative advantages, and increase the participation of Latin American countries in the global economy. The experiences of OECD countries and Asian developing countries, however, are worth recalling.

It is noteworthy that, although private firms are the main actors in the innovation process, all OECD Governments are involved, in different degrees and by different means, in the upgrading of indigenous technological capacity. Japan is the most clear case of a national system of innovation aimed at increasing the competitiveness of the economy by an unusual combination of government intervention and strong private sector participation (at both the conglomerates and small and medium-size firm levels). In the United States, except in critical strategic sectors like defence and semi-conductors, the government role in relation to industry and technology has been chiefly concerned with competition and trade policies in the United States. In contrast, more mixed solutions involving government intervention and/or the concerted actions of private agents have generally been attempted in Europe (OECD, 1987).

Subsidies to industries in trouble, jointly with non-tariff measures, were widely used in OECD countries throughout the 1970s and peaked in the early 1980s. In some cases, trade adjustment assistance has also been provided. The results achieved, in terms of regaining competitiveness, are not easily assessed (Lawrence, 1988). In addition to programmes for declining industries, more focused policy instruments have been used to support high-tech sectors; however, the concept, risks, and implications of "strategic" policy interventions are at issue (Krugman, 1986 and OECD, 1990b). In Europe, attempts to facilitate the entry into high-tech industries by supporting national champions have had uneven success. At the same time, policies to support high-tech industries have been increasingly made at regional levels and are an integral part of the European integration process. In addition to the crucial role played by the Department of Defense in promoting high-tech ventures (though in some cases with doubtful commercial results), there is a lively ongoing debate in the United States about the role that the Government should play in these matters.

Although measures in declining and emerging activities are still applied in most OECD countries, a clear shift in policies related to industry is visible. The new policy directions are clearly oriented towards increasing the competitiveness of the industrialized economies through the support for investment in know-how and by fostering the internationalization process of enterprises (OECD, 1990a). A variety of programmes aimed at providing support for intangible investments have been put in motion in many OECD countries, jointly with a number of activities for promoting the application of microelectronics and of advanced manufacturing technology (OECD, 1989 and 1991). Government policies have been significant regarding information and awareness of such technologies, especially in the early stages of diffusion, the provision of advisory and consultancy services and setting up of different training schemes. Several aid programmes with the purpose of encouraging the internationalization of industrial enterprises have been established in recent years. Emphasis is placed on the international procurement of technology, cross-border co-operative R&D (where the EU has been particularly active), and on promoting FDI investment aimed at upgrading domestic competitiveness. In fact, one of the main purposes of the European internal market is to enhance the competitiveness of European firms in the high-tech industries through harmonization of national procurement policies, technical standards and rules on subsidies for R&D (Tussie and Casaburi, 1991).

In East Asia, with the exception of Hong Kong that is closest to the neo-liberal paradigm, a variety of trade, industrial and innovation policies have been used to foster industrialization on the basis of dynamic comparative advantages. In the Republic of Korea low protection for mature industries has been combined by selective intervention in capital and technology intensive industries, relying on high rates of protection, restriction to FDI inflows and subsidized and highly selective finance. The well developed local design and innovation capabilities have been fostered by high efforts in training adequate manpower and growing R&D expenditures (Pack and Westphal, 1986; Amsden, 1989; Westphal, 1990). Taiwan Province of China, has also been active in offering its industries high rates of protection and generous fiscal incentives. It has been more open to FDI than the Republic of Korea and less interventionist in promoting heavy industry. Public companies have been very important in several industries, however, and the Government has established several research and service organizations to promote technological and managerial upgrading in industry (Wade, 1988). Finally, FDI in manufacturing and services has been extremely important in the rapid development of Singapore's economy. After an initial period of import substitution, very liberal trade and FDI policies have been successfully applied. The State has, however, been quite active in the development of infrastructure and manpower training, as well as in curbing trade unions and implementing extensive labour market interventions (Fong, 1987).

These experiences are not directly transferable to Latin America, but they do provide a basis to question the conventional wisdom, according to which the entrepreneurial spirit will sooner or later flourish and productive investment will pick up as market forces fully operate in a stable macroeconomic environment. It is possible that, if economic agents learn to operate in a more open and predictable economy, some Latin American countries may enter into a sustainable growth path and revert the previous marginalization from the dynamic forces of the world economy. In this scenario, however, resource enhancing investments and the creation of dynamic competitive advantages cannot be necessarily expected.

Macroeconomic stabilization without stagnation is a necessary, but not a sufficient condition, to facilitate better allocation of human and physical resources. Enforcing competition may provide a stimulant for adopting and creating technological and organizational innovations in so far as the right institutional framework is beginning to be developed.

Most firms in Latin America, however, have not been able to increase investment in manufacturing and services. Consequently, they have generally not upgraded their process technologies, which has hindered upgrading into more value-added production. The international competitiveness of Latin American goods and services thus remains very fragile.

To make the adjustment to the new conditions, existing companies not only need a predictable macroeconomic framework and the threat of international and domestic competition. They also need time and stimuli both in the trade and in the innovation policies areas.

Trade liberalization policies should be implemented in a gradual manner with an adequate foreign exchange policy and with well-designed anti-dumping devices to protect domestic producers against unfair competition. At the same time, a clear system of incentives should be designed to foster export-generating activities. Subregional trade agreements or custom unions may also facilitate the restructuring process by expanding the relevant markets.

To induce firms to allocate resources to upgrade their structural competitiveness, other macro-organizational policies are needed. The provision of adequate financial and fiscal schemes, consulting services, retraining and training of personnel, support services and linkages between research institutes and firms, as well as between firms, are among the most relevant activities governments should take care of and/or initiate and support appropriate institutions for that purpose.

Financial and fiscal schemes and time-bound trade protection for an eventual entry into new activities should be used. While in the past these incentives were generally given without any *quid pro quo*, the new context of greater competition should assure a better spillover out of this resource allocation.

Innovation policies should be applied on a selective basis both at the level of some key sectors (the less competitive and/or the more promising ones, without necessarily entering into the difficult process of picking winners) and at a more horizontal level for some types of firms or specific regions.

Different forms of TNC activity and technology transfer should become important channels in helping Latin American economies catch up with international advances in product and process technologies. If these imports are used to complement domestic technological efforts, the chances of indigenous firms in mastering such technologies are likely to be greater.

Given that structural reforms are already in motion in most Latin American countries, the debate on how to put in motion innovation policies and how to link them with trade policies (and eventually competition and FDI policies) cannot be postponed. As discussed in the present paper, the received literature and experiences from other regions are solid enough to start working on these issues.

To promote a more constructive debate, and develop more specific innovation policies and institutional arrangements for implementation, however, it is important to fill a few critical gaps.

First, more information is needed on how domestic and foreign companies have adjusted to the significant structural changes (especially trade liberalization) that have been taking place and the role played by FDI and technology imports and development in such adjustment process. Country studies would aid in identifying the sort of assistance private firms may need from government or other institutions to increase their competitiveness.

Second, there is need to clarify at a conceptual and empirical level the kind of spillovers that can be expected from the activities of TNCs operating in manufacturing and producer services, in the context of greater domestic and international competition.

Third, an assessment should be made of the availability of external and internal finance for productive and intangible investment and on the respective roles to be played by the private sector and public sector in stimulating innovatory capacity in Latin American countries. It would be important to take stock of the experiences available in the region regarding the financial and fiscal schemes for promoting innovatory activities, diffusion of innovations, provision of technical and consultancy services and of the role of institutions concerned with these instruments.

Finally, governments and international organizations need to follow and improve the management of trade policies, including the implementation of subregional integration schemes and the negotiations of free trade zones with the United States. In addition to the various traditional trade policy issues, attention should also be paid to trade in services, intellectual property rights and access to technology.

Notes

1. International or structural competitiveness is used in the sense discussed by ECLAC (1990) and especially by OECD (1992).
2. In so far as industrial restructuring and technological modernization require not only innovation, but also financial competition, industrial and technological policies, innovation policies are used in the present paper as a general term to refer to this complex policy set. For some elements of this new policy set, see ECLAC (1990) and SELA (1991).
3. In contrast to earlier approaches in which innovations were treated as single events resulting from linear research, innovation is now conceived as a complex process characterized by continuous and numerous interactions and feedbacks, both within and between firms and the science and technology environment in which they operate (that is, the chain-linked model as discussed by Kline and Rosenberg, 1986). The ability to master technical knowledge is developed cumulatively over time through the acquisition of skills, production experience, learning by doing and by using, imitation and R&D expenditures. Since part of this knowledge is tacit (that is, ill-defined and uncodified), the cumulative nature of technology is, to some extent, firm-specific. It is this proprietary nature of technological innovations that is one of the key assets of the innovating firm and a main source of the ownership and internalization advantages that characterize TNCs.
4. Williamson (1990) defines Washington consensus as "the political Washington of Congress and senior members of the administration and the technocratic Washington of the international financial institutions, the economic agencies of the US Government, the Federal Reserve Board, and the think tanks" (p.7).
5. In some agroindustrial activities, however, the Chilean experience suggests the importance of incorporating technical progress in traditional exports. In this respect the activities of the Chile Foundation have been significant (Huss, 1991).
6. In addition to removing most non-tariff barriers, existing tariffs with an average of 35 per cent and extreme rates between 0 and 105 per cent have been reduced in a gradual manner since 1991, to reach in 1994 a range between 0 and 40 per cent with a mean and modal tariff rate of 20 per cent. A 40 per cent rate is only reserved for products to be especially protected for technological learning or other criteria fixed by the government. Tariff for non-produced goods and inputs were reduced to zero in the second half of 1990.
7. Frischtak *et. al.*, 1990, p. 5.

8. TNCs like Nestlé, Campbell, Nabisco, Parmalat, Philip Morris and Swift have been investing in some Argentine agroindustrial segments.
9. In the case of the large domestic conglomerates, it would be advisable to study ways of legalizing a process that has already started the internationalization of their activities. While some of these activities, however, may bring important externalities to the investing countries (for example, "strategic alliances" in developing new technologies – or other less ambitious technological activities – with partners from other advanced developing countries and/or from industrialized countries) others may simply be means to transfer financial resources abroad.
10. The whole question of financing productive investment and sharing the risk of innovatory activities is an extremely important policy issue hardly yet discussed in the financial reform in progress in developing countries.
11. EMPRETEC is a programme developed by UNCTC to help start up companies. It began as a pilot project in Argentina in March 1988 with funding from the Government of Italy. EMPRETEC is also operational in Chile, Ghana, Nigeria, Uruguay and Zimbabwe.

References

Amsden, A. (1989). *Asia's Next Giant. South Korea and Late Industrialization.* New York: Oxford University Press.

Basualdo, E. and M. Fuchs (1989). Nuevas formas de inversión de las empresas extranjeras en la industria argentina, Buenos Aires: CEPAL.

Bergsman, J. and W. Edisis (1988). Debt-equity swaps and foreign direct investment in Latin America. Discussion Paper No. 2, Washington, D.C., International Finance Corporation.

Bielschowsky, R. (1992). Transnational corporations and the manufacturing sector in Brazil. Santiago: CEPAL. (mimeo).

Blomström, M. (1991). Host country benefits of foreign investment, National Bureau of Economic Research Working Paper No. 3615, Cambridge, Massachusetts.

Calderón, A. (1992). Inversión Extranjera Directa en América Latina y el Caribe 1970-1990. Santiago: CEPAL (mimeo).

Casson, M.C. (ed.) 1991. *Global Research Strategy and International Competitiveness*, Oxford: Basil Blackwell.

Chudnovsky, D. (1992). The future of hemispheric integration: the Mercosur and the Enterprise for the Americas Initiative. Centro de Investigaciones para la Transformación (CENIT), Buenos Aires. In W. Fritsch (ed.), *Latin America in the Global Economy*, North South Institute, Miami, Florida. (forthcoming).

Correa, C. (1989). Propiedad intelectual, innovación tecnológica y comercio internacional. *Comercio Exterior* (Mexico DF.) diciembre.

Dunning, J. (1993). Multinational enterprises and the global economy. Wokingham, Berkshire: Addison Wesley.

ECLAC (1990). *Changing Production Patterns with Social Equity*, (United Nations, publication, Sales No. E.90.II.G.6).

151

Fanelli, J.M., R. Frenkel and G. Rozenwurcel (1990). Growth and structural reform in Latin America. Report prepared for UNCTAD, CEDES, Buenos Aires.

Fong Pang Eng (1987). Foreign investment and the state in Singapore. In V. Cable and B. Persaud, eds. *Developing with Foreign Investment*. London: Croom Helm.

French-Davis, R., P. Leiva and R. Madrid (1991). *Trade Liberalization in Chile: Experiences and Prospects*. Trade Policy Studies No. 1 (United Nations publication, Sales No. 91.II.D.18).

Frischtak, C. with B. Hadjimichael and U. Zachau (1990). *Competition Policies for Industrializing Countries*. Washington, D.C.: The World Bank.

Fritsch, W. and G. Franco (1991). *Foreign Direct Investment in Brazil. Its Impact on Industrial Restructuring*. OECD Development Centre, Paris.

Granstrand O., L. Håkanson and S. Sjölander, eds. (1992). *Technology, Management and International Business*. Chichester and New York: John Wiley and Sons.

Huss, T. (1991). Transfer of technology: the case of the Chile Foundation. *CEPAL Review* (April).

Kell, G. and S. Marchese (1991). Developing countries' exports of textiles and metals: the question of sustainability of recent growth. *UNCTAD Review*, vol. 1, No. 3 (October).

Kline, S. J. and N. Rosenberg (1986). An overview of innovation. In R. Landau and N. Rosenberg, eds. *The Positive Sum Strategy*. Washington, D.C.: National Academy Press.

Krugman, P. (ed.) (1986). *Strategic Trade Policy and The New International Economics*. Cambridge, Massachusetts: The MIT Press.

Lall, S.(1990). *Building Industrial Competitiveness in Developing Countries*. Paris: OECD. Development Centre.

Lawrence, R. (1988). Structural adjustment policies in developed countries, UNCTAD/ITP/8.

_____ (1987). *Structural Adjustment and Economic Performance*. Paris: OECD.

_____ (1989). *Government Policies and the Diffusion of Microelectronics*. Paris: OECD.

_____ (1990a). *Industrial Policy in OECD Countries. Annual Review 1990*. Paris: OECD.

_____ (1990b). Support policies for strategic industries: systemic risks and emerging issues. A forum for the future conference. Paris: OECD.

_____ (1991). *Managing Manpower for Advanced Manufacturing Technology*. Paris: OECD.

_____ (1992). *Technology and the Economy. The Key Relationships*. Paris: OECD.

Ominami, C. and R. Madrid (1989). *La Inserción de Chile en los Mercados Internacionales*. Dos Mundos, Santiago de Chile.

Ostry, S. (1990). *Governments and Corporations in a Shrinking World: Trade and Innovation Policies in the United States, Europe and Japan.* New York: Council of Foreign Relations.

Ozawa, T. (1991). The dynamics of Pacific Rim Industrialization. How Mexico can join the Asian flock of flying geese. In Riordan Roett (ed.). *Mexico's External Relations in the 1990s.* Boulder, Colorado and London: Lynne Rienner.

Pack, H. and L. Westphal (1986). Industrial strategy and technological change. Theory versus reality. *Journal of Development Economics* (June).

Patel, P. and K. Pavitt (1989). Do large firms control the world's technology. Science Policy Research Unit (SPRU), United Kingdom. Discussion Paper (mimeo).

Peres Nuñez, W. (1990). *Foreign Direct Investment and Industrial Development in Mexico.* Paris: OECD Development Centre.

_____ (1992). Latin America's experience with technology policies. Current situation and prospects. (mimeo).

Porta, F. (1991). Apertura comercial e integración regional en América Latina. Diagnóstico y escenarios alternativos. Buenos Aires: CENIT.

Porter, M. (1990). *The Competitive Advantage of Nations.* New York: The Free Press.

Rodrik, D. (1990). How should structural adjustment programs be designed? *World Development* (July).

Saborio S. *et al.* (1992). *The premise and the promise: free trade in the Americas.* New Brunswick, New Jersey: Overseas Development Council, Transaction Publishers.

SELA (1991). *Desarrollo Industrial y Cambio Tecnológico. Políticas para América Latina y el Caribe en los noventa.* Caracas: Editorial Nueva Sociedad.

Tussie, D. and G. Casaburi (1991). Los nuevos bloques comerciales: a la búsqueda de un fundamento perdido. *Desarrollo Económico,* Buenos Aires (Abril-Junio).

UNCTAD (1988). Technology related policies and legislation in a changing economic and technological environment, TD/B/C.6/146, Geneva.

_____ (1989). *Trade and Development Report.* UNCTAD/TDR/9 (United Nations publication, Sales No. 89.II.D.14).

_____ (1994). *World Investment Report, 1994: Transnational Corporations Employment and the Workplace* (United Nations publication, Sales No. E.94.II.A.14).

_____ (1995a). *Trade and Development Report.* UNCTAD/TDR/15 (United Nations publication, Sales No. E.95.II.D.16).

_____ (1995b). *World Investment Report 1995: Transnational Corporations and Competitiveness* (United Nations publication, Sales No. E.95.II.A.9).

UNCTC (1988). *Transnational Corporations in World Development" Trends and Prospects* (United Nations publication, Sales No. E.88.II.A.7).

_____ (1992). Foreign direct investment and industrial restructuring in Mexico. *Current Studies,* No.18, United Nations, New York.

Wade, R. (1988). State intervention in "outward -looking" development: neoclassical theory and Taiwanese practice. In G. White (ed.). *Developmental States in East Asia.* Hong Kong: Macmillan Institute of Development Studies.

Westphal, L. (1990). Industrial policy in an export-propelled economy: South Korea. *Journal of Economic Perspectives* (Summer).

Williamson, J. (1990). *Latin American Adjustment. How much has happened?.* Washington, D.C.: Institute for International Economics.

World Bank (1991). *World Development Report 1991.* Washington, D.C.: World Bank.

5

Globalization and development in Africa

John Cantwell

Globalization and the trend in the international division of labour run against Africa's resource-based economies. For that reason, as well as a variety of internal constraints, the potential for substantial new foreign direct investment in Africa is limited in the immediate future. Nevertheless, FDI plays a significant role within many African economies and transnational corporations can be basic catalysts for development in Africa.

Foreign direct investment in Africa

Most recent studies of economic development in Africa, and of the role of TNCs within such development, have tended to take a rather pessimistic overall view of current trends and future prospects, while pointing to some occasional brighter spots and advancing some more positive policy recommendations (see, for example, Stewart, Lall and Wangwe, 1992, and UNCTAD, 1995a). There can be no question that, since the 1960s, the main growth areas for TNC investments in the developing world have been in East Asia and to a lesser extent Latin America, and not Africa. Historically, however, Africa has been an important investment location for European TNCs and for these firms

Africa remains significant even if new investment has been limited (Cantwell, 1991). The continuing importance of investment in Africa is especially true of British and French TNCs, and to a lesser degree German and Italian companies, which have had traditional historical links with Africa. European TNCs have continued to dominate inward direct investment in Africa, just as other similar regional clusters have been established by the leading role of the United States TNCs in investment in Latin America, and by Japanese TNCs in East Asia (UNCTC, 1991).

In 1981, 12.7 per cent of the total stock of foreign direct investment in developing countries of firms of the eight major industrialized countries was located in Africa (Cantwell, 1991). This excludes South Africa, which is normally counted among the developed countries. In the mid-1970s, inward FDI flows into Africa continued to be sufficient to maintain its share of FDI stock in the developing countries, with flows into Africa accounting for 17.1 per cent of the total flow of FDI to developing countries in 1974-1978. As investment in the newly industrialized countries took off in the late 1970s, however, Africa's share of FDI inflows into developing areas fell back to 8.9 per cent from 1979-1983. Although in the aftermath of the Latin American debt crisis Africa's share of new FDI was restored to a level almost sufficient to maintain its existing share of FDI stocks (at 12.1 per cent of inflows into all developing countries from 1981-1990), following recovery in Latin America, Africa's share of FDI inflows slipped right back to 4.9 per cent in the period 1991-1994 (UNCTAD, 1995b).

It is also clear from table 1 that, where new investment in Africa has taken place in more recent years, it has been quite highly concentrated in a relatively narrow range of countries. Much of this investment has been directed to the North African economies of Egypt, Morocco and the Libyan Arab Jamahiriya, while in sub-Saharan Africa the more attractive locations have been Nigeria, Angola, Zambia, Namibia, Côte d'Ivoire, and Swaziland (UNCTAD, 1995a). Burkina Faso, Cameroon and Zaire received significant investments in the late 1970s and early 1980s (Dunning *et al.*, 1987), but they have fared badly since that time. It is perhaps no accident that the sub-Saharan African countries with the best industrialization records have been the Côte d'Ivoire, Kenya, Gabon and Zimbabwe (Lall, 1992), a group of countries that overlap quite closely with those that have tended to attract the greater involvement of TNCs. While Zimbabwe is the one country in this group that has induced little

Table 1.   Annual average flow of inward foreign direct investment, 1982-1994
(In millions of United States dollars)

Country	1982-1985	1986-1990	1991-1994
Algeria	-13.3	6.8	9
Angola	141.3	69.8	386
Benin	0	0.6	10
Botswana	40	61	40
Burkina Faso	1	1	0.3
Burundi	1.5	1.2	1
Cameroon	165	-9.2	-38
Cape Verde	n.a.	0.4	0
Central African Republic	6	4	-3
Chad	9	11.2	2.8
Comoros	n.a.	3	2.3
Congo	35	17	4
Côte d'Ivoire	34	52	63
Djibouti	0	0.2	1.8
Egypt	673	1068	435
Equatorial Guinea	1.3	3.8	27.5
Ethiopia	0	0.4	4.3
Gabon	67	75	56
Gambia	-0.8	3.2	7
Ghana	7	6	22
Guinea	0.5	13.5	20.5
Guinea-Bissau	0.8	0.8	2
Kenya	17	39	9
Lesotho	3.8	11.8	8.5
Liberia	26	239	9
Libyan Arab Jamahiriya	562.5	1067.8	434.8
Madagascar	3.3	11	18
Malawi	11	14	8
Mali	4.5	-1	-2.8
Mauritania	8	4	4
Mauritius	8	25	16
Morocco	48.3	95.6	442
Mozambique	0.3	5	26
Namibia	0	7	75.8
Niger	5.3	11.6	0.3
Nigeria	364	723	780
Rwanda	15.5	16.2	4
Senegal	2	2	8
Seychelles	10	21	22
Sierra Leone	-5	-14	16
Somalia	-6.3	-3.4	-4.8
South Africa	98.3	-1.8	-7

/...

(Table 1, cont'd)

Country	1982-1985	1986-1990	1991-1994
Sudan	7.3	-3.2	-0.3
Swaziland	-0.8	49.8	57.8
Togo	6	7	2
Tunisia	186.3	74.2	263.3
Uganda	-0.5	-0.6	2.3
United Republic of Tanzania	7	0	12
Zaire	-40	-15	4
Zambia	34	113	97
Zimbabwe	-1	-13	15

Source: UNCTAD, *World Investment Report 1995* (United Nations publication, Sales No. 95.II.A.9).

n.a. = not available

new FDI since the establishment of democratic majority rule, this may be a temporary feature of the period of political transition, as the country retains a substantial stock of FDI from the past (Clarke, 1980) and a large expatriate population.

Even considering just the new investment in Africa, much is associated with firms that have historical roots in Africa, and especially with European companies. The interest of these firms often began from colonial ties, particularly for a range of British companies in resource-based areas (mining and agricultural plantations), in allied trading activities, as well as in the provision of basic infrastructure (such as the construction of railway systems). A list of some of these early investors is set out in table 2. The list includes the British-owned firms Rio Tinto Zinc (RTZ) in mining in Zimbabwe, Imperial Tobacco in Kenya and Zimbabwe, Lever Brothers in coconut and palm oil plantations in Nigeria, Mitchell Cotts in the export of primary products from Kenya, and the British South Africa Company in railways in Zimbabwe. French TNCs also concentrated on mining, plantations and trade, including Schneider-Cruesot in iron ore mining in North Africa, as well as Elf Acquitaine in oil and various trading companies in Gabon (Cantwell, 1991).

In that respect, Africa's position in the international division of labour has not changed very much in recent years. Most African economies remain largely oriented towards resource-based activities,

Table 2. Historically significant foreign direct investors in Africa

Company name	Home country	Host country	Date of establishment	Sector
Anglo-French Sisal Co.	UK/France	Kenya	1931	Sisal growing
Ass. Portland Cement	UK	Kenya	1933	Building materials
BAT (Imperial Tobacco)	UK	Kenya	1907	Tobacco
BAT (Imperial Tobacco)	UK	Zimbabwe	1917	Tobacco
BOC	UK	Zimbabwe	1930s	Industrial gases
BP (APOC)	UK	Kenya	Interwar	Oil distribution
BSA	UK	Zimbabwe	Pre-1914	Railways, plantations
Balfour Beatty	UK	Kenya	1922	Power generation
Bird and Co.	UK	Kenya	1920	Merchant trade
Brooke Bond	UK	Kenya	1924	Tea and coffee processing
Brooke Bond	UK	Tanzania	Interwar	Tea and coffee plantations
Brooke Bond (Liebigs)	UK	Zimbabwe	Pre-1914	Cattle ranching
Brooke Bond (Liebigs)	UK	Kenya	1935	Metal processing
James Finlay	UK	Kenya	1924	Tea manufacture
Firestone	USA	Liberia	1920s	Rubber plantations
Foote Minerals	USA	Zimbabwe	Pre-1914	Chrome mining
Forestal Land and Timber	UK	Kenya	1932	Wattle bark
Gibson and Co.	UK	Kenya	1920	Merchant trade
Guggenheim Enterprises	USA	Congo	Pre-1914	Diamond mining, rubber plantations
ICI	UK	Kenya	1911	Soda extraction and processing
Ind Coope Ltd.	UK	Kenya	1922	Beer manufacture
Mitchell Cotts	UK	Kenya	1906	Export of primary products
RTZ	UK	Zimbabwe	1929	Mining
Schneider-Creusot	France	North Africa	Pre-1914	Iron ore mining
Shell	UK	Nigeria	1951	Oil
Shell	UK	Tunisia	1951	Oil
Sinclair	USA	Angola	1920s	Oil exploration
Sinclair	USA	Ghana	1920s	Oil exploration
Société Générale	Belgium	Congo	Pre-1914	Metal mining
Tate and Lyle	UK	Zimbabwe	1940s	Sugar plantations
Turner and Newall	UK	Zimbabwe	1917	Asbestos mining
Unilever (Lever Bros.)	UK	Congo	1910	Vegetable oil trading
Unilever (Lever Bros.)	UK	Nigeria	1910	Coconut & palm plantations
Unilever (Utd. Africa Co.)	UK	Kenya	1924	Food machinery

Source: J.A. Cantwell, "Foreign multinationals and industrial development in Africa", in P.J. Buckley and L.J. Clegg (eds.), *Multinational Enterprises in Less Developed Countries* (London: Macmillan, 1991).

159

and in these fields Africa continues to play host to substantial TNC investments. While, as already stated, 12.7 per cent of the total FDI stock in developing regions in the early 1980s was located in Africa, as much as around 40 per cent of the stock of resource-based FDI in the less developed countries was directed to Africa (Cantwell, 1991). Today these investments in Africa are concentrated more in mining and in oil, rather than in plantations, as in colonial days. In the case of investment from the United States, the emphasis is on oil, which sector accounted for more than two-thirds of the total stock of United States FDI in Africa in 1993, compared to about 15.9 per cent of the equivalent United States investment in all developing countries considered together.

The primary sector received a major share of European investors as well. Eighty-seven per cent of French investment and 68 per cent of investment from the Netherlands went into the primary sector. The corresponding figures for Germany and the United Kingdom were a bit lower with 42 per cent of German investment and around 30 per cent of the United Kingdom investment going to this sector. For the United Kingdom, the share of the primary sector in FDI stock in Africa has fallen in part owing to the industrial diversification of a number of United Kingdom-owned mining TNCs in Africa, but in any case the share of resource-based investment seems to have somewhat recovered again recently, judging by data on the United Kingdom FDI flows to Africa since 1987. For many European TNCs, Africa is crucial for mining. Much of the substantial investment of British mining companies is situated in Zimbabwe, including that by firms such as RTZ, Lonhro, Falcon Mines and Turner and Newall (Clarke, 1980).

While mining in the larger countries (Zimbabwe and Nigeria) has been reasonably broadly based, the shift away from the traditional mining of gold and diamonds towards the extraction of metallic ores has created some mono-export economies. For example, in 1989, ores and metal represented 83.4 per cent of Zambia's exports (UNCTAD, 1993) and 87 per cent of Guinea's exports in the mid-1980s (Yachir, 1988). Of the four most important minerals mined by TNCs in Africa, the production of bauxite (chiefly in Guinea) and uranium (in Gabon, Namibia, and the Niger) has developed mainly since the 1970s, while, owing to the state of world demand, the production of copper (in Zambia and Zaire) and iron ore (especially significant in Liberia and Mauritania) has contracted somewhat over the same period.

Table 3. Sectoral distribution of the stock of foreign direct investment in Africa, for the largest home countries in the most recent year

(Percentage)

Country	Year	Primary	Secondary	Tertiary
France	1989	87	3	10
Germany[a]	1990	42	20	15
Japan[b]	1993	10	4	86
Netherlands	1989	68	22	10
United Kingdom	1992	30	37	33
	1989-1992[c]	56	24	20[d]
United States	1993	66[e]	12	22

Source: UNCTAD, *Foreign Direct Investment in Africa* (United Nations publication, Sales No. E.95.II.A.6).

[a] Does not add up to 100, owing to 23 per cent being unallocated.
[b] Principally investment in shipping in Liberia, related to flags of convenience.
[c] Flows.
[d] Financial services only.
[e] Oil investment only.

Table 4. Sectoral distribution of foreign direct capital stock in selected countries, 1982

(Percentage)

Country	Primary	Secondary	Tertiary
Developed areas	18.7	43.7	37.6
Developing areas	22.6	54.1	23.3
Africa (except South Africa)	52.1	28.1	19.8
Botswana	92.6	3.7	3.7
Burkina Faso	18.8	47.1	34.1
Cameroon	10.6	89.2	0.2
Central African Republic	33.9	40.7	25.4
Congo	21.3	28.7	50.0
Egypt	86.6	3.1	10.3
Gabon	70.0	28.4	1.6
Kenya	14.3	50.5	35.2
Liberia	72.4	13.8	13.8
Libyan Arab Jamahiriya	94.6	2.9	2.5
Malawi	54.9	32.8	12.3
Morocco	12.6	38.5	48.9
Nigeria	46.7	31.6	21.7
United Republic of Tanzania	8.3	72.7	19.0
Zambia	14.1	52.3	33.6
Zimbabwe	31.6	34.7	33.7

Source: J.A. Cantwell, "Foreign multinationals and industrial development in Africa", in P.J. Buckley and L.J. Clegg (eds.), *Multinational Enterprises in Less Developed Countries* (London: Macmillan, 1991).

As shown in table 4, overall the primary product sector (mining, oil and agriculture, forestry and fishing) took about 52 per cent of the total inward FDI stock in Africa in the early 1980s, a share that is much higher than in any other region. In contrast, the extraction of natural resources accounted for just 19 per cent of FDI stock in the industrialized countries, for 21 per cent in Latin America, and for only 12 per cent on average in Asia. Particularly high shares of primary product investments in national FDI stocks are evident in Botswana (93 per cent, and still 88 per cent by 1989, as shown in table 5), Egypt (87 per cent, including over 70 per cent in oil), Gabon (70 per cent, including 39 per cent in oil and 28 per cent in other mining and quarrying), Liberia (nearly 73 per cent, comprising 43 per cent in mining, 16 per cent in forestry and 14 per cent in the production of crude rubber), the Libyan Arab Jamahiriya (95 per cent, mainly in the oil sector), and Malawi (55 per cent in agriculture, mainly in sugar and tea plantations). As suggested earlier, investments in the larger economies of Nigeria and Zimbabwe are also quite strongly resource-oriented, taking account of their size. In Nigeria about 31 per cent of FDI stock in the early 1980s was in oil, and 16 per cent in other mining, while in Zimbabwe 32 per cent of investment was in extractive ventures, including 22 per cent in mining. Table 5 shows that by 1988, despite some retreat, still 31 per cent of FDI stock in Nigeria was in the primary sector as a whole.

The higher share of FDI in Africa in primary products is also indicative of the slower pace of post-war industrialization in Africa, by comparison with Latin America or Asia. At the same time, Africa has, if anything, tended to become more attractive as a centre of mining activity.

Table 5. Share of the primary sector in foreign direct capital stock, late 1980s

(Percentage)

Country	Year	Share of Primary Sector
Botswana	1989	88
Cameroon	1986	6
Morocco	1988	9
Nigeria	1988	31

Source: *Foreign Direct Investment in Africa* (United Nations publication, Sales No. E.95.II.A.6).

For example, the mining of bauxite has been switched away from the Caribbean (Jamaica and Guyana) and relocated in Africa (Guinea) despite a fall in the world demand for aluminium (Yachir, 1988). To the limited extent industrialization has taken place in Africa, it has tended to follow the Latin American model of import substitution rather than the East Asian export-oriented growth (Lall, 1992). Correspondingly, manufacturing FDI in Africa has been of an import-substituting kind (Swainson, 1980), especially in the larger and more developed African economies.

On average just over a quarter of the total FDI stock in Africa is in manufacturing, compared with about a half in Asia and Latin America (table 4). Just as the industrialization of Africa has built upon the local natural resource base as well as been of an import-substituting kind (Lall, 1992), so too has manufacturing FDI tended to be more resource-related than in other regions. The manufacturing sectors that feature most prominently in the inward investment records of most African countries are metal products (often linked to mining), food products (linked to agriculture), wood products and paper products (linked to forestry), textiles and rubber products. Countries in which the share of manufacturing investments in the total FDI stock is high by African standards include Cameroon (a share of 89 per cent, including significant investments in food products, wood products, metals, textiles, building materials and some chemicals), Gabon (28 per cent, including metals, textiles, wood products, building materials and oil-related chemicals), Kenya (51 per cent, including a substantial foreign presence in the food processing sector), Nigeria (32 per cent, including food products, rubber products and chemicals), Zambia (52 per cent, including food products and textiles and clothing), and Zimbabwe (35 per cent, including not only food products, wood and paper products, and textiles and clothing, but also investments in some heavier industries partly encouraged by restrictions on capital withdrawal – which compelled local reinvestment – and the strong import-substituting regime of the sanctions economy). Also notable is the case of Mauritius, different from the general African pattern in being a small export-oriented economy, but similar in that inward investment has been concentrated in the textiles and clothing sector (which accounted for 83 per cent of employment in the country's Export Processing Zone in 1982 - see Currie, 1986).

Rather like Hong Kong firms in Mauritius, whose investments have been partly motivated by the preferential trade agreements enjoyed by Mauritius (which contrast with the quotas imposed upon Hong Kong), so in a similar special case German and Italian firms have located export-oriented investments in the textiles and clothing sector in North Africa (Frobel, Heinrichs and Kreye, 1980; Acocella, Sanna-Randaccio and Schiattarella, 1985). French TNCs, however, do not seem to have moved so readily from their traditional style of operations in Africa. Apart from their involvement in food processing linked to agribusiness they have only diversified to a limited extent into the resource-based building materials (cement crushing) and metals (canning) sectors, and have only developed slowly in the areas of textiles, plastics and car assembly (Savary, 1984).

Potential development paths

It seems fairly clear that, in terms of the changing international division of labour, and of plausible regional shifts in the location of global productive activity, Africa will not attract the level of FDI flows that are directed to Asia and Latin America, at least not in the foreseeable future. Africa's share of the world stock of FDI is likely to continue to fall slowly for some time to come. This general forecast holds more or less irrespective of the various investment policies and incentives that governments in different developing countries decide to adopt. The lower average wage rates of Africa are also not, by themselves, a major point of attraction for inward direct investment; instead what matters is the ratio of wage rates to local productivity, and this ratio (the unit costs of production) tends to be lower in countries in which productivity is rising faster, generally linked to innovation (Cantwell, 1989). In this context, and in the case of developing countries, the most important issues are the suitability of local forms of work organization, the local capacity for organizational and related innovation, and the existence of an appropriate infrastructure of supporting activities. In these respects, with a few exceptions, African countries remain well behind the leading Asian and Latin American countries. In Africa, TNCs serving local markets often have to become more directly involved in distribution and after-sales servicing than they would elsewhere, due to less satisfactory local infrastructure. This may extend to the need for product adaptation, because for example of inadequate local storage facilities (Quelch and Austin, 1993).

One brighter spot on the horizon is the likely future economic regeneration of South Africa, which in turn is likely to create major new opportunities for trade-related development in other African countries, especially those in the Southern part of the continent. The basis for such new regional trade and investment might become an expanded Southern African Development Coordinating Conference (SADCC), despite the fact that previous efforts to increase inward investment and trade through regional integration in Africa have proved disappointing (Cockcroft, 1992). Yet it would surely be mistaken to expect a substantial new wave of investment to occur quickly in South Africa, just as it proved unrealistic to believe that the recent social, economic and political reforms in Eastern and Central Europe would lead to an immediate upsurge in inward direct investment. One reason is that economic and social institutions take time to change. Another related reason is that bringing about such changes is normally associated with a marked degree of political resistance and instability, and the atmosphere of uncertainty with which this is associated reinforces the natural caution of potential investors. As a general rule, the early phases of new investments are likely to involve only a small or incremental expansion of existing activity. Investments are then gradually increased and eventually lead to a take-off phase if local institutional changes and internal corporate learning processes succeed.

While it is necessary, however, to acknowledge that, in the immediate future, the potential for new FDI in Africa is limited in that current trends in the international division of labour are likely to continue to run against Africa, it is no less important to appreciate that FDI still plays a significant role within the African economies; and that even though development in Africa is likely, on average, to be quite slow, the investments of TNCs will continue to be one of the basic catalysts for such development that does take place. The globalization of economic activity implies that strategies of national economic independence are even less viable than they were in the past, as the trade and investments of TNCs and inter-firm agreements with TNC partners provide the means by which the capacity for changing the methods of production, and improving old products or creating new ones is transmitted more rapidly around the world. While there may be some scope for varying the institutional form of the involvement of TNCs in different countries,

TNCs cannot be excluded entirely from any development path that is likely to be successful.

In considering more precisely the place of TNC investments in national paths of economic development, Africa differs from East Asia in that most inward investment that has moved into manufacturing activities has been import-substituting rather than export-oriented, and much less associated with the capacity for dynamic improvement and local productivity growth. At the same time, Africa differs from Latin America inasmuch as foreign-led import-substituting industrialization has been far more tied to the previously established structure of existing FDI in extractive sectors. Given the strong resource base of most African countries, it seems likely that the future course of development will be resource-oriented for some time to come, and that in this process much of the investment of TNCs will continue to be of a resource-related kind.

Three highly stylized stages of national economic development are suggested in table 6, each stage corresponding to the degree of sophistication of local technological competence. Most African countries remain in the first stage, in which most of the leading local firms have basic engineering skills, and organizational routines and structures that complement these basic skills and allow them to be mobilized effectively.

Table 6. Technological accumulation and the national course of inward direct investment

| | Stages of national development | | |
	(1)	(2)	(3)
Form of technological competence of leading indigenous firms	Basic engineering skills, complementary organizational routines and structures	More sophisticated engineering practices, basic scientific knowledge, more complex organizational methods	More science-based, advanced engineering, organizational structures reflect needs of coordination
Types of inward direct investment	Early resource- or market-seeking investment	More advanced resource-oriented or market-targeted investment	Research-related investment and integration into international networks
Industrial course of inward direct investment	Resource-based (extractive TNCs or backward vertical integration) and simple manufacturing	More forward processing of resources, wider local market-oriented and export-platform manufacturing	More sophisticated manufacturing systems, international integration of investment

Thus, the typical target for African economic development — which is likely to be associated with successful industrialization, but not industrialization at any cost (Lall, 1992) — is the second stage, in which the leading local firms develop more sophisticated engineering practices and more complex organizational methods, while acquiring some basic scientific knowledge related to the new engineering skills. It should be noted that in this stylized depiction of the course of economic development some elements of earlier stages are preserved and not completely replaced in later stages; that is, while the leading indigenous firms are making the transition from the first to the second stage, many other local firms would be just coming to achieve the standards of the first stage, through improved organization and the acquisition of some basic skills.

These different phases of technological accumulation and development tend to be associated with equivalent phases of TNC involvement in a national economy and, as argued above, the linkages between development and TNC involvement have tended to become closer and less avoidable as economic activity has become more globalized.[1/] As described in the previous section, so far most inward direct investment in Africa has been of a resource-seeking kind, with some import-substituting, market-seeking manufacturing investment in the larger and the more successful African economies. Naturally enough, many of these investments were due to TNCs based in oil, mining, agriculture and food, or forestry and wood products, together with some manufacturing firms backwardly, vertically integrating into resource-based ventures in Africa. To the extent that there has been an evolution away from these areas, it has typically taken the form of a limited downstream diversification into simple resource-related manufacturing. This pattern of TNC involvement is a function of Africa's early stage of development (the first stage), together with the resource-based character of that development.

The further progression of this kind of development can easily be envisaged. In the African case the next stage is likely to focus upon more advanced resource-oriented TNC investments, moving into a more extensive local forward processing of resources, and some export-platform manufacturing especially in the smaller countries. The widespread agricultural, forestry and mineral resources in Africa all provide scope for downstream manufacturing investments in which there is some hope that local as well as foreign firms can become involved, thereby ensuring against an enclave development. Apart from the TNCs that have held a traditional presence in Africa and may wish to diversify their local operations, there are two potential sources of new investment. One is the firms of resource-rich countries, such as Sweden or Canada, which have a substantial experience in resource-related development, but a home base that has already been thoroughly exploited. The other potential source is the firms of resource-scarce countries that are themselves industrializing rapidly, and encountering resource supply constraints as a result (Ozawa, 1979).

In both of these cases, firms have an interest in relocating their less sophisticated types of resource-related but downstream production to resource-abundant countries at an earlier stage of development, as production in their home economies is steadily upgraded. Although these companies still possess the technological and organizational know-how to sustain the simpler activities that lie downstream from the original extraction of resources, it may become more profitable to do so abroad, and to concentrate on higher value-added activities in the now more developed home environment. The driving force behind this process is the rise in wage and other costs with industrial development which render less economic the older activities characterized by lower labour productivity. This is often accompanied by greater environmental pressure at home as the full consequences of earlier industrial expansion are better appreciated.

Apart from higher labour costs, the costs of energy provision have risen in the more developed countries. This may have created an opportunity in African countries such as Guinea or Zaire that are well equipped with hydro-electrical resources, which may become a significant locational advantage. Relative transport costs also tend to favour a shift towards local downstream processing activities. Transport costs are responsible for 27 per cent of the price of imported iron ore, but only 12 per cent in the case of steel products; while two tons of bauxite are needed to produce one ton of aluminium (Yachir, 1988). A similar comparison holds for ore concentrates as against blister or refined copper; or for agricultural produce as against processed food.

As mentioned already, however, there are other factors that are working against Africa, and which suggest that the pace of such local resource-based development is likely to be slow and uneven.

Technological change in established industries may reduce the cost advantages of relocation, and reduce the extent of pollution associated with them. Indeed, in some instances even the underlying extractive activity may be displaced from Africa by, for example, the development of the resources of the seabed closer to the industrialized countries. It may also be that foreign trade barriers are higher in the case of finished or semi-finished products than for raw materials, and that coordination with user firms favours a developed country location. The future for the local development of downstream processing depends to a large extent on the overall state of demand: a number of steel projects proposed for Africa were put on ice when world demand dropped. Perhaps the most important qualification is that new manufacturing facilities (and even new resource development) will only be established where the country has a suitable supporting infrastructure, and only countries that have already attained the first stage of development in table 6 and whose firms become actively engaged in production-related technological effort, capability development and the promotion, as well as the use of skills (Lall, 1992), will be able to achieve the second stage, and to attract the kinds of inward investment that are associated with it. Only certain African countries have the potential to attract new FDI at all, and only a rather small sub-set of these (those with the better industrialization records to date) can hope to attract the more dynamic types of investment associated with the second stage of economic development.

It should perhaps be emphasized again that, while there are some African countries that have not even attained the first stage of development in table 6, and quite a number are currently in this first stage, there are none at all in the third stage (the most advanced). Those that have reached the second stage are the few African countries with the more successful records of industrialization mentioned earlier (that is, Côte d'Ivoire, Kenya, Gabon, Mauritius, South Africa and Zimbabwe). Those countries are still at best consolidating their position in the second stage of development, and only South Africa has any realistic prospect of moving towards the third stage in the foreseeable future. With respect to the contribution of TNCs in development, this implies that there will not be strategic asset acquiring FDI in Africa, linked to research and sophisticated manufacturing systems, except perhaps to a very limited extent in South Africa. It is just possible, however, that some of the currently local market-oriented investments in the more advanced countries of Africa may become somewhat more rationalized or integrated (say, between South Africa and Zimbabwe) if South Africa becomes a pole of attraction for regional development. This possibility would certainly be enhanced if regional integration takes off around the SADCC, as mentioned earlier.

The notion that FDI should be given the role of gradually but systematically assisting in the upgrading of the productive capacity of a developing country, in accordance with the existing capabilities of local firms and the stage of development so far achieved is familiar from the literature on FDI in Asia (see, for example, Kojima, 1978, and Koo, 1985). In cultivating resource-related FDI, Africa can learn from the development strategies of the East Asian countries. This holds especially true for the regions more recent success stories, such as Malaysia and Indonesia, which are rich in natural resources. They provide a good indicator for a successful development path for many African countries.

Transnational corporations and resource-based development in Africa

In order to assess more precisely the potential for extending the activities of TNCs already present in Africa, and for attracting new investment, and to appreciate the likely linkages between these investments and local development, it is advisable to divide the African countries into groups, since, owing to their differences, they are likely to follow different development paths. The TNCs likely to be involved in each group of countries also have distinct characteristics. Leaving aside those countries which, due to their backwardness or remoteness, have little chance of attracting any significant investments, the remaining African countries can be divided into three groups as set out in table 7. In the table, these groupings are organized with reference to the established pattern of TNC involvement in each case, which can be traced back to its historical roots.

As should be clear from the evidence presented previously, the most important for Africa is the first grouping, consisting of countries rich in natural resources, and in which resource-based TNCs have already invested heavily in extractive ventures. This group includes the large countries Nigeria, South Africa and Zimbabwe, and small countries such as Gabon, Guinea, Liberia, Namibia, Zaire and Zambia. Countries in other parts of the world that have enjoyed a similar type of resource-based development, recently or in the past, include the large economies of Brazil, Canada and the United States, and smaller countries such as Indonesia, Malaysia, the Philippines and Sweden. In these countries, the dominant form of the earliest foreign involvement was resource-oriented, together with some local market-oriented investments in the large economies, especially where (as in post-war Africa and Latin America) they operated in an import-substituting regime.

The second group comprises large countries without an abundance of natural resources, but in which local production, because of its scale, tends to be resource-intensive and thus dependent upon imports and on the trading linkages established by local or foreign firms. In Africa, Kenya is the case in point, while elsewhere Argentina, the Republic of Korea, Japan and the United Kingdom might also be placed in this category. The earliest inward direct investment in these countries tended to be

Table 7. Variations in the early stages of inward direct investment across different types of country

Categorisation of national development	Examples of countries		Dominant form of earliest foreign involvement	Type of foreign firm
Resource-abundant	Brazil Indonesia Malaysia Philippines Canada Sweden United States (oil)	Gabon Guinea Liberia Namibia Nigeria South Africa Zaire Zambia Zimbabwe	Resource-oriented, and local market-oriented in large countries (see below)	Former colonial firms Resource-based firms Manufacturing firms, backwardly integrating
Resource-scarce large countries (with resource-intensive production)	Argentina Korea, Republic of Japan United Kingdom	Kenya	Local market-oriented, trade-related	Expatriate firms Trading companies Manufacturing firms, serving local markets
Resource-scarce small countries (with non-resource-intensive production)	Hong Kong Singapore Belgium Netherlands Switzerland	Arab States of North Africa Mauritius	Export-oriented, service-based	Offshore producers Service firms (trade, shipping, finance)

local market-oriented or trade-related. In addition, in Kenya, foreign entrepreneurs and expatriate firms developed a major presence, and constitute an important linkage between TNCs and localities.

The third group is more of a special case in the African context, and especially in sub-Saharan Africa. These are resource-scarce small countries (of which there are certainly a number in Africa), but which have managed to develop the skills and organizational effectiveness needed to mount an export-led expansion (of which there are unfortunately very few in Africa). This group consists of some of the Arab States of North Africa together with Mauritius, which are attempting to follow the kind of path so successfully achieved previously by countries such as Belgium, Hong Kong, the Netherlands, Singapore and Sweden. The earliest TNC investments in those countries involved either the export-oriented activities of offshore producers, or the trading, shipping and financial activities of service companies.

For the purposes of charting the future prospects for the further development of TNC involvement and local industrialization, it is worth also considering a fourth group of countries as suggested in table 8. The fourth group — which is listed as the third in this table — is made up of large countries that might have previously appeared under the first or second groups, but which now lack the technological effort and organization that are needed to push ahead towards the next stage of development, a lack of capability that is often reinforced by a greater social and political unrest and instability than in the past. Small countries that have fallen into this position are unlikely to attract any new investment at all, even if they are well endowed with natural resources. Large countries in this state, however, may continue to attract some mild TNC interest owing mainly to the size of their markets, and TNC involvement may increase slowly in line with a gradual increase in domestic demand. This might be the prognosis, for example, for present-day Nigeria. In this scenario, development has little impetus, because it is not associated with any serious restructuring or upgrading of the nature of local activity.

Thus, in what remains, attention is focused upon those countries in each of the other three groups that do have the potential for the technological effort and organizational effectiveness that is needed to at least move towards the next stage of development. This is principally the countries mentioned previously as having had the best industrialization records to date - namely, the Côte d'Ivoire, Kenya, Gabon, Mauritius, South Africa and Zimbabwe. Of these, those that belong to the first group, the resource-abundant countries, fall into the most important category in Africa, which includes the cases of South Africa and Zimbabwe, the countries that perhaps have the best prospects for the longer-term future. As argued already, the likely path of development will continue to be resource-oriented in this group of countries. TNCs and their local partners may undertake related diversification (for example, from one kind of mining to another, which may in turn encourage the emergence of a new industry), and greater downstream processing, including a range of simpler manufacturing activities previously conducted elsewhere. This is likely to include the further development of the metal processing, mechanical engineering, agribusiness and food products, wood products and oil-related chemicals sectors.

Table 8. Potential development paths for inward direct investment and their association with local industrialization across different types of country

Categorization of national development	Link between domestic development and the growth of foreign involvement	Type of new foreign firm
Resource-abundant	Related diversification (for example, from mining), downstream processing (for example, metal processing, wood products, oil-related chemicals, agribusiness), with some other upgrading of industry in large countries (see below)	Firms from resource-rich countries Firms from resource-scarce newly industrialized countries
Resource-scarce large countries (with broader range of local competence and skills)	Industrial upgrading and export growth (as wages rise following productivity growth), and extension of local infrastructure	Manufacturing firms, in new areas Construction and local service firms
Large countries (lacking the capability for sustained export expansion)	Slower expansion of an essentially similar industrial structure	Local market-seeking manufacturing firms
Resource-scarce small countries	Shift away from simpler manufacturing activity to some industrial upgrading, but more towards a greater service-orientation	Newly industrialized country firms relocating activity International service groups

John Cantwell

In the resource-abundant countries, in addition to the extension of activity by established TNCs, two other types of foreign firms might be particularly attracted. One type is firms from resource-rich industrialized countries, such as Canada and Sweden in the case of wood and paper products, which have developed ownership specific advantages that can be utilized beneficially in timber-rich developing countries. The other kind is Third World TNCs, principally from the newly industrialized countries, which have steadily built up experience in production in a variety of Third World conditions, whether from origins in resource-based production at home (as in Indonesia or Malaysia) or from supplying the primary products needed by a resource-scarce home economy (as in the Republic of Korea). These companies tend to be organizationally innovative and technologically adaptive in traditional small-scale industries, in which they have well developed managerial and marketing skills (Lall, 1983; Tolentino, 1993). They have advantages that are well suited to extracting the greatest benefits from the resource-related potential of some of the better developed African economies.

While large traditionally established TNCs in mining, agribusiness and oil may lead development in the metal processing, food products and chemical sectors, respectively, perhaps the likeliest source of new FDI in the wood products sector is newer and smaller TNCs, often originating from faster growing countries. The firms of higher growth countries have begun an especially rapid international expansion in recent years. Much of this has been in innovative activity in the industrialized world, but resource-based firms have also been seeking investment opportunities in developing countries. Ozawa (1979) explains this through the use of a Ricardian growth model in which expansion relies upon the alleviation of resource constraints through the import of raw materials supported by resource-based export-oriented outward FDI. This resource-based type of outward investment is likely to be most important either in countries that are industrializing rapidly (Japan in the 1960s, the East Asian newly industrialized countries today), or whose own resource-based development path has created an industrial structure in which indigenous firms have their greatest advantage in resource-related areas (as in the Canadian case).

Other kinds of local industrial upgrading are also feasible in the large countries of the first, resource-abundant group, and of the second resource-scarce category (which includes Kenya). These depend upon the achievement of an active indigenous technological effort and the extension of local infrastructure, which would promote productivity and export growth, and an industrial restructuring as wages gradually rise in the wake of productivity growth. Apart from new investments by TNCs already established in these countries, some additional foreign manufacturing firms may be attracted to involve themselves in the new (higher grade) areas of development, while construction and service-based TNCs are likely to bid for contracts associated with the expansion of local infrastructure. In any event, in these countries new FDI in the metal products and food processing sectors would be in part local market-oriented as well as export-oriented, depending upon the degree of international vertical integration which characterizes the product concerned (iron and steel, for example, are different from copper or aluminium).

The export-oriented feature of the investment potential in these larger more developed countries, however, is especially important, as the objective of development would be to increase the local value added in a vertically integrated chain that usually ends in marketing in the industrialized countries. These higher grade activities may involve the TNCs with traditional interests in Africa, perhaps under contractual arrangements more favourable to local firms than have prevailed in the past. In areas like engineering and food processing there is evidence from the larger African countries that TNCs with existing operations in Africa do have an incentive to attempt to diversify into higher value added downstream activities in the local economy (Clarke, 1980: Swainson, 1980). In the case of resource-based production in general, new forms of cooperative ventures with local partners also seem to have worked better and to have led to greater commitment on the part of foreign firms - including, for example, the management contracts and technical assistance set up by Booker McConnell in some quite sophisticated forms of food processing in Kenya (Cantwell and Dunning, 1985). The scope for encouraging vertical linkages between foreign and local firms in developing countries has been further discussed by Lall (1980) and Landi (1986).

In the final group of resource-scarce small countries with a significant local skills base, Third World TNCs are likely to be important in increasing productivity in the textiles sector and related local activity. The relocation of textiles production from Hong Kong to Mauritius has had an additional motive besides the general advantages of shifting simpler activity to a country at a lower stage of the development ladder which has the organizational capacity to follow in the footsteps of the source country. That is, trade policy within the industrialized countries has imposed quota restrictions on textile exports from Hong Kong, which have compelled firms based there to diversify home production, moving in the direction of more sophisticated articles, while relocating the more basic lines in Mauritius, which enjoys more favourable conditions of access to industrialized country markets (Currie, 1986; Chen, 1983). The prospects for the further upgrading of industrial production in Mauritius, however, are limited due to its small size. In Hong Kong too, development has moved more in the direction of an increasing provision of international services rather than continued industrial upgrading of the kind that has characterized the larger economies of the Republic of Korea and Taiwan Province of China. Some international service groups might be attracted by the export-orientation of Mauritius, and perhaps more generally by the legal and tax advantages that are sometimes offered by such small but rather more developed countries.

A policy footnote

With respect to the role of governments in encouraging TNCs to make a contribution towards local development, the discussion suggests that they should adopt policies of targeting investment in sectors that are most conducive to the national path of development most likely to succeed in their own case, rather than catch-all policies aimed at attracting inward investment in general. Probably the most important criterion in selecting sectors in which to seek out greater foreign participation is the need to encourage development in sectors in which indigenous firms already have some potential, or have potential in related and complementary sectors. The objective is that the entry or expansion of foreign firms should set in motion a process of positive interaction with local companies, and hence a more rapid development of the industry in question. If this happens, then forced partnerships and regulations to prevent the monopolization of local industry are unnecessary and unhelpful. TNCs are then also likely to make a greater contribution to exports than they have so far in Africa, and are better able to bridge the gap with local small- and medium-sized firms (Cockcroft, 1992).

The adoption of a sector-specific FDI policy with chosen target sectors requires differentiated policies designed to meet the needs of particular local industries. It also requires a flexible approach towards inward direct investment as the priorities for economic development change, including the need to relate FDI strategies to the provision and adaptation of an appropriate supporting infrastructure. It is also possible that policies would need to be adapted if regional integration based around growth in South Africa becomes an important source of endogenous (African propelled) development in future (Quelch and Austin, 1993); although, as argued earlier, this is still likely to be some way off. The limits to what FDI policy can achieve, however, must also be clearly understood so that governments do not become easily disillusioned. Policies can only promote investments in areas in which there is already an incipient potential in the local economy. At a general level in Africa the greatest current potential seems to be in the development of resource-based simple manufacturing activity. Given the historical presence of TNCs in extractive sectors in Africa, and given the desires for international expansion of many newer resource-based TNCs, this seems the likeliest way in which to involve foreign firms in the further development of African countries.

Note

1. See Ozawa, 1992 and Dunning, 1993 for similar schemes for representing the linkage between foreign participation and national development.

References

Acocella, N., F. Sanna-Randaccio, and R. Schiattarella (1985). *Le Multinazionali Italiane*. Bologna: Il Mulino.

Cantwell, J.A. (1989). *Technological Innovation and Multinational Corporations*. Oxford: Basil Blackwell.

_____ (1991). Foreign multinationals and industrial development in Africa. In P.J. Buckley and L.J. Clegg (eds.), *Multinational Enterprises in Less Developed Countries*. London: Macmillan.

_____ and J.H. Dunning (1985). *The New Forms of International Involvement of British Firms in the Third World*, Report submitted to OECD (January).

Chen, E.K.Y. (1983). *Multinational Corporations, Technology and Employment*. London: Macmillan.

Clarke, D. (1980). *Foreign Companies and International Investment in Zimba-bwe*. Gwelo: Mambo Press.

Cockcroft, L. (1992). The past record and future potential of foreign investment. In F. Stewart, S. Lall and S. Wangwe (eds.), *Alternative Development Strategies in Sub-Saharan Africa*. London: Macmillan.

Currie, J. (1986). Export-oriented investment in Senegal, Ghana and Mauritius. In V. Cable (ed.), *Foreign Investment: Policies and Prospects*. London: Commonwealth Secretariat.

Dunning, J. H. (1993). *Multinational Enterprises and the Global Economy*. Wokingham, Berkshire: Addison Wesley.

_____ and J. Cantwell (1987). *IRM Directory of Statistics of International Investment and Production*. New York: New York University Press.

Frobel, F., J. Heinrichs, and O. Kreye (1980). *The New International Division of Labour: Structural Unemployment in Industrialised Countries and Indus-trialisation in Developing Countries*. Cambridge: Cambridge University Press.

Kojima, Kyoshi (1978). *Direct Foreign Investment: A Japanese Model of Multinational. Business Operations*. London: Croom Helm.

Koo, B.-Y. (1985). Korea. In J.H. Dunning (ed.). *Multinational Enterprises, Economic Structure and International Competitiveness*. Chichester: John Wiley.

Lall, S. (1980). Vertical inter-firm linkages in less developed countries: an empirical study. *Oxford Bulletin of Economics and Statistics,* vol. 42, No. 3, pp. 203-226.

_____ (1983). The theoretical background. In S. Lall (ed.), *The New Multina-tionals: The Spread of Third World Enterprises*. Chichester: John Wiley.

_____ (1992). Structural problems of African industry. In F. Stewart, S. Lall and S. Wangwe (eds.), *Alternative Development Strategies in Sub-Saharan Africa*. London: Macmillan.

Landi, J.H. (1986). Vertical corporate linkages. *University of Reading Discus-sion Papers in International Investment and Business Studies,* No. 94 (April).

Ozawa, T. (1979). *Multinationalism, Japanese Style: The Political Economy of Outward Dependency*. Princeton, New Jersey: Princeton University Press.

_____ (1979). A newer type of foreign investment in Third World resource development. *Rivista Internazionale di Scienze Economiche e Commerciali,* vol. *29,* No. 12 (December), pp. 1133-1151.

_____ (1992). Foreign direct investment and economic development. *Transnational Corporations,* vol. 1, No. 1, pp. 27-54.

Quelch, J.A. and J.E. Austin (1993). Should multinationals invest in Africa? *Sloan Management Review*, Spring, pp. 107-119.

Savary, J. (1984). *French Multinationals*. London: Frances Pinter.

Stewart, F., S. Lall, and S. Wangwe, eds. (1992). *Alternative Development Strategies in Sub-Saharan Africa*. London: Macmillan.

Swainson, N. (1980). *The Development of Corporate Capitalism in Kenya, 1918-1977*. London: Heinemann.

Tolentino, P.E.E. (1993). *Technological Innovation and Third World Multinationals*. London: Routledge.

UNCTAD (1993), *Handbook of International Trade and Development Statistics* (United Nations publication, Sales No. B.94.II.D.24).

‗‗‗‗‗ (1995a), *Foreign Direct Investment in Africa* (United Nations publication, Sales No. E.95.II.A.6).

‗‗‗‗‗ (1995b), *World Investment Report 1995; Transnational Corporations and Competitiveness*: (United Nations publication, Sales No. E.95.II.A.9).

UNCTC (1991), *World Investment Report 1991: The Triad in Foreign Direct Investment* (United Nations publication, Sales No. E.95.II.A.12).

Yachir, F. (1988). *Mining in Africa Today: Strategies and Prospects*, London: Zed Books.

Part III
Investment and trade

6

Investment, trade and international competitiveness

Louka T. Katseli

Introduction

In the present chapter, the linkages between foreign direct investment (FDI), competitiveness and trade performance in developing countries are investigated. While this topic has been extensively discussed by economists and policy makers for many decades, interest has recently been revived largely owing to the globalization of economic activity and to the recognition that transnational corporations (TNCs) play an increasingly important role in trade and the promotion of competitiveness.

The emphasis on the role of TNCs in providing equity capital and in acting as catalysts for trade promotion and structural change is based not only on the large number of firms that have created international operations — some 39,000 (UNCTAD, 1996) — and on the spread of home countries of such firms, but more importantly on the increasing importance of TNCs in the growing world trade and in the international transfer of technology. In fact, TNCs trade to a large extent internally, as subsidaries trade between each other and the parent firm (UNCTAD 1995).

The process of globalization has been underpinned by the explosion of technological innovation. The rapid introduction and diffusion of new technologies has led to the creation of new products, has transformed production processes, has driven unit costs down and lowered barriers to entry in existing markets (Stevens and Andrieu, 1991 and Dunning 1994). Moreover, in the fast growing, technologically advanced industries, the growing fixed capital cost of research and development (R&D) and capital equipment, as well as accelerating technological obsolescence, have increased production risks and costs and have contributed to a consolidation of oligopolistic structures. Thus, as TNC activities expanded in high-technology sectors, in complex manufactures and technology-based services, their global operations have tended to create significant externalities for host countries. These are associated with the use and diffusion of technology, with the extent and direction of knowledge-transfers regarding production, management or distribution, and with the ability of host countries to enter established, regional or global, finance-related or trading networks.

These trends have altered the sources of comparative and competitive advantages for firms and national economies alike. Competitiveness of a country appears to be increasingly affected not only by the host country's natural and created assets or the productivity of its indigenous firms, but by its ability to gain access to and use effectively TNC-related products and services. Access and effective use of these products or services in turn determine a country's ability to upgrade its products, to penetrate new markets and to improve its trade performance.

Given the dynamic effects of TNC activities on competitiveness, private capital flows to developing countries might resolve two problems at once: (a) increase the total flow of saving in their economies through the substitution of non-debt creating private flows for bank lending and official development finance, which have been on the decline since the mid-1970s; and (b) improve their trade performance, increase their competitiveness and restructure their economies in the process.

A small number of developing countries are participating in globalization through a process of industrial restructuring which exploits linkages between FDI, trade and competitiveness. Those linkages, as well as their effects on host countries, are analysed in the chapter. The analysis suggests that trade and foreign investment can be either substitutes or complements depending on the motives for and kind of international production undertaken by TNCs. While TNCs can act as catalysts for export promotion and the restructuring of an economy's productive base, the process is not an automatic one. Inflows of FDI in a country or in a region will not be sustained, either in small export-based economies or in large relatively protected markets, unless national policies ensure that the basis for international production and exchange is supported by improvements in infrastructure, skills, services and the political and business environment.

Comparative versus absolute advantage

The "conventional wisdom" regarding the expected direction of factor movements between countries at different stages of development is more often than not misleading. According to this view, developing countries possess locational advantages as host countries for manufacturing investment due to their relatively lower labour costs. In fact, the presence of other factors in developing countries complicate the story to the point that the opposite tendencies are observed.

In the simple neoclassical growth model, if barriers to international factor movements are removed, capital will tend to flow to those areas or countries where the ratio of capital to labour used in the production process is relatively low, that is, from developed to developing countries. The scarcity of capital relative to labour in most developing countries implies that the rental-wage ratio in those countries is higher than in developed countries so that capital owners will find it profitable to invest there. As investment takes place, the capital-labour ratio is raised, increasing per capita incomes and real wages. Firms are expected to continue to invest in developing countries as long as the productivity of their resources and capabilities increases faster than real wages, and will cease to do so once productivity improvements are no longer easier to achieve. Capital-rich areas or countries, on the other hand, are expected to experience a decline in investment and a fall in the amount of capital employed per worker. As a consequence, the relative rental-wage ratio is expected to increase in those areas. Under these very simplified assumptions, incorporated in the standard neoclassical growth model, the liberalization of capital and/or labour movements brings about convergence of relative and even absolute factor returns across capital-rich and capital-poor areas.

Three sets of factors stand out, however, as impediments to such a convergence through capital movements: (a) risk and uncertainty regarding capital returns in developing regions or countries; (b) the low productivity of capital and the high costs associated with production in those countries; and (c) market externalities.

The simple model assumes that the prospective returns to investment are known with sufficient certainty to persuade investors to divert resources and capabilities towards those areas. In practice, uncertainty in doing business in most developing countries make the returns to investment at best highly risky. Accordingly, as capital restrictions are removed, capital may not necessarily flow in the direction predicted, at least not on a sufficient scale to have a marked effect on capital/labour ratios, on productivity and on real income levels.

The most important obstacle to foreign investment flowing to developing countries, however, is the high effective cost associated with doing business in those countries, in connection with the low productivity of factors of production. Production costs encompass not only labour costs, which are relatively lower, but also transportation, telecommunication and distribution costs. Productivity is low due to lack of labour training, inappropriate work organization, poor quality of administration, inadequate availability of business services etc.

In the presence of footloose factors of production (capital or other traded inputs), production and trade patterns are decided not only by comparative advantages, but also by absolute advantages, that is, not only by differences between countries that affect industries in a differential fashion (for example, relative labour costs), but also by each country's absolute level of efficiency of inputs. This is because resources and capabilities that are footloose (for example, many intangible assets) will be attracted to the country offering the highest return. The maximum return that a country can offer, however, depends not only on final-goods prices and on comparative advantages in the form of relative labour costs, but also on all national characteristics that affect the absolute productivity of those footloose factors. Thus, as set out in chapter 1, the level of taxation, the "business culture" and the overall availability of economic and social infrastructure are important determinants of the absolute productivity of capital and FDI. Improvements in any of those determining factors can relocate international production as capital is redirected to the country offering, *ceteris paribus,* the highest real return on its investment.

Finally, a firm's productivity depends on the actual and expected size of the market in which it operates. This is because it usually takes a minimum cluster of business activities and sufficient business networking to generate a new climate for business, to change the attitudes of the workforce, to attract pools of skilled workers etc. (Danthine, 1991; Diamond, 1982). Considering whether to invest in a given area, investors take into account their expectations of how fast other investors will follow suit. They may then decide to wait until enough investors have jumped in. Such behaviour usually leads to a situation where no investment is undertaken, thus fulfilling everyone's *a priori* hypothesis that the situation was not ripe to begin with.[1]

These factors, namely uncertainty, the absolute level of efficiency of inputs and "thick-market externalities" above and beyond more traditional factors, such as market size and growth, help explain why FDI tends to concentrate in developed areas. They also explain why some developing countries are consistently left out of investors' plans despite their relatively low level of wages even in comparison to those developing countries which are traditional host countries for FDI.

Foreign direct investment and trade linkages

The linkages between FDI and trade critically depend on the type of FDI involved and the underlying motive for the international exchange. At least five types of FDI activities can be distinguished,[2] with corresponding direct and indirect effects on trade and competitiveness.

When most international exchange involves the trading of finished, relatively cheap, consumer goods (clothing, footwear etc.), differences in comparative advantage, that is, differences in relative factor returns, provide the standard basis for international production and trade. In these cases, captured by the standard Heckscher-Ohlin model of international exchange, capital will tend to flow to relatively capital-poor, labour-abundant countries and the conventional wisdom described earlier would apply. If markets are large, then FDI usually takes place for market-penetration purposes, that is, it is import substituting. If markets are small, then the country can be used as an export base, that is, FDI is export promoting. Whether or not international exchange takes place through production in the foreign market or through trade depends on the prevalence of market barriers or market imperfections, including tariffs, export subsidies, transportation costs, and exchange rate movements that affect the relative final prices of traded goods and hence the country's overall comparative advantage. Thus, differences in relative factor endowments that are an important source of differences in comparative advantage, in combination with market imperfections, help explain the initial gravitation of FDI to the large Latin American markets, such as Brazil and Mexico, and to the relatively small South-East Asian economies, including Hong Kong, Singapore, Taiwan Province of China and the Republic of Korea.

Whether geared to the domestic or to the international market, FDI in these cases is largely a substitute for trade in the sense that trade and international production, being alternative means of delivering goods to foreign markets, will have identical effects, in the long run, on capital-labour ratios, on relative factor returns and on real incomes. Thus, whether through trade or through FDI, relative wages in the capital-poor countries will tend to increase and relative factor returns will tend to converge to the level of the trading partner or the home country. Under such assumptions both free trade and freedom of capital movements are expected to be beneficial for both developed and developing countries.

From a policy perspective, however, what should be noted is that in a multi-country world and in the presence of footloose factors, the basis of comparative advantage in any given country can be quickly eroded. In other words, as labour returns increase in the host country, footloose activities will tend to contract in the original countries and be transplanted to more profitable locations. Given this process, policy makers should realize early on that the cheap pool of labour will eventually be exhausted. Policy should thus provide incentives for the channelling of export earnings to the expansion and restructuring of the productive base so that a new upgraded basis for international exchange is created.

As development proceeds and incomes increase, the basis for international exchange is altered.[3/] As there is greater demand for variety, international exchange involves the trading of more expensive consumer goods and differentiated products. In the case of horizontal investments in large domestic markets, local production facilities enable firms to penetrate these markets and to adapt products to foreign demand conditions. Thus, product differentiation is a characteristic of exchange between more developed markets. Product differentiation implies that consumers can import some brands from abroad while exporting some varieties to others. In this case, a large proportion of trade usually takes place between parent companies and affiliates or between TNC affiliates. For example, as FDI has concentrated within the Triad, an increasing portion of trade appears to be intra-industry and even intra-company trade (Julius, 1990, UNCTAD 1995). Industries that fall into this category are those which are characterized by differentiated products such as automobiles, consumer durables, pharmaceuticals etc. There is little foreign investment in industries with undifferentiated products (paper, steel etc.) or with substantial production scale economies (aircraft etc).[4/]

In the case where exchange is in differentiated products, FDI does not necessarily displace existing trade, but gives rise to new trade flows between national entities across countries. Thus, from the host country's point of view, FDI in these types of industries tends to be trade-creating as it expands consumption possibilities and imports while, at the same time, it adds a factor-endowment basis for expanded exports. In this case, therefore, FDI and trade become complementary activities in contrast to the traditional case of Heckscher-Ohlin trade.

Contrary to the previous production models, in this case, the basis for international production resides in differences in technology characteristics associated with the presence of increasing returns to scale. It is the joint presence of the desire for variety and of increasing returns that leads to markets in which a large but finite number of differentiated products emerges, each product serving some segment of a national or world market. Furthermore, as exchange in differentiated products takes place, there is no presumption that relative factor returns and real incomes of the trading countries will tend to converge. The returns to the specific factors used in the production of the traded commodity are likely to increases but no generalization at the macroeconomic level can be made.

Component-outsourcing FDI falls in between the first and second category mentioned above. Whereas the basis for domestic production tends to be the availability of cheap labour, this labour-seeking investment is attracted to countries which possess not only comparative, but also absolute advantages in production and trade. This type of investment involves more expensive commodities so that the return required to attract capital in the production process is determined not only by relative labour costs, but also by the productivity of factors. Thus, whereas small, unskilled labour-abundant countries might be able to attract FDI in traditional labour-intensive activities, the development of economic infrastructure, the provision of adequate labour training and discipline, and a relatively risk-free environment are important determinants of component-outsourcing FDI.

Trade related to component-outsourcing FDI mostly consists of intra-firm trade, where components produced in one or more countries are assembled in the same or in a different country. Thus, as with trade in differentiated products, component-outsourcing FDI is trade-creating and FDI and trade are complementary to each other.

Whereas the major motive behind labour-seeking, market-seeking, assembly- transplanting or component-outsourcing FDI is ensuring the profitability of total operations of the investing firms, resource-seeking FDI is usually undertaken to ensure availability and to reduce uncertainty and risk in the provision of raw materials. In this case, international mobility of factors and, more specifically, capital movements is a prerequisite for commodity trade as these resources would otherwise have remained unexploited.

The concentration of FDI activity in more advanced sectors, where firms possess more sophisticated ownership specific advantages (Dunning 1992a) relative to firms in traditional sectors, implies that the locational advantages of countries required to attract FDI become even more difficult to attain. Cheap unskilled labour, traditional trade distortions etc., become neither necessary nor sufficient conditions for the attraction of this type of FDI. Minimum infrastructure standards, a disciplined and/ or skilled labour force, quality control, political stability and certainty in delivery time become important locational advantages. Thick market externalities play an increasingly important role as a determinant of FDI and as a major factor behind the volume and direction of trade. Thus, whereas these factors are of little significance for elementary stages of cheap labour-seeking or resource-seeking FDI, they are crucial for assembly-transplanting FDI or for component-outsourcing investment in technologically advanced sectors.

Finally, in the case of services-related FDI, the linkages between FDI and trade are more complex. FDI in services involves capital accumulation in what is usually called the non-traded or non-tradable sector of the economy. Foreign investment in business services, in construction or in financial activities, cannot be directly traded as are primary or manufacturing commodities. It is access and effective use of those services usually provided by TNCs, however, that determine a country's ability to upgrade its own products, to penetrate new markets and to improve its export performance. FDI in services critically affects the host country's absolute advantage and competitiveness in two ways: (a) it raises the productivity of capital and enables host countries to attract new capital under more favourable terms, thus shifting the basis of international production in their favour, and (b) it can be used as a strategic input by the host country's traditional export sectors to expand the volume of its trade, as well as to upgrade its productive capabilities through process and product innovation. From a policy perspective, FDI in services raises a number of interesting issues.

Given that FDI in services is usually driven by market size and thickness and is geared to the domestic market, the challenge for host countries is not only to liberalize services, but to integrate effectively those TNC activities with the home-based productive sectors of the economy. In most developing countries where markets tend to be "thin", TNCs in services attempt to penetrate industries where monopolistic profits are possible, most notably in transportation, telecommunications and construction. These are usually sensitive areas for public policy, since those services tend to be provided by a few domestic, usually public, firms. Thus, to attract FDI, complex arrangements need to be worked out that involve either direct privatization of companies or joint ventures by domestic and foreign firms. Given the monopolistic structure of small markets, however, the issue of regulation in such cases almost always arises. From a policy perspective, therefore, the regulation costs involved in monitoring foreign business operations in those areas have to be weighed against sizeable potential "knowledge-transfers", as well as against the externalities associated with the presence of large TNCs in the country. Much FDI in services thus affects trade only indirectly through its effect on competitiveness.[5/]

Effects on competitiveness and trade

This brings us to a more general point regarding FDI and trade linkages, namely, that FDI has both direct and indirect effects on trade. On the one hand, resource-extracting, labour-seeking, or efficiency-seeking FDI influences trade directly as TNC activities give rise to production and exchange of commodities across borders. For example, FDI in resource extraction gives rise to imports of machinery and to exports of raw materials. Similarly, horizontally based rationalized or component-outsourcing FDI usually induces imports of capital goods and/or intermediate products and exports of other intermediate or final consumer goods. On the other hand, FDI has indirect microeconomic and macroeconomic implications for the host country concerned. More specifically, FDI affects the competitiveness of domestic firms, the business environment, the market structure and finally national competitiveness as a whole.

Foreign investment is usually undertaken by established companies that are substantial sellers in their home country's markets. In that process, companies have acquired ownership advantages, namely, managerial and technological know-how, trading expertise, patents, trademarks and other intangible assets. Having been acquired while the firm built a position in the domestic market, those assets become available for use elsewhere and give firms monopolistic advantages over local firms in the host country's markets. As long as FDI promotes the diffusion of these ownership advantages in the host country's economy, TNCs affect indirectly the competitiveness of domestic firms, namely, their entrepreneurial, managerial and technical capacity to set up and operate industries efficiently over time (Lall, 1987, 1989, 1990). Furthermore, the presence of foreign firms increases competitive pressures in the domestic market, forcing domestic firms to reduce mark-ups, to modernize their operations, and to produce more efficiently. The presence of FDI thus alters both the business environment and the market structure (Frischtak and Newfarmer, 1993).

These indirect effects are stronger in the case of FDI in technologically advanced manufactures and in tradable services. In these cases, FDI is associated with significant pro-trade externalities that involve knowledge transfers as well as organizational economies usually through the provision of upstream and downstream business services. FDI into more technologically advanced sectors increases the productivity of capital invested in the country and induces both process and product innovation. As industrial processes become more efficient or new goods and services are introduced, the volume of exports relative to imports, as well as productivity in the traded-goods sector of the economy are expected to increase. Similarly, FDI in services, if integrated properly in the host economy's productive system, enables existing domestic firms to upgrade not only their own production, but also their distribution and marketing networks.

Thus, overall national structural competitiveness, defined to be a country's ability to enhance collective techno-economic capabilities in the world market-place, appears to be increasingly determined not only by relative prices and the productivity of factors of production but by its ability to gain access to and use effectively a range of TNC-related products and/or services, that is, modern information technology, telecommunication services, modern managerial and accounting methods, banking services etc.[6]

Trade and competitiveness are also affected indirectly through the effects of FDI on the level of domestic activity, notably employment, income, consumption and domestic prices in the host country. Growth and trade literature have shown that the effects of capital accumulation on the volume of trade depend on the combined behaviour of consumption and production in the economy. Thus, if the average propensity to consume importables is increased (decreased) as a consequence of FDI, then FDI has a pro-trade (anti-trade) consumption effect. Similarly, if, as a consequence of FDI, domestic production becomes skewed towards exportables (importables), then the production effect is pro-trade (anti-trade). Thus, the direction of FDI in individual sectors of the economy and its effects on the overall production and consumption of exportables and importables are of critical importance for the pro-trade or anti-trade bias of FDI.

In general, market-seeking FDI tends to be import-substituting and thus tends to have an anti-trade production bias as it reduces the need for importables. The increase in employment and incomes, however, is expected to increase overall consumption of importables and thus create a pro-trade consumption effect. FDI for the purpose of using the home country as an export platform tends to have pro-trade production and consumption effects. Labour-seeking FDI is also expected to lead to pro-trade production and consumption effects as production of exports and consumption of imports are expanded. Resource extraction can have a pro-trade or an anti-trade net bias depending on whether it increases exports by more than it reduces imports. In this case, the production and consumption effects are probably biased in opposite directions and the total effect cannot be easily predicted (Chacholiades, 1978). Component-outsourcing FDI, on the other hand, tends to have both pro-trade production and consumption effects as some intermediate products are imported, assembled and reexported from the host country. The same can be said for horizontal efficiency-seeking FDI which has pro-trade effects both on production and consumption.

The effects of FDI on domestic prices and hence on price competitiveness and the real exchange rate should also be taken into account.

Effects on the real exchange rate

In the case of developing countries, which are price-takers in world markets, price competitiveness has to be defined as the relative price of traded to non-traded commodities. Price competitiveness is enhanced as the relative price of traded goods increases or, put differently, if the real exchange rate depreciates.

If capital inflows are prompted by domestic financial deregulation so that only investment in financial assets is increased, then capital inflows will raise domestic spending power and demand for both traded and non-traded goods, worsening both competitiveness and the trade account. This is because the excess demand for commodities raises the price of non-traded goods in the economy, while the price of traded goods is determined by the world market. This shift in relative prices, which is equivalent to a real exchange rate appreciation, leads to a deterioration in price competitiveness as resources are pulled away from tradables towards non-tradables (housing, construction etc).

If the capital inflow is used to finance capital accumulation rather than domestic consumption, then such capital inflows are expected to enhance in the future the productivity of the economy. In such a case, however, the orientation of FDI towards the tradable or the non-tradable sector of the economy is of critical importance for real exchange rate movements. Thus, if capital accumulation is concentrated in the traded goods sector, then, over time, the supply of traded goods will increase, allowing for an improvement in the trade account. This pattern of adjustment will produce a real exchange rate appreciation, but the worsening of price competitiveness in that case can be sustained without a policy problem.[7/] If instead, capital accumulation is oriented towards the non-tradable sector (domestic utilities etc), then the trade account will deteriorate and the real exchange rate is likely to depreciate as prices of non-tradeables will tend to fall. Even though the gradual improvement in price competitiveness will eventually pull resources towards tradables and in so doing restore equilibrium in the trade account, the short-run effects on the trade account are quite different than in the previous case.

Patterns of investment and trade linkages

The main points of the analysis of direct and indirect linkages presented so far are summarized in table 1, which relates the nature of FDI activity to its expected trade and competitiveness effects.

The first column of the table lists the five different types of FDI activities described earlier, namely, (a) labour-seeking investment, (b) resource-extracting investment, (c) component-outsourcing investment, (d) horizontal investment in differentiated products and (e) services-related investment. It also describes the basis for the international exchange that takes place. Comparative advantage refers to relative labour costs across countries augmented by differential tariffs, transportation costs etc. Absolute advantage refers to the overall productivity of capital in any given host country, which determines, *inter alia*, the real rate of return to foreign capital. Resource-extracting investment is usually driven by the availability of natural resources under profitable extracting conditions and the need to secure raw materials. Finally, increasing returns to scale and "thick-market" externalities provide the basis of production and exchange for technology intensive and more sophisticated products and services.

The second column describes the key characteristics of FDI and trade flows by type of FDI activity. Thus, labour-seeking investment channelled to small markets is directly linked to export promotion. Investment in large markets is undertaken for the purpose of satisfying domestic demand, thus being linked to import substitution. Since international exchange can be promoted either through trading or through FDI activity, in both cases FDI and trade are gross substitutes. Resource-extracting investment generates new export flows (trade creating) as exports of extracted resources are expanded, but has ambiguous consumption effects as imports of machinery and other intermediate inputs tend to increase but imports of resources decline. In most real

Table 1. Foreign-direct-investment-trade linkages

FDI activity	FDI-trade characteristics	Trade effects	
		Production and income	Price[b]
1. Labour-seeking investment (clothing, footwear, etc.) Basis: comparative advantage[a]	Export promotion in small markets Import substitution in large markets Gross substitutability	Pro-trade production effects Pro-trade consumption effects Anti-trade production effects Pro-trade consumption effects	Appreciation of real exchange rate (RER)
2. Resource-extracting Basis: availability of natural resources; security of raw materials	Trade creating FDI prerequisite for trade	Pro-trade production effects Anti-trade consumption effects	Appreciation of RER
3. Component-outsourcing Basis: comparative and absolute advantage, increasing returns	Intra-firm trade Trade creating Gross substitutability	Pro-trade production effects Pro-trade consumption effects	Appreciation of RER
4. Horizontal investment in differentiated products (automobiles, consumer durables, pharmaceuticals)	Intra-industry or intra-firm trade Trade creating Gross complementarity	Pro-trade production effects Pro-trade consumption effects	Appreciation of RER
5. Services-related investment Basis: thick- market externalities		Pro-trade production effects Pro-trade consumption effects	Depreciation of RER

[a] Defined as low relative labour costs augmented by differential tariffs, transportation costs, etc.
[b] Defined as relative price of traded to non-traded goods.

cases, extensive TNC investment activities precede trade flows so that FDI appears to be a prerequisite for trade.

Efficiency-seeking FDI is similarly trade-creating and consists largely of intra-industry and, often, intra-firm trade. In the case of product differentiation, investment does not usually displace trade, but expands trade as both domestic consumption and exports tend to increase. Thus, in this case, trade and FDI tend to be complementary activities.

The third column describes the trade effects associated with each type of investment, including the production effects, the consumption effects and the real exchange rate effects. As was noted earlier, appreciation of the real exchange rate is associated with a deterioration in price competitiveness. It should be observed that only investment in services which expands the production of non-tradables generates an improvement in price competitiveness. In all other cases capital inflows tend to worsen price competitiveness, at least in the short-run.

In conclusion, table 1 makes it clear that the linkages between FDI and trade depend not only on the basis of international production and exchange, which shift as development proceeds, but also on the implied substitutability or complementarity of trade and FDI, which is, in turn, dependent on the type of FDI.

From a policy perspective, it becomes apparent that, as the composition of FDI changes from labour-seeking or assembly-based investment to component-outsourcing and services, the locational advantages required to attract FDI become more demanding. Thus, the liberalization of trade and capital movements and the maintenance of relatively low wages are necessary, but not sufficient conditions for attracting FDI to developing countries. Absolute advantage does matter and so does risk, thick-market externalities and the availability of business services. Even in labour-seeking and/or in assembly-based FDI, there are sufficient economies of scale in production and distribution to require the support of an effective infrastructural network.

Table 1 can also be interpreted as an evolutionary pattern of FDI-trade linkages that correspond to different stages of development (see also Ozawa 1992 and Dunning 1993, chap. 10). According to such interpretation, one can distinguish five stages of FDI-driven development, each associated with a specific set of ownership and locational advantages.

Stage A. Prior to any FDI activity, trade is organized on the basis of Heckscher-Ohlin comparative advantage, that is, the country tends to export goods which use intensively the country's abundant factors of production, such as agricultural products and/or unskilled labour-intensive commodities.

Stage B. As output and exports increase, labour-seeking FDI takes place for the purpose of using the country as an export base for unskilled labour-intensive commodities and for organizing production on a more efficient basis. FDI is associated with pro-trade production and consumption effects. (The ownership advantages of firms include patents, trading networks etc; the main locational advantages of countries reside in their natural resources.)

If the host country is large, market-seeking FDI takes place for the purpose of serving the domestic market. FDI is associated with anti-trade production effects and probably pro-trade consumption effects. (Locational advantages include actual or expected trade barriers, high transport costs, etc.)

If the host country possesses raw materials, resource-extracting FDI takes place for export purposes. FDI is associated with pro-trade production effects and probably anti-trade consumption effects. (Here the locational advantages relate to the availability, and security of supply, of raw materials.)

Stage C. Labour-intensive processes in industries where vertically disarticulated investment is technically possible (electronics/automobiles), are transferred to host countries. (Ownership advantages include patents, trademarks, technological and marketing know-how; and locational advantages relatively cheap, but disciplined labour in an organized productive system; low political, economic, foreign exchange risk factors; more advanced infrastructural requirements and service networks.)

If the country is large, horizontal investment takes place in differentiated products with pro-trade production and consumption effects.

Stage D. FDI in services takes place due to increased demand for upstream, instream and downstream business services generated by established firms to strengthen trading networks and networks of cooperative subcontracting arrangements. Host country tends to become home country of industries of Stages A, B and probably C. (Locational

The Republic of Korea, however, has had access to considerable official net resource flows as opposed to private capital.[13/] FDI accounted for a considerable share of gross domestic capital formation in Singapore (on average 23.9 per cent between 1986 and 1989), but a minuscule share in the Republic of Korea (less than 0.5 per cent in 1992 (UNCTAD, 1994)).

Both countries have experienced rapid growth rates of exports and have assumed specific roles in the Asian regional market. While Singapore appears to have transformed itself into a regional service centre, the Republic of Korea has continued to specialize in relatively labour-intensive, assembly-based, subcontracting-dependent mass manufacturing. In Singapore, by 1992 more than nearly 60 per cent of the total inward stock of FDI was in services and about a quarter in what can be described as complex or advanced manufacturing. The bulk of FDI in the Republic of Korea is still directed to the secondary sector, especially in chemicals and electrical and transport equipment. These are medium- and high-technology industries where the scope for "unpackaging" in the form of licensing activities is limited.[14/] It is only in the last 15 years or so that the share of investment in services has increased from 19 per cent in 1976 to 38 per cent in 1992.

Japan's share of FDI stock remains relatively small in Singapore, while FDI from the United States increased in the 1980s as strategic alliances across regional clusters emerged. Other South-East Asian economies, most notably Hong Kong and Malaysia, are principal investors in Singapore. Japan, on the other hand, is the dominant investor in the Republic of Korea, controlling more than 50 per cent of the total stock of FDI in the country.

The composition of exports of the two countries testifies to their specialization within the group. Singapore's exports are concentrated in chemicals and metal manufacturing (around 70 per cent). The Republic of Korea's industrial production and exports are more diversified across textiles, chemicals, basic metals and metal manufacturing. Singapore, being a regional centre, not only invests in other regional members, but trades extensively with them. Singapore's investment accounted for 24 per cent of the total FDI stock in Malaysia in 1987, and for 5 per cent of the total FDI stock in Thailand in 1988. Almost 20 per cent of its exports and imports are directed to those countries, most notably to Malaysia (UNCTC 1992c).

The Republic of Korea, on the other hand, appears to be loosely attached to other group members, but firmly attached to global trading networks, trading mostly with Japan and the United States.

The other two members of the group, namely Malaysia and Thailand, are clearly at earlier stages of the evolutionary growth and integration process described earlier. In 1992, around 30 per cent of Malaysia's inward FDI stock was in labour-intensive or resource-extracting industries, although that in the higher technology manufacturing sector and in services is currently (1994) expanding the most rapidly. Around 20 per cent of Thailand's inward FDI stock is in more complex manufactures, while the bulk of investment in services is in trading and construction. The composition of their exports corresponds to their stage of development and integration within the regional cluster (stages B and C).

Labour-seeking or resource-extracting investment has generated exports and export earnings, which have then been used to restructure the domestic base either towards more complex manufacturing activities, as in the case of the Republic of Korea, or towards services as in the case of Singapore. As footloose, labour-intensive operations have relocated in the less developed countries of the area, component-outsourcing FDI and FDI in services have been attracted to the fast-growing original host countries.

As the complexity and technological level of industries is upgraded, inter-industry trade is replaced by intra-industry trade. Thus, by 1990 most trade between majority-owned United States foreign affiliates and the United States is conducted on an intra-firm basis, especially in the chemical, non-electrical, and electrical industries. Intra-firm trade with Asia, especially with the newly industrializing economies, appears to be dominant in those industries (over 90 per cent of total trade between affiliates and the United States), where semi-skilled labour and a predictable investment environment have provided incentives for United States downstream processing and assembly-based FDI.[15/]

A very different pattern of FDI-trade linkages emerges in Latin America. Each country in the area, pursuing more inward-looking strategies than the Asian developing countries, has lured FDI largely into protected import-substituting industries mostly from the United States and the European Union. The presence of large markets has mainly attracted horizontal investments in differentiated products to satisfy domestic market requirements.

As expected with this type of investment, trade is mostly intra-industry and/or intra-firm, as opposed to inter-industry. Industries which are characterized by product differentiation and for which intra-firm trade is particularly dominant include non-electrical machinery and transport equipment.[16]

Contrary to the Asian experience, there is no strong evidence pointing to the emergence of an integrated United States-Latin America regional cluster. If anything, most countries appear as independent players in capital markets. This is quite evident in the case of Brazil, which accounts for almost a quarter of the total FDI inflows in Latin America, attracting FDI mostly from Europe and less so from the United States and Japan. The United States' share in Brazil's inward FDI stock has, in fact, fallen from 38 per cent in 1971 to 28 per cent in 1990. Similarly, the share of Brazil's exports and imports to and from the United States has returned to its early 1970s level. FDI serves largely the internal market. Exports of United States majority-owned foreign affiliates in 1989 accounted for only 17 per cent of total sales. Exports consist of food and beverages, chemicals and metal manufacturing.

The pattern of FDI-trade linkages is quite different in Mexico, which, by the end of the 1980s, became the largest host country in Latin America. The United States and Canada have a dominating role in Mexico. They accounted for 64.3 per cent of the total inward FDI stock in Mexico in 1991 (UNCTAD 1994b), absorbed 71.7 per cent of Mexico's exports, and provided for 65 per cent of its imports (UNCTAD 1994c). United States affiliates in Mexico accounted for two-thirds of the total 1987-1988 growth in employment by developing-country affiliates of United States TNCs.[17] Further, although there is a lack of empirical data at this stage, it can be assumed that the NAFTA agreement has increased TNC related Mexican-United States trade even more.

After the second oil crisis, most of the increase in United States FDI flows to Mexico was in resource-extractive industries. About 60 per cent of Mexico's exports are still concentrated in that sector. Already by the late 1960s, however, Mexico's large domestic market, its proximity to the United States, the availability of cheap unskilled labour and finally the establishment of assembly plants (*maquiladoras*) along the United States-Mexican border controlled by TNCs, created the basis for labour-seeking, as well as for component-outsourcing investment. Recently, Mexico has emerged as a key host country for many United States TNCs in more advanced sectors, including Ford, IBM, Hewlett Packard and General Electric. As the basis for international exchange has evolved over time and thick-market externalities have been achieved, FDI in services and in more technologically advanced sectors has increased. The share of services in FDI has doubled between 1970 and 1992 to support and serve the business activities located in the area.

In terms of the evolutionary pattern of FDI-trade linkages discussed earlier, Mexico is entering Stage D. Whether or not it will emerge in the 1990s as the centre of a regional cluster including other adjacent Latin American countries will depend on the strategic behaviour in the region of the United States TNCs, on outward investment-incentive policies by potential host countries and on coordinated efforts to redress the external and internal macroeconomic imbalances of the region. Given the predominance of United States TNCs in the area and their traditional tendency to invest in import-substituting, high-technology activities to maximize economic rents arising from superior technology, the development of such a regional cluster appears rather unlikely.

Due to Mexico's locational advantages as well as its market size, FDI in the country has increasingly been serving not only the domestic, but also the United States market. While in 1982, exports of United States affiliates accounted for only 11 per cent of total sales, in 1986, that share increased to 34 per cent serving almost exclusively the United States market.[18] United States affiliates accounted in the 1966-1986 period for almost 30 per cent of Mexico's export growth in manufactures as opposed to 17 per cent in Brazil and in Singapore and only 1 per cent in the Republic of Korea.[19]

Proximity to the United States market appears to be an important determinant of Mexico's evolutionary process of stage-based sequential growth, triggered by FDI and promoted through FDI-trade linkages. Low transportation costs in conjunction with the establishment of *maquiladoras* have increased Mexico's comparative advantage as an export-base for the United States market. These proved to be particularly important locational advantages in the early stages of FDI-trade linkages, when investment was dominated by labour-seeking or assembly-based footloose operations. Their importance has lessened over time as Mexico's host market has expanded. The same process is observed in

Asia as regionalization has reduced the importance of the original locational advantages. In both cases, the absolute advantage of the country or of the region and the presence of thick-market externalities have ensured the profitability of TNC operations in the area.

Contrary to Mexico's experience, Nigeria has not managed to move forward from stage B. The country is the largest African host country attracting 25 per cent of FDI inflow, or 21 per cent of FDI stock in 1994 in Africa (UNCTAD 1995). Foreign investment is mostly resource-seeking, as Nigeria remains a major oil-exporting country. Almost 42 per cent of its inward FDI stock comes from European Union countries and 24 per cent from the United States. By the early 1980s, 95 per cent of its exports consisted of oil. Even though this has probably declined somewhat, industrial restructuring via FDI-trade linkages is altogether absent. So is any systematic effort by policy to reinvest export earnings in order to diversify the productive base, and to create the absolute advantages necessary to lure FDI into new manufacturing activities. In fact Nigeria is a good example of what has come to be known in economics as a "Dutch-disease problem", where the existence of a booming sector has increased domestic liquidity with adverse consequences for competitiveness and manufacturing exports. Thus, given the uncertainty in Nigeria's growth prospects coupled with its distance from home countries, and the lack of a forward-looking development strategy, the presence of a large domestic market of more than 100 million people has not been a sufficient condition to lure FDI into manufacturing activities.

The lack of any systematic relationship between FDI and export performance is testified, in the case of Nigeria, by a low and negative correlation coefficient between the FDI/GDP ratio and the export/output ratio throughout the 1970s and 1980s. This has to be contrasted with a very high positive coefficient for Mexico (0.8) and a relatively high positive coefficient for Singapore (0.6), the Republic of Korea (0.5) and Brazil (0.5).[20/]

Similarly, while in Nigeria there does not appear to be any systematic relationship between FDI and structural competitiveness measured by the export/import ratio, positive correlation coefficients in Singapore and the Republic of Korea indicate that FDI in those countries is associated with export expansion and with pro-trade production effects. On the other hand, the high negative correlation coefficient between the

FDI/output ratio and the export/import ratio in Brazil is consistent with the anti-trade production effects and the pro-trade consumption effects expected from import-substituting FDI in large host countries.

Policy implications

The main conclusion that emerges from the preceding analysis is that increased flows of FDI to developing countries cannot be assumed to take place simply on grounds of traditional comparative advantages and outward-oriented liberalization policies. As the composition of FDI shifts towards more complex manufactures and services, only a few developing countries will possess the "absolute" advantages, the "thick-market externalities" and the business environment and networking required to attract and sustain modern FDI inflows.

These are the countries which have successfully exploited past FDI inflows to develop the appropriate infrastructure and their local absorptive capacities. They have done so by reinvesting export receipts to augment their locational advantages and restructure their productive base. Especially in South-East Asia and more recently in Latin America, the countries which are likely to receive FDI in the 1990s are those countries whose forward-looking development policies in the past have allowed TNCs to act as "interstate arbitragers of economic development" (Ozawa, 1992), thus expanding not only trade, but, at the same time, their technological and productive capacities. In these countries, policies have capitalized on FDI-trade linkages to ignite a "virtuous circle of development".[21/]

The geographic concentration of FDI in a few developing countries can thus be explained as a by-product of policies which aim at matching ownership and locational advantages. This concentration is not inevitable, however. It could change significantly if developing countries, wishing to attract and sustain FDI, follow an appropriate set of policies depending on their location, the size of their economy and their development stage. The reduction of uncertainty inherent in doing business in developing countries is a prerequisite for attracting FDI. It is thus important for any country to stipulate observable investment rules, if it is to present a credible long-term programme for infrastructure and human resource development, to set policy guidelines for the operation of credit and labour markets and to adopt consistent macroeconomic policies.

This is especially true for those developing countries that face major internal and external imbalances and/or are over-indebted. In such cases, credibility is enhanced and uncertainty is reduced if the Governments involved are perceived to follow a steady course of economic adjustment that addresses effectively their macroeconomic imbalances. In the absence of foreign capital transfers to underpin development, this implies that Governments must be able to increase domestic saving to finance increased investment. This should be done in a manner that does not stifle growth or produce such political and social upheaval that it undermines the continuation of stabilization programmes. Even though the design of stabilization programmes that promote economic adjustment with growth is beyond the scope of the present study, it is important to realize that productive restructuring is conditional upon a favourable macroeconomic environment and a credible public sector.

The importance of absolute advantages for attracting TNC activities and footloose capital implies that there are certain programmes that should be placed outside the annual ups and downs of budget approvals. The following three such programmes are singled out.

(i) <u>Public investment</u>. Investment in physical capital and in infrastructure has to be maintained at a pace consistent with a satisfactory path of development. The very nature of the programmes and the need to support the credibility of the development process require that they should be immune to the vagaries of short-term demand management.

(ii) <u>Education, training and health</u>. Programmes relating to education, training and health should not bear the brunt of adjustment. They provide services that relate not only to basic human rights, but also critically affect human capabilities and national competitiveness.

(iii) <u>Basic needs</u>. Programmes designed to satisfy the basic needs of the poorer segments of the population should not be cut back. However austere a stabilization programme might be, it should not go as far as denying the right to survival.

While these programmes may appear to be self evident, they have often been the main victims of stabilization plans, partly because they have gained support from relatively weak political constituencies. If these matters can be removed from the agenda of day-to-day politics, and if multilateral development institutions support this view, there is a good chance that adjustment programmes will gain wider support and may become sustainable in the long term.

The absence of "thick-market externalities" can be corrected through "networking policies" that aim (a) at linking domestic firms with each other through information-exchange or subcontracting agreements, (b) at participating in established global trading networks, (c) at strengthening the linkages between domestic and foreign firms, and (d) at developing policies for attracting a cluster of foreign firms into the domestic economy. The programmes and policies adopted by the European Community aimed at strengthening the cohesion of member States through effective networking, provide an interesting experience for developing countries to study.

Development can also be facilitated in small countries by the creation of cooperative business networks within a wider region that promote horizontal and vertical integration and would enlarge the market size sufficiently to give rise to thick-market externalities. As the combination of rising investment costs and shorter product life cycles has increased the risks associated with new investment in new locations, participation in regional clusters can substantially reduce market risks through cooperative arrangements.

The augmentation of locational advantages requires a concerted domestic effort to increase investment in physical and human resources, to improve infrastructure, to promote networking and to generate favourable business conditions. FDI can act as a catalyst for industrial restructuring only if local absorptive capacities are simultaneously expanded so that domestic firms can upgrade their production through product and process innovation, penetrate new markets and improve their competitiveness and trade performance.

To achieve those targets, government macroeconomic and organization policies should be aimed at translating FDI productivity-enhancing domestic investment, while minimizing its (short-term) consumption effects. Given the limited mobility of factors across sectors at early stages of development, policies should channel FDI to the traded-goods sectors of the economy, preferably to the export sector, even if that implies a temporary worsening of price competitiveness. The channelling of FDI into non-tradables, most notably in construction activities and in services, before markets function properly and relative prices adequately serve their purpose as efficient signals for resource allocation, runs the risk of exacerbating the pro-trade consumption effects as opposed to the pro-trade production effects of FDI.

The overall policy implication of the analysis presented is that, in an environment where economic activity is becoming increasingly globalized, development strategies should aim at augmenting the domestic basis for international production and exchange by exploiting FDI-competitiveness and trade linkages.

The experience of Asian developing countries and of Mexico has shown that this process is eminently feasible. All those countries have followed a similar evolutionary strategy of stage-based sequential growth and development by channelling FDI initially into unskilled labour-intensive or resource-extracting industries and subsequently into more complex manufactures and services.

As the source of comparative advantage was eroded in the original locations and footloose operations were transplanted to adjacent profitable locations, a regional cluster was formed, supported by extensive networking across complementary business activities. The integration of the smaller Asian market economies into regional clusters has expanded the boundaries of national markets, created thick-market externalities and has further increased the profitability of TNC operations in the area through reductions in transaction costs.

This pattern of integration based on FDI-trade linkages is only now emerging in Latin America. The removal of barriers to trade and FDI across countries in the region and the adoption of policies that would promote integration of the region based on inter- and intra-industry specialization, would induce further FDI inflows and facilitate industrial restructuring through FDI-trade linkages. It would also enable traditional host countries in the area, such as Mexico and Brazil, to diversify their economies and their role in the region and to ease in that way their external and internal imbalance problems.

The response of developing countries to the globalizing economy of the 1990s will not solely depend on upgrading their indigenous capabilities, and providing the right kind of incentives to FDI. An issue that is often downplayed, but critical for the effectiveness and speed of adjustment, is the appropriate selection of development agents in a society. In most developing countries, the centralization of authority and the lack of intermediate development institutions have hindered development initiatives and have weakened entrepreneurship. One of the central tasks of government macro-organizational strategy, therefore, is to create a network of institutions, agencies or mechanisms that would support the functioning of markets, mobilize human resources and reward entrepreneurial activities. The restructuring of public administration systems according to modern organizational and management practices, the development and deepening of capital markets and the modernization of banking sector activities are important steps in that direction.

The European experience has shown that the creation of semi-autonomous regional development agencies that provide not only information, but also technical and organizational support to entrepreneurial initiatives, can mobilize resources more effectively and at less cost than central authorities. Regional agencies can also act as intermediaries between TNCs and local enterprises facilitating and promoting the creation of networks and linkages.

Finally, the creation of development-oriented political coalitions is a precondition and not a consequence of development. The presence of a "development block" can effect the required shift in the consumption-saving mix and sustain an austere path to development. Tinkering with productive restructuring with the wrong political formation in the background is an exercise in futility.

Development coalitions need to be pursued not only at the national, but also at the international level. The globalization of productive activities suggests the need to establish regional or global forums to promote a dialogue among national Governments, multilateral finance and development agencies, the private sector of the countries concerned and transnational corporations. Such a dialogue would promote the adoption of more coordinated and effective policies for the successful management of structural change.

Notes

1. See Danthine (1991), p. 4.
2. For a review of the literature, see Dunning (1993).
3. For an excellent analysis of the relationship between economic development, trade and investment, see Ozawa (1992). See also Dunning (1993), chap. 10.
4. See Caves, Frankel and Jones (1990), p. 201.
5. Exceptions include trade in intermediate services and information. The advent of the information highway, for example, is having a major impact on trade in telecommunications hardware and software.

6. For a recent review of the ways in which FDI might upgrade a host country's competitiveness, see Dunning (1994).
7. Centre for Economic and Political Studies, Macroeconomic Policy Group (1990). "Convergence and real exchange rates in the European monetary system", Brussels. p. 21.
8. T. Ozawa. "Foreign direct investment and economic development", *Transnational Corporations*, vol. 1, No. 1 (February), pp. 27-54.
9. Hong Kong, the Republic of Korea, Singapore and Taiwan Province of China.
10. Blomström (1990), p. 29.
11. Ibid.
12. Hill and Johns (1985), p. 358.
13. Ibid., p. 357.
14. Ibid., p. 373.
15. Blomström (1990), p. 53.
16. Ibid., p. 52.
17. UNCTC (1991), p. 50.
18. Blomström (1990), p. 29.
19. Ibid., p. 24.
20. For the complete statistical analysis, see *Foreign Investment and Trade Linkages in Developing Countries* (United Nations publication, Sales No. E.93.II.A.12).
21. See Ozawa, op. cit., pp. 27-54.

References

Blomström, Magnus, I.B. Kravis and R.E. Lipsey (1989). Multinational firms and manufactured exports from developing countries, National Bureau of Economic Research (NBER), Working Paper, No. 2493.

———— (1990). *Transnational Corporations and Manufacturing Exports from Developing Countries* (United Nations publication, Sales No. E.90.II.A.21).

Bohn-Young Koo (1985). In *Multinational Enterprises, Economic Structure and International Competitiveness* J.H. Dunning, ed., Geneva: John Wiley and Sons.

Caves, R.E., J.A. Frankel and R.W. Jones, (1990), *World Trade and Payments: An Introduction,* 5th ed. Glenview, Illinois: Scott, Foresman and Company.

Centre for Economic and Political Studies (CEPS), Macroeconomic Policy Group (1990). Convergence and real exchange rates in the European monetary system, Brussels: CEPS.

Chacholiades, M. (1978). *International Trade Theory and Policy.* New York, McGraw-Hill.

Chan, Steve, Cal Clark and David R. Davis (1990). State entrepreneurship, foreign investment, export expansion and economic growth. *Journal of Conflict Resolution,* vol. 34, No. 1 (March), pp. 102-129.

Danthine, J.P. (1991), Wage subsidies or investment incentives: What are the options for public intervention in the East German economy? Centre for Economic and Political Studies (CEPS), Economic Policy Group. Unpublished.

Datta Chaudhuri, Mrinal (1982). The role of free trade zones in the creation of employment and industrial growth in Malaysia. Asian Employment Working Papers, Bangkok, Thailand.

Diamond, P. (1982). Aggregate demand management in search of equilibrium. *Journal of Political Economy*, vol. 90, No. 5 (October), pp. 881-894.

Diaz-Alejandro, C.F. (1981). Southern cone stabilization plans. In *Economic Stabilization in Developing countries*, W.R. Cline and S. Weitraub, eds. Washington, D.C.: Brookings Institution.

Dunning, J. (1988). *Explaining International Production*. London, Unwin Hyman.

_____ (1991). European integration and transatlantic foreign direct investment: the record assessed. Unpublished.

_____ (1993). International enterprises and the global economy. Wokingham, England: Addison Wesley.

_____ (1994) Re-evaluating the benefits of foreign direct investment, *Transnational Corporations*, vol. 3, February, pp. 23-52.

Frischtak C. and R. Newfarmer (eds.) (1993). *Transnational Corporations: Market Structure and Industrial Performance*. United Nations Library on Transnational Corporations, vol. 15. London and New York: Routledge.

Hill, Hal and Brian Johns (1985). The role of direct foreign investment in developing East Asian countries. *Weltwirtschaftliches Archiv*, vol. 121, pp. 355-381.

Julius, De Anne. (1990). *Global Companies and Public Policy: The Growing Challenge of Foreign Direct Investment*. London: Chatham House Papers.

Katseli, L. (1984). Real exchange rates in the 1970s. In *Exchange Rate Theory and Practice*, J. Bilson and R. Marston, eds. Chicago, Illinois: NBER and Chicago University Press.

Kojima, Kiyoshi (1977). *Japan and a New World Economic Order*. London: Croom Helm.

Lall, S. (1987), *Learning to Industrialize: The Acquisition of Technological Capability by India*. London: Macmillan.

_____ (1989). Human resource development and industrialization, with special reference to Africa. *Journal of Development Planning*, vol. 19, pp. 129-158.

_____ (1990). *Building Industrial Competitiveness in Developing Countries* Paris: OECD.

Lecraw, D. (1985). Singapore. In *Multinational Enterprises, Economic Structure and International Competitiveness*, J.H. Dunning, ed. London: John Wiley and Sons.

Lee, Kyu-Uck (1990). International trade and industrial organisation: the Korean experience. Seoul, Korean Development Institute. Unpublished.

Ozawa, T. (1985). Japan. In *Multinational Enterprises, Economic Structure and International Competitiveness*, J.H. Dunning, ed., London: John Wiley and Sons.

_____ (1991). Multinational corporations and the flying-geese paradigm of economic development in the Asian Pacific. University of Colorado, unpublished.

_____ (1992). Foreign direct investment and economic development. *Transnational Corporations*, vol. 1. No. 1 (February), pp. 27-54.

Porter, M. (1990). *The Competitive Advantage of Nations*. New York, Macmillan Free Press.

Reich, R. (1991). *The Work of Nations: Preparing Ourselves for 21st-Century Capitalism*. New York: Alfred A. Knopf, pp. 301-315.

Stevens, B. and M. Andrieu (1991). Trade, investment and technology in a changing international environment. In *Trade, Investment and Technology in the 1990s*. (Paris: OECD.

UNCTAD (1993a). *World Investment Report 1993: Transnational Corporations and Integrated International Production* (United Nations publication, Sales No. E.93.II.A.14).

_____ (1993b). *Handbook of International Trade and Development Statistics* (United Nations publication, Sales No. E/F.94.II.D.24).

_____ (1994a). *World Investment Report (1994): Transnational Corporations, Employment and the Workplace* (United Nations publication, Sales No. E.94.II.A.14).

_____ (1994b). *World Investment Directory, Volume IV: Latin America and the Caribbean* (United Nations publication, Sales No. E.94.II.A.10).

_____ (1995). *World Investment Report 1995: Transnational Corporations and Competitiveness* (United Nations publication, Sales No. E.95.II.A.9).

_____ (1996). *World Investment Report 1996: Investment, Trade and International Policy Arrangements* (United Nations publication, Sales No. E.96.II.A.14).

UNCTC (1988). *Transnational Corporations in World Development: Trends and Prospects* (United Nations publication, Sales No. E.88.II.A.7).

_____ (1991). *World Investment Report 1991: The Triad in Foreign Direct Investment* (United Nations publication, Sales No. E.91.II.A.12).

_____ (1992a). *The Determinants of Foreign Direct Investment: A Survey of the Evidence* (United Nations publication, Sales No. E.92.II.A.2).

_____ (1992b). *World Investment Report 1992: Transnational Corporations as Engines of Growth* (United Nations publications, Sales No. E.92.II.A.19).

_____ (1992c). *World Investment Directory Volume I: Asia and the Pacific* (United Nations publications, Sales No. E.92.II.A.11).

United States Department of Commerce (1992). *U.S. Direct Investment Abroad, 1992*. Washington, D.C.: Government Printing Office.

7

Attracting investment in an integrating world economy

Stephen Thomsen

Regional integration within a general liberalization of trade can play a strong role in stimulating investment into and, more important, within each region. By creating large, more open markets, regional integration may also have the additional advantage of restraining any monopolistic tendencies on the part of investing firms. This competitive pressure, in turn, enhances the potential spillovers from FDI. Enhanced spillover effects should be one of the most important aims of any policy, and certainly more significant than simply attracting footloose firms.

Developing countries and globalization

How do developing countries fit into the overall global strategy of TNCs? The answer lies in the pattern of production and sales of TNCs. Unfortunately, few countries provide such information except for the United States. Although United States TNCs clearly dominate world investment flows, their role is diminishing over time, and they may steadily become less representative of TNCs. Nevertheless, the information provided on United States TNCs is unparalleled.

We will begin by looking at export sales of American affiliates abroad in 1989 as set out in figure 1. Where regional integration is sufficiently advanced, the affiliate is also likely to export a large share within the regional market. Over 40 per cent of intra-firm imports to the United States parents from their majority-owned foreign affiliates come from Canada. Almost two-thirds of these imports consist of transport equipment. The 1965 Auto Pact has given rise to a high level of integrated production in automotive goods between the two countries (United States Economics and Statistics Administration, 1992). Mexican affiliates have also become significant exporters to the United States after the implementation of the North American Free Trade Agreement (NAFTA). Similarly, affiliates in Europe export $144 billion on a regional basis, but only $28 billion back to the United States.

American affiliates in developing countries are not as concentrated on the region in which they are located. With the exception of Mexico, affiliate exports are divided fairly evenly between the United States and the rest of the world. Given the state of regional integration in many developing regions and the overall minimal level of intraregional exports, it should not be surprising that very little South-South trade has yet arisen from American affiliates in those countries. But the exports back to the United States or to other Triad markets are not particularly impressive given all the hyperbole about the global factory. In 1992, affiliates of United States TNCs in developing countries exported $38 billion back to the United States, almost one half of which comes from Singapore and Mexico alone. Another 30 per cent came from Brazil, Hong Kong, Malaysia, Taiwan Province of China, Nigeria and Thailand.[1]

Figure 1. Sales of United States manufacturing affiliates in developing countries

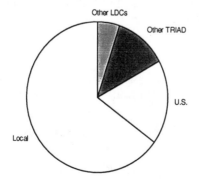

Other LDCs

Other TRIAD

U.S.

Local

The most consistent characteristics of sales patterns of United States owned affiliates in 1992 is the importance of the local market. In developed countries, 63 per cent of affiliates sales are in the domestic market of the affiliate. The corresponding figure for developing countries is 56 per cent.[2/] These figures, together with the significance of regional exports in relatively well-integrated regions, suggests that American firms are primarily market seekers. They produce in large and fast-growing markets. Their market is global in scope, but their production is national and increasingly regional in orientation.

The significance of this regional strategy will become clear later in the present chapter. For the moment, what evidence do other countries provide on their own firms? Japanese affiliates abroad sell 84 per cent of their output to the local market in which they are located. Even in Asia the share is 64 per cent and is likely to increase rather than decrease in the future as more and more Japanese TNCs indicate a growing interest in the regional market itself (as discussed in chapter 3).

We have little information about the activities of European firms, but, as can be seen from table 1, their choice of location for investment mirrors that of American and Japanese firms, and one can only deduce that the motives for such investment are similar. For the top ten hosts for individual home countries, seven are mentioned in at least three cases. These countries are Brazil, Singapore, Mexico, Malaysia, Hong Kong, the Republic of Korea and Taiwan Province of China. Brazil alone accounts for between 17 per cent of American,[3/] and over 30 per cent of German[4/] FDI stock in developing countries. There is a slight regional bias for American FDI and a much stronger one for Japan. British investors are more likely to choose former colonies. But all investors as a group seem to be following similar strategies with respect to developing countries regardless of their origin.

Discussions of FDI and globalization are usually confined to firms from Triad markets, but a growing share of investment now emanates from within the developing world itself. For host countries starved of capital and technology and with little information about exporting opportunities, this investment is at least as important, if not more, than that from the Triad. The Republic of Korea has been a net overseas direct investor since 1990 and Taiwan Province of China since 1988. China is already the major outward investor among developing countries

Table 1. Principal host developing countries by home country investors[a]

United States Millions of $ (1993)		United Kingdom Millions of £ (1993)		Germany Millions of DM (1994)		Japan Millions of $ (1994)	
Brazil	16 908	Singapore	3 702	Brazil	10 582	Indonesia	16 981
Mexico	15 413	Hong Kong	3 592	Mexico	4 127	Hong Kong	13 881
Hong Kong	10 457	Brazil	1 935	Argentina	1 977	Singapore	9 535
Singapore	8 782	Malaysia	1 751	Singapore	1 925	Brazil	8 849
Indonesia	5 031	Nigeria	817	Hong Kong	1 794	China	8 729
Argentina	4 355	Zimbabwe	255	Malaysia	743	Thailand	7 184
Taiwan Prov. of China	3 096	India	..	Rep. of Korea	721	Malaysia	6 357
Rep. of Korea	3 001	Indonesia	..	Libyan Arab Jamahiriya	656	Korea Taiwan Prov.	5 268
Thailand	2 893	Mexico	..	Thailand	477	of China	3 997
Chile	2 869	Kenya	..	India	450	Philippines	2 817

Sources: United States Commerce Department, *Survey of Current Business*, August 1994. Ministry of Finance of Japan, 1995. Deutsche Bundesbank, May, 1995, United Kingdom Central Statistical Office, Overseas Direct Investment 1993, 31 January, 1995.

[a]   Excludes tax havens. Countries are ranked by size of FDI stock.

(UNCTAD, 1995). Some of this investment has flowed to the Triad markets in search of technology and markets, but some has also gone to low wage neighbouring countries. At one stage, the biggest investor in Malaysia was Taiwan Province of China. Hong Kong firms have also been investing in southern China as described in chapter 3. Intraregional FDI in the developing countries of Asia sometimes exceeds investment from Triad countries. In Malaysia and China, over one half of recent flows have come from NIEs in the region.[5/] In the Philippines and Indonesia, NIE investments exceed those from Japan or any other individual Triad member. Such intraregional investments are also starting to appear in Latin America, as recent Chilean investment in Argentina testifies.

Table 2 provides total inflows for selected countries in Asia and Latin America over the period 1982-1994, thus permitting one to judge the importance of different host countries for all TNCs as a group. The story is much the same except that China becomes far more important than was indicated from OECD investments, primarily because investment in China is channelled through Hong Kong. For almost all countries listed in table 2, inflows in the last five years of the period were substantially higher than those in the preceding eight years which followed the eruption of the debt crises. More than one half of total inflows into the two regions over the whole period were accounted for by only three countries: Singapore, Mexico and China.

What do all of these countries have in common? They are all either large or fast growing markets, or they possess the requisite skills and training to fit into the global production strategies of TNCs. These are precisely the variables that figure prominently in regression analyses of the determinants of FDI (see, for example, UNCTC 1992a and Dunning 1993). In particular, market size is consistently significant, even when one is looking at where TNCs locate production for export (Kravis and

Table 2. Inflows of foreign direct investment for selected developing countries, 1982-1994

(Annual average)

Developing countries	1982-1994 Millions of $	Share percentage
China	7 314.1	20.8
Singapore	3 699.6	10.5
Malaysia	2 205.2	6.3
Hong Kong	1 367.2	3.9
Thailand	1 199.2	3.4
Indonesia	946.6	2.7
Taiwan Province of China	780.4	2.2
Republic of Korea	525.8	1.5
Philippines	318.5	0.9
Pakistan	184.9	0.5
ASIA (10 countries)	18 541.5	52.7
Mexico	3 105.1	8.8
Argentina	1 560.6	4.4
Brazil	1 457.8	4.1
Chile	743.8	2.1
Colombia	577.7	1.6
Venezuela	399.4	1.1
Peru	257.1	0.7
Trinidad and Tobago	134.1	0.4
Costa Rica	132.5	0.4
Dominican Republic	101.3	0.3
LATIN AMERICA (10 countries)	8 469.4	24.1
DEVELOPING COUNTRY TOTAL	35 215.5	100
Africa	2 568.7	7.3
South, East, and South-East Asia	18 991.7	53.9

Source: UNCTAD/DTCI 1995.

Lipsey, 1982). Given the preponderance of local sales in total sales, the significance of this market size variable should not come as a surprise. India, China, Brazil and other developing countries with a large domestic market are likely to attract TNCs with nothing more than a liberal investment regime. India, for example, implemented the Programme of Economic Stabilisation and Restructuring in 1991, which included the opening of previously closed areas of the economy to foreign direct investment. As a result, FDI flows into India increased from $113 million in 1991 to $1.7 billion in 1995 (UNCTAD, 1995).

Other, smaller countries do not have the same options. Without a sufficiently large market of their own, they are unlikely to attract TNCs even if their intention is to export. For this reason, regional integration among developing countries may hold the key to greater FDI in countries that do not otherwise offer much of interest to TNCs by allowing them to attach themselves to larger neighbours. Countries such as Mexico, Brazil, India, Indonesia or South Africa could all serve as potential magnets. Smaller countries are far more likely to serve as export platforms for the regional market than they are for the global market. Within the European Union, for example, United States TNCs in Ireland export more to the rest of the European Union than do their counterparts in Italy, a country nearly 20 times the size of Ireland.

Trade liberalization in developing countries

Trade liberalization can take several forms: unilateral, bilateral, regional and multilateral. The trade-off is between the deeper levels of integration that can be achieved among smaller groups and the discrimination that preferential market access implies. In general, the less an agreement distorts the pattern of trade and investment, the more beneficial it is likely to be for the world economy as a whole. The principle of non-discrimination is enshrined in the WTO articles, and thus multilateral liberalization should remain the priority of all governments. Triad markets remain the most important markets for many developing countries, and there are clearly sectors, such as textiles, where further liberalization of Triad markets would be welcomed by the developing world. At the same time, it seems unlikely that multilateral liberalization will be enough to fulfil the export wishes of most developing countries.

While countries such as the Asian newly-industrializing countries (NICs: Singapore, Republic of Korea, Taiwan Province of China and Hong Kong), have been able to export vast quantities of goods on both an arm's-length and intra-firm basis to the Triad markets, it is simply not possible for all developing countries to be equally export-oriented towards those same markets. The demand for goods produced in developing countries is not infinite in the Triad markets, nor is the demand for intra-firm imports from TNC affiliates located in those countries. The export-led development strategies of Asian countries have proved to be a remarkable success and, in many cases, TNCs have contributed substantially to that success. But host countries in other regions need to be realistic about their ability both to export to Triad markets and attract TNCs for that purpose. As the similarities between intra-firm and arm's-length exporting patterns indicates, it is not the inability to attract TNCs that relegates these countries to the sidelines within the global economy, but their general unsuitability as locations for production. Countries that have problems exporting to the Triad markets are likely to find it equally difficult to entice investors to locate their export platforms there for many of the same reasons: inadequate infrastructure, distance from the principal markets, poor skills etc. Any multilateral market opening by Triad markets will probably not benefit smaller, poorer countries more than proportionately. Given that in 1992 the four Asian NICs accounted for more than two-thirds of developing country exports to the Triad, equiproportional increases in exports will not fulfil the export-led growth ambitions of the remaining developing countries.

Efforts to increase the share of individual countries through bilateral or regional deals with the nearest Triad will almost always involve some investment diversion away from other locations. The links which are most likely to be forged are Mexico with the United States, Asia with Japan, and Eastern Europe with the European Union. At best, this will have a neutral effect on smaller, more remote developing countries outside of the region if, for example, it increases outward FDI from the Triad country to regional bases beyond what would have occurred in the absence of integration. At worst, regional integration centred on a Triad market may divert FDI away from these distant countries which otherwise might have had a comparative advantage in producing goods now manufactured within the integrating region. Even under the NAFTA Agreement, where the signatories are already what has been termed "natural trading partners", some investment in Mexico has represented a clear diversion away from other locations.

As has been shown in chapter 6, all forms of trade liberalization are likely to affect FDI flows. Some of the latter will be created, while others will merely be diverted from other locations. Bilateral deals are most likely to be diversionary, and the pressure on other developing countries to follow suit may strengthen the negotiating hand of the Triad country, just as the need to attract investment gives more power to the investor, that is, the TNC. Furthermore, as more and more such agreements are reached with the Triad, they may well serve to return the situation to the status quo ante.

After multilateral liberalization, regional integration among developing countries is perhaps least likely to cause trade diversion, especially if external tariffs do not change or even are lowered. Such integration has been attempted before, but has failed to live up to expectations. The reason may simply be that previous attempts were made during an era of import substitution policies. In the new liberal climate, in which developing countries often unilaterally dismantle barriers as well as privatize and deregulate their economies, the pessimists may yet be proved wrong.

Transnational corporations and a regional division of labour

As both Triad and indigenous TNCs organize production on a regional basis, they will in turn help to bring about the gains from that integration. In this way, trade policy liberalization and FDI create a mutually reinforcing process or symbiosis.

The automobile sector, with its constant striving for economies of scale, has long been one of the most keen proponents of such integration. Other sectors have often pursued more national or multi-domestic strategies. But once again, the European experience is replete with examples of rationalization and integration in other sectors. Unilever, the food giant from the Netherlands and England, trimmed its operations in Europe from nine plants to four in advance of the Single Market. While such rationalization inevitably implies that some factories will be closed, it is nevertheless accompanied by an increase in the overall investment activities of TNCs in the region as a whole. Indeed, the experience of European integration over the past four decades suggests that greater investment in and within the region vastly overwhelms such divestment. Virtually all European countries enjoyed more inward investment in the late 1980s than at any time previously (Thomsen and Woolcock, 1993).

Such rationalization within regions is also starting to occur through indigenous firms. Although some TNCs from developing countries have invested abroad to gain access to technologies or markets, particularly in the Triad markets, much of the regional investment appears to represent an incipient regional division of labour. Chapter 3 has documented the rising importance of investment by Asian NICs in the rest of the region. This division of labour is already starting to show up in the trade statistics in Asia where intraregional trade, some of it intra-firm, is booming. Foreign direct investment by NICs in Asia has been encouraged by rising wage costs and currency appreciation in NICs, together with their loss of GSP status.

The gains from inward investment

A firm is made up of employees, capital, goods, services, technology and various other intangible assets. When the firm establishes an affiliate abroad, it is in effect transferring these various components as a package. While internalization theory has focused on the question of why such components need to be transferred internally within the firm rather than in the external market, there is no reason a priori to expect the welfare consequences of that transfer to differ whether or not it is internalized. In other words, much of the gain from investment stems from the transfer of capital and technology to the host country and not from the fact that they were transferred through the TNC.

Not only are the effects likely to be similar, but so are the determinants. We have already seen with respect to trade, that intra-firm exports from affiliates tend to be complementary to arm's-length exports from the same location. Indeed, Blomström has shown that, where affiliated exports of United States TNCs grew most quickly, arm's-length exports grew at an even faster rate.[6] Furthermore, with only two exceptions, those developing countries which are already the largest exporters to the United States play an even bigger role in the offshore production of TNCs.

And FDI also tends to complement other forms of development finance. Both direct investment and debt flows to developing countries declined in the early 1980s and then grew in the second half of the decade. Although direct investment now exceeds international lending, they often tend to go to the same countries. TNCs invest in those countries, which are also candidates for bank lending, as economic growth raises the return for investors and lowers the risk for lenders.

Foreign direct investment is not only complementary with other forms of international capital flows, but it has been suggested that it may also serve to complement local capital in the host country.[7] Even in-house technology transfer and external mechanisms of technology transfer can be complementary in the sense that both affect the capability of the host country to utilize and to absorb technologies. Because of this complementarity, all policies which attempt both to hire capital, technology etc., or to increase exports will probably affect both inward investment and arm's-length transactions. Any policy which seeks to attract TNCs, but which is not viewed as beneficial in its own right − such as by increasing arm's-length transfers − must be viewed with suspicion.

Policies towards inward investment

As shown in chapter 8, developing country policies need to be judged not only by the number of firms that they attract, but also by the technological and other spillovers from that investment. Many existing policies seem to fail on this criterion. In contrast to the general distrust of TNCs that prevailed in the 1970s, all manners of virtue are now attributed to inward investment. Direct investment can contribute greatly to the development strategies of developing countries, but it is important to recognize both the limitations of policies that rely on TNCs and the need to focus on the potential benefits from that investment rather than the investment itself. Too often, policies are designed to attract firms through incentives or protected markets, which erode or even negate the potential gains from that investment. The United States Commerce Department (1994) found in a survey of United States-owned affiliates abroad that 26 per cent of affiliates had been offered tax concessions, 16 per cent tariff protection, and 9 per cent subsidies.[8] Recognizing that such incentives might be harmful, Governments of the host countries compound their error by stipulating performance requirements: local sourcing, employment or export guarantees etc. The same survey found that from 3 to 15 per cent of affiliates had been subjected to one of the following: minimum level of exports or employment, maximum level of imports, equity limits or technology transfer requirements.

While the net effect on this mix of carrot-and-stick policies may be neutral from the point of view of the investor's profits, it is not neutral for the host country. In extreme cases, incentives negate any benefit from the investment. As OECD reported concerning the effect of Irish incentives on the role of investment:[9]

> "The most striking development has been the emergence of a dual industrial economy. On the one hand, foreign firms have expanded output and exports rapidly and enjoy very high levels of productivity. On the other hand, the indigenous sector has only recently halted its rapid decline in domestic market share, and productivity levels are low despite recent improvements. Moreover, *foreign-owned firms have developed few linkages with the indigenous economy, little in the way of local research or technological inputs, and depend heavily on important raw materials and components* (italics added)."

The report goes on to argue that a large share of profits are repatriated, that generous fiscal and financial capital incentives distort the pattern of factor costs by making labour relatively more expensive and provide little tax revenue to the Exchequer.

Distortions induced by policies are not confined solely to incentives. In an era when developing countries are all interested in pursuing export-led development strategies similar to those that were so successful in the Asian NICs, TNCs are seen as a way of increasing the export potential of the host country. Traditionally, FDI for export is deemed to complement the comparative advantage of the host country thus improving resource allocation and hence growth. FDI designed to serve the local market is equated with import substitution and a misallocation of resources, as argued by Johnson (1967) and Brecher and Diaz-Alejandro (1977) in the context of capital inflows into a protected sector. Wells and Encarnation (1986) looked at a number of investments by TNCs and found that those cases where the investment had a negative effect on the local economy were related to the degree of protection afforded to the investor. That FDI may make a country worse off in this situation is not the fault of the investing firm.[10] It is the fault of trade policy. Such a resource flow into a protected sector in which the country does not enjoy a comparative advantage could just as easily come from within the host country.

The problem with focusing only on export-oriented investment, even if all trade distortions are removed, is that it does not look at the potential productivity gains, only at the static benefits from export expansion. In the extreme case, export processing zones provide little in the way of spillovers in the host country. Export platforms, which perform a small and narrowly defined process within a vertically integrated firm in a high technology industry are unlikely to contribute more than employment to the host country. Disappointing results were described from export platforms in Malaysia.[11] Reuber *et al* found in a study of 80 investment projects by TNCs that the export-oriented ones sourced only half as large a proportion of their input locally as did other projects, and that TNCs held a higher portion of the equity in export projects.[12] Local linkages may be more prevalent with market-based FDI as they are more likely to involve joint ventures and TNCs may be more willing to adapt production to local conditions.[13]

Regional integration and technological spillovers

The unique benefit of FDI is not in improved resource allocation: trade policy alone can achieve that. Rather FDI improves resource *efficiency* through a transfer of technology and a more competitive environment. To ensure that these efficiency improvements arise and that they do not lead to a magnification of existing distortions, FDI must be accompanied by trade liberalization. It is not necessary, however, that the TNC invest in the export sector as long as open trade policies remove the scope for misallocation of resources. Investment by TNCs which improves the efficiency of the non-tradable are clearly inputs into the export sector, and greater efficiency in providing those inputs could free up resources which could then be devoted to exporting. For similar reasons, It has been argued by Bhagwati that developing countries should welcome free trade in services, because it will make their own tradable sector more efficient.[14]

The argument for allowing inward investment even when it is to serve the domestic market does not imply either that under all circumstances is it beneficial or that countries should adopt inward looking development strategies. Investment in the non-tradable sectors will only contribute to efficiency if the TNC is not allowed to achieve monopoly power in that market by virtue of its greater competitiveness or financial power. Open trade policies combined with regional agreements are an important ingredient in maintaining a competitive domestic market. Any potential monopolistic tendencies on the part of the investor will be restrained not only by import competition, but also by other firms within the market. The larger the market, the more firms and TNCs that can operate efficiently. The more competitive the environment, in turn, the more TNCs will be forced to transfer technology and other intangible assets in order to remain competitive. Transnational corporations will only transfer as much technology as they need. By forcing firms to compete in the larger regional market, they will be compelled to transfer more and more technology in order to ensure its competitive lead.

Until now, investment from the Triad market has been emphasized. But one of the most likely outcomes of regional integration, as can already be seen in Asia, the Americas and even more clearly in Europe, is greater intraregional direct investment. Some authors have also argued that such investments are more likely to benefit the host country because the technology that is transferred is most appropriate for that economy. Lecraw has argued that the competitive advantage of developing country firms lies in their knowledge of small-scale, labour-intensive production techniques.[15/] These techniques are often viewed to be those most appropriate for the labour abundant developing world. Furthermore, Lecraw finds in his sample that developing country TNCs are more likely to have local partners in order to provide knowledge of local marketing and the local economic environment. The participation of a local firm is widely considered to enhance potential technological spillovers. Finally, Lecraw adds that these developing country TNCs were less likely than Triad firms to reduce their investment under adverse circumstances. Technology and ideas do not originate solely in the Triad. Chilean investment in Argentina's privatisation process demonstrates how expertise can also flow through intraregional direct investment.

Regional integration is not just about trade liberalization. It represents a package of reforms of which trade flows are only one part.

As in the European Union, labour and capital mobility are also important components. Eventually, some institutional framework similar to the European Commission might be envisaged which could provide a mechanism to prevent countries from offering incentives designed to entice TNCs away from other countries. Such "beggar-thy-neighbour" policies greatly limit the potential gains from inward investment. Since most of the competition for investment is likely to occur on a regional rather than a global basis, regional institutions may be best placed to monitor investment incentives which give away too much to potential investors.

Another area beyond trade liberalization where regional integration can prove beneficial is with greater factor mobility. Restrictions on capital flows and on take-overs of local firms by outside investors restrict the potential for greater intraregional investment and the attendant rationalization. Here, once again, the efforts of the European Union provide an example not only of the institutional steps that can be made towards liberalizing factor movements, but also the tremendous benefit that flows from the heightened investment activity. In many sectors, mostly those offering services, but also some in manufacturing, effective competition can only come about through FDI. Because such competition is vital in order to stimulate technology transfer, it is essential that reforms be extended to include direct investment and cross-border mergers and acquisitions as well as trade. Blomström and Persson find a positive relationship between the efficiency of domestic firms and foreign participation in that sector across a broad range of Mexican industries.[16/]

Conclusion

No judgement can be made about FDI without an understanding of the policy context in which the investment is made. The gains from FDI arise from the transfer of capital, technology and other intangible assets, from the dynamic effect on competition in the host market and from the role of TNCs in regional and global structural adjustment. The benefits of FDI cannot be measured by either the number of TNCs or the level of exports of those firms.

The evidence both of a growing regional division of labour and of market seeking FDI in developing countries suggests that regional integration may well increase the flows of FDI both into and within the region. More importantly, it may enhance the potential spillovers from that investment. Because FDI is likely to complement other forms of capital, technology etc., the recommendations set forth must be judged in the wider context than just TNC involvement in host economies. Furthermore, regional integration must be accompanied by a package of reforms at both a macroeconomic (for example, the exchange rate) and a microeconomic (such as by improving worker skills) level.

In a world of global products and globally integrated TNC production, such regional integration might be superfluous, but with few exceptions that stage has not yet been reached. National and regional markets still matter, as indicated by the very high share of output of United States TNCs which is sold in the local market of the affiliate. Amidst all the hyperbole of globalization, it is easy to forget this reality. Developing countries ignore it at their peril.

Notes

1. US Direct Investment Abroad, 1994, table II H, pp. 22 and 23.
2. Ibid, table III F 2.
3. United States Commerce Department, *Survey of Current Business*, August 1994, and Deutsche Bundesbank, May, 1995.
4. Deutsche Bundesbank, May 1995.
5. Part of Hong Kong investment in China represents indirect investment by third countries, though some of this is in turn from Taiwan so the NIE share would still probably remain the largest even if one could adjust for this discrepancy.
6. M. Blomström (United Nations publication, Sales No. E.90.II.A.21), p. 23.
7. Linda Lim and Pang Eng Fong, "Foreign investment and industrial restructuring", December 1989, p. 77. OECD Development Centre.
8. Op. cit., *Survey of Current Business* (August 1994).
9. OECD, *Country Survey 1984/1985: Ireland*, p. 45. Paris, OECD.
10. Some TNCs have requested tariff protection as a precondition for investment in a market which would otherwise be too small to support a profitable level of production, so in this sense TNCs may have contributed to the problem.
11. Linda Lim and Pang Eng Fong. "Foreign investment and industrial restructuring: The experience of Malaysia, Singapore, Taiwan Province of China and Thailand. OECD Development Centre, December 1989, pp. 97-100.
12. G.L. Reuber, H. Crookell, M. Emerson and G. Gallis-Hamonno. *Private Foreign Investment*, 1973, Oxford, Clarendon Press.
13. Richard Caves. *Multinational Enterprises and the Global Economy*. Cambridge University Press, 1987. chap. 9.
14. Jagdish Bhagwati, "Trade in services and the multilateral trade negotiations", *World Bank Economic Review*, September 1987, pp. 549-570.
15. Donald Lecraw, "Direct investment by firms from less developed countries", *Oxford Economic Papers*, vol. 29, No. 3, 1977, pp. 442-457.

16. Magnus Blomström and H. Persson. "Foreign investment and spillover efficiency in an underdeveloped country: Evidence from the Mexican manufacturing industry", *World Development*, June 1983.

References

Bhagwati, Jagdish (1987). Trade in services and the multilateral trade negotiations. *World Bank Economic Review*, September, pp. 549-570.

Blomström, Magnus and H. Persson (1983). Foreign investment and spillover efficiency in an underdeveloped economy: Evidence from the Mexican manufacturing industry. *World Development*, June.

Blomström, Magnus (1990). *Transnational Corporations and Manufacturing Exports from Developing Countries* (United Nations publication, Sales No.E.90.II.A.21).

Brecher, Richard and Carlos Diaz-Alejandro (1977). Tariffs, foreign capital and immiserizing growth. *Journal of International Economics*, vol. 7, pp. 317-322.

Caves, Richard (1982). *Multinational Enterprise and Economic Analysis*, Cambridge, England: Cambridge University Press.

Dunning, J.H. (1993). *Multinational Enterprises and the Global Economy*, Wokingham, Berkshire, United Kingdom, Addison Wesley.

Johnson, Harry G. (1967). The possibility of income losses from increased efficiency or factor accumulation in the presence of tariffs, *Economic Journal*, March, pp. 151-154.

Kravis, Irving and Robert Lipsey (1982). The location of overseas production and production for export by US multinational firms, *Journal of International Economics*, vol. 12, pp. 201-23.

Lecraw, Donald (1977). Direct investment by firms from less developed countries, *Oxford Economic Papers*, vol. 29, No. 3, pp. 442-457.

Lim, Linda and Pang Eng Fong (1989). Foreign investment and industrial restructuring: The experience of Malaysia, Singapore, Taiwan Province of China and Thailand. OECD Development Centre, December.

Organisation for Economic Cooperation and Development (1985), *Country Surveys 1984/85: Ireland*. Paris:OECD.

Reuber, G.L. with H. Crookell, M. Emerson, and G. Gallis-Hamonno (1973). *Private Foreign Investment in Development*. Oxford: Clarendon Press.

Thomsen, Stephen and Stephen Woolcock (1993). *Direct Investment and European Integration: Competition among Firms and Governments*. London: Chatham House Papers Series, Royal Institute of International Affairs.

UNCTAD (1993). *World Investment Directory, Vol. III, Developed Countries* (United Nations publication, Sales No. E.93,II.A.9).

_____ (1994). *World Investment Report 1994: Transnational Corporations, Employment and the Work Place* (United Nations publication, Sales No. E.94.II.A.14).

229

_____ (1995). *World Investment Report 1995: Transnational Corporations and Competitiveness* (United Nations publication, Sales No. E.95.II.A.9).

_____ (1996). *World Investment Report 1996: Investment, Trade and International Policy Arrangements* (United Nations publication, Sales No. E.96.II.A.14).

UNCTC (1991). *World Investment Report 1991: The Triad in Foreign Direct Investment* (United Nations publication, Sales No. E.91.II.A.12).

_____ (1992a). *The Determinants of Foreign Direct Investments: A Survey of the Evidence* (United Nations publication, Sales No. E.92.II.A.2).

_____ (1992b). *World Investment Report 1992: Transnational Corporations as Engines of Growth* (United Nations publication, Sales No. E.92.II.A.19).

United States Economics and Statistics Administration (1994). *U.S. Direct Investment Abroad: Operations of U.S. Parent Companies and their Foreign Affiliates.* Washington, D.C.: United States Economics and Statistics Administration, June.

Wells, Louis and Dennis Encarnation (1986). Evaluating foreign investment. In T.H. Moran (ed.), *Investing in Development: New Roles for Private Capital.* Washington, D.C.: Transaction Books, for the Overseas Development Council.

Xiaoning James Zhan (1993). The role of foreign direct investment in market-oriented reforms and economic development: The case of China. *Transnational Corporations*, vol. 2, No. 3, 1993.

Part IV
Investment and technology

8

Investment, technology and international competitiveness

Sanjaya Lall

Introduction

This chapter examines the relationship between investment flows (IF) and technology transfer (TT) to developing countries in a globalizing world economy. The main form of IF considered here is foreign direct investment (FDI). It has traditionally been the dominant form of resource and technology transfer from developed to developing countries. It is the most packaged form of TT, combining the provision of capital with technical know-how, equipment, management, marketing and other skills. In its classic form, it also entails control over the operation by the foreign investor. The significance of such classic investment-related transfer of technology has grown dramatically in complex, high technology industries in the advanced industrial countries. Over the past decade, after a period of relative decline, it also seems to have grown in the developing world in industrial TT more generally.[1/] The chapter explores what this may mean for indigenous technology development in the developing countries concerned, and how this might help them in their bid for global markets.

Equity involvement by foreign firms is, of course, only one means of transferring technology between countries. Since the 1960s, a number of other means of TT, such as minority joint ventures (with local control), licensing, turnkey projects, management contracts, subcontracting, strategic alliances and the like, have become more important.[2/] Traditional overseas investors have become more willing to enter into these "new forms" of involvement in their less valuable technologies, often responding to the desire of many developing countries to establish independent industrial bases. Various technologies have matured and seen the development of new intermediaries and suppliers, specialized sellers of engineering, consultancy and equipment that have little interest in investing in equity overseas. In addition, sources of technology to developing countries have diversified as new firms and countries (generally more willing to enter into "new forms") have entered the international arena. To some extent, therefore, the traditional link between IF and TT has been loosened. It should be noted, however, that transnational corporations from the developed world have been the main sources of TT in both new and traditional forms.

The recent resurgence in the importance of FDI to the developing world, noted above, may be traced to several factors. The share of world innovation, production and trade accounted for by TNCs has grown steadily, making it essential for industrializing countries to establish closer contacts with them. This has become increasingly evident throughout the developing world (even the least industrialized countries), where there is widespread disillusionment with earlier strategies based on import substitution and national ownership. This general move towards "structural adjustment", emphasizing market forces and fuller integration into the global economy, requires, among other things, the upgrading of technologies and human resource development in the manufacturing and some service sectors. Investment flows by TNCs may provide quickly and effectively the necessary technologies, skills and access to foreign markets. Moreover, with growing constriction in commercial lending and aid flows to developing countries, the financial component of IF has assumed considerable importance. Finally, several newly industrializing countries (for example, the Republic of Korea, Taiwan Province of China and Hong Kong) have themselves emerged as important overseas investors, with their activities providing a dynamic means of TT between developing countries. Thus, as has been shown in chapter 1, more fully, the environment for IF has changed enormously over the last decade, and developing countries with very different levels of development and political systems are welcoming it as a valuable input into their technological development process.

While IF is clearly a powerful and important mode of technology transfer, the relationship between IF and indigenous technological development is not always straightforward and linear. There are several stages between the import of technology and the development of local technological capabilities. A body of recent work on the innovatory strengths of developing countries suggests that the process of becoming and remaining technologically efficient (that is, competitive in world markets) is complex.[3/] It often involves far more than allowing access to international technology flows (via IF or any other means), though clearly such access remains vital. The assimilation, adaptation and further development of the imported knowledge usually requires a process of building new capabilities that do not exist in developing countries. Capability development is determined, at the national level, by the policy regime on trade and industry, and by investments in skills, information flows, infrastructure and supporting institutions. At the micro level, it is the outcome of firm level efforts to build new organizational and technical skills, its ability to generate and tap information, the development of an appropriate specialisation *vis-à-vis* other firms, and the striking up of linkages with suppliers, buyers and institutions. Furthermore, because of widespread externalities in the creation of skills and technologies, the social benefits of enterprise efforts to develop capabilities may far exceed the individual benefit to the firms themselves.

In this context, the mode of technology transfer (that based on IF and others) and its relationship to the various determinants of capability development can have important effects on the nature and pace of indigenous capability development and the restructuring of economic activity. In the present chapter an attempt will be made to try to clarify some of these effects, and to place them in the setting of the rapid technological changes that are taking place in the manufacturing industry, and in the light of the changing international division of labour. Given the complexity of the issues involved, it may be best to proceed in stages, addressing a sequence of questions in turn. These questions are:

(a)   What determines the choice of the mode of technology transfer?

(b)   Given the role of IF as a mode of TT, what determines the nature and direction of investment flows?

(c)   What is the contribution of TT by this mode to local capability development, and the path of that development?

(d)   How does the acquisition of technological capabilities affect a country's position in the global economy and its comparative advantage in trade and international investment?

(e)   What are the impacts of recent technological changes on the domestic and international competitiveness of developing countries?

Clearly the range of issues is very large, and it will only be possible to highlight the main points involved. The following sections will treat each of these issues in turn.

Modes of technology transfer

There exists a large spectrum of modes of TT according to the intensity, duration and nature of the relationship between the suppliers and buyers of technology.[4/] For present purposes, only two broad categories are distinguished: internalized and externalized forms of technology transfer. Internalized forms refer to investment associated TT, where control resides with the foreign partner (generally, but not necessarily, associated with majority or full equity ownership); these transfers are normally funded by way of FDI. Externalized forms refer to all other forms, such as joint ventures with local control, licensing strategic alliances and international subcontracting — these may be referred to as non-IF forms of TT.

The distinguishing feature between these two modalities of resource transfer is that in internalized TT the transferor has a significant and continuing financial stake in the success of the affiliate, allows it to use its brand names and to have access to its global technology and marketing networks, exercises control over the affiliate's investment, technology and sales decisions, and sees the affiliate as an integral part of its global strategy. Externalized forms lack one or all of these features, with repercussions on the TT process. Over time, the array of TT arrangements has diversified and particular modes have also become more flexible. Thus, the dividing lines between externalized and internalized modes are becoming less easy to draw.[5/] Strategic alliances and *Keiretsu* relationships, in particular, represent a grey area where all sorts of intermediate arrangements are possible. Thus, there is an element of simplification involved in the following discussion that should be borne in mind.

Four sets of factors affect the correct choice of the mode of TT: the nature of the technology; the strategy of the seller; the capabilities of the buyer; and the policies of the Government of the host country (see figure 1). As far as the *nature of the technology* is concerned, the choice of mode is determined by the inherent complexity of the technology, its speed of change, its novelty, the degree of centralization of R&D, and whether the technology is product or process based. In general, the higher the degree of complexity (and so the greater the need for continuous personal interaction of transferor and transferee), the faster the speed of change, the newer and more valuable the technology and the more centralized the R&D on which it is based, the more will TT take internalized forms. Process technologies are, however, more readily transferable in externalized forms, with even the latest vintages available from engineering firms and equipment suppliers. Product technologies (machinery, electrical, transport and electronic) are more demanding of skills, and less available, at least in their latest versions, at arm's length prices.

The *seller's strategy* is determined by the size of the firm (large firms prefer internalised modes for their valuable technologies and are more capable of handling transnational operations); product concentration (more diversified firms are more willing to externalize non-core technologies); dependence on proprietary brand names (more valuable names call for greater internalization); the firm's experience of TT (less exposure to international operations induces more externalization); and individual strategic considerations, for example, the need for additional technological capacity or access to markets, some of which are influenced by the corporate culture of the home country of the seller (countries that are new entrants to the international investment scene have tended to have firms that favour externalized modes).

Buyers' capabilities have a mixture of effects on the preferred mode of TT. On the one hand, a more capable buyer needs fewer elements to make the transfer successful and implies less effort and cost to the seller; thus, there is less need to internalize the transfer on these grounds. On the other hand, a more capable buyer poses a greater potential threat to the supplier, especially if it is oriented to world markets. Unless it has some technology to offer in return, therefore, the seller may prefer internalization, or a sale at very high prices and with many conditions

Figure 1. Determining the choice of mode of TT

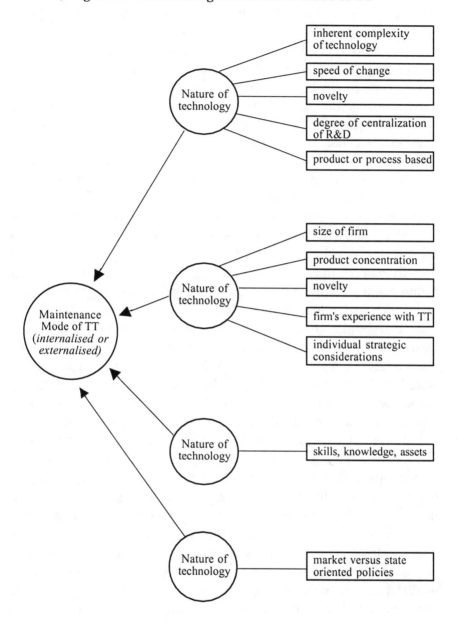

attached. In these cases, the outcome is usually settled by a bargaining process, and is affected by the skills, knowledge and assets that the parties can muster.

The above conditions are based on the assumption of freely functioning markets. In developing countries, most governments seek to intervene in the TT process to lower the costs of, and improve the conditions for indigenous production. Until recently, the thrust of *government policies* has been to encourage externalized TT in order to boost local technological capability, often behind high protective barriers. The shift to more market- oriented policies has reduced this bias in many countries, and the emerging tendency is to leave the choice to the parties concerned. Some governments still confine internalized TT to high tech or export oriented activities, while others actively promote internalized TT over other forms because of associated capital flows and the commitment entailed.

In general, internalized technology flows can be a very efficient means of transferring a package of capital, skills, technology, brand names and market access to developing countries. The economic value of such transfer depends, however, on the costs and effects of alternative means available of effecting the transfer. For some frontier technologies, internalized TT may be the only mode possible; even if the technology were for sale, internalization may be the most efficient way of transferring the knowledge and skills involved. If the technology were changing rapidly, internalization would again be preferable, as it would be if exports based on the technology require an established brand or a vertically integrated production structure across several countries. Even for simple technologies, if the recipient lacked the complementary skills and organization to utilize them efficiently, internalization would be the best mode. Inbound direct investment does have its costs, however, and profits are realized on the total value of the package transferred. If the host country already has some elements of the package, it may be cheaper to buy only the missing elements. In general, the more standardized and diffused the technology, and the more capable the buyer, the more economical will be the externalized modes. Even for more complex technologies, the existence of learning benefits and externalities may tilt the choice in favour of externalization. These issues are taken up below.

Determinants of foreign direct investment flows

International direct investment flows are determined by a number of political, policy-related and economic factors. The significance of political stability, appropriate and transparent policies, efficient administration and the like are evident, and need not be discussed here. On the economic determinants, a broad consensus has emerged on the factors that affect the content and direction of international production.[6/] These are placed under three headings: ownership, location and internalization factors. Under these headings, respectively, fall the consideration of factors that decide which industries and firms are likely to undertake direct overseas investment, where these investments will be located, and what organizational form the investment (or transfer of technology or other intangible assets) will take. Internalization factors have already been mentioned, and the focus of this section will be on ownership and location factors.

Ownership factors: If all firms had access to the same technology, skills and markets, there would be no reason for foreign direct investment, and capital flows would take the form of portfolio investments or loans. No firm would be able to bear the extra costs of operating in foreign countries if it did not have an ownership specific advantage over its competitors. The growth of direct investment is thus dependent on the existence of some intangible advantages that accrue to particular firms and that can be transferred abroad at a low enough cost to make such investments profitable. These intangible assets are also those that allow some firms to grow, and so give rise to concentrated industrial structures within given countries. These are similar to the "barriers to entry" to new competition that are the basis of much industrial economics, except that the barriers that give rise to overseas expansion are more characterized by transferable firm-specific assets like technological and marketing advantages rather than plant-level economies of scale.

Ownership advantages arise in technology and marketing because, in both, firms can create proprietary assets to which competitors are denied access, either because of legal (intellectual property) protection, or because they arise from investments in specific skills, knowledge and organizational capabilities. The scale of these investments may create barriers to contestable markets. The more important barriers, however, may arise from the nature of the "learning" and innovation process, in which new knowledge and skills reside in particular individuals and groups. Others cannot gain these without investing in a similar, often prolonged and risky process. It is the ability to generate such intangible assets that allows firms to grow within and across countries. Physical economies of scale become important only if large firms (and TNCs) have privileged access to capital markets - they often do, but this is a permissive rather than a driving force in international investment. Similarly, the very fact of being transnational can give rise to advantages (of communication, knowledge, supply sources, organization and so on) that facilitate further IF, but the exploitation of these advantages depends ultimately on the continuous creation of a competitive edge in technology and marketing.

Technological and marketing advantages thus explain which industries and, within them, which firms, are likely to undertake significant IF. A large body of empirical research shows that transnational activity is closely associated with industrial propensities to invest in R&D and product differentiation. Firms that lead IF are large enterprises with strong technological and brand name assets; the bulk of the world's enterprise R&D is accounted for by a relatively small number of transnational firms.[7/] The national ability to foster these activities also helps explain why some countries produce more than others - and most noticeable, those that have the human capital, technological resources and supporting infrastructure, and which generate intensive inter-firm competition.[8/] This is not to argue that firm-specific strategies are unimportant. Clearly they are. Firms have their own perceptions of their competitive advantages and how best to enhance and exploit them. In this, as in technology, they have their own "learning" trajectories, influenced by chance, history and experience. There are sufficient common elements, however, that allow us to make some generalizations about industrial and national determinants.

While technology and marketing (and the associated skills and organizational structures) are the engines of growth of IF, the process of investment *per se* does not imply that all technologies and skills get equally diffused internationally. Transnational firms may not deploy their latest technologies, or set up innovative functions in all the locations where they produce abroad. The technological and other functions that are transferred to particular locations depend on the factor endowments and other conditions there (see below), but the nature of the innovation process also affects the process of technology and innovation transfer. In the earliest stages of the product development cycle, it is imperative to have intense interaction between research, production and marketing functions within firms, as well as close linkages with sophisticated science and technology infrastructures and supplier networks.[9] As TNCs grow better established abroad, the innovation process extends itself to other locations and the product cycle does shorten. But the transfer of innovation, because of its skill and linkage requirements, tends to be confined to a few other advanced countries, and the home country still remains the main base of innovation even in the most internationalized of firms.[10]

As far as developing countries are concerned, some NIEs are benefiting from the shortening of the product cycle, because they have the complementary factors necessary to make new, advanced technologies work efficiently. These countries, notably those in East Asia, are also attracting substantial inbound investment, and engaging in networking with TNCs pursuing global strategies.[11] Other countries are still at the lower end of the cycle, and technological trends may be keeping them there. These issues are discussed in the following paragraphs.

Locational Factors. The choice of where to place an investment abroad is determined, on the *host country side*, by market size, factor endowments and costs, infrastructure, trade policies and other policies that affect macroeconomic stability, competition, entry and exit, ownership, employment and so on. National government policies are also important influences on the attractiveness, risk and cost of each location, and tend to be particularly significant in developing countries. They are not, however, directly germane to the present chapter, and will be generally ignored in the discussion. On the *side of the investor*, location is affected by the nature of the technology concerned, individual corporate strategies and perceptions of risk and reward. Again, only the technology factor is relevant here and will be discussed below.

Market size has an obvious effect on the location of domestic market-oriented investments, whether or not these are stimulated by protectionist policies of the Government of the host country. While protection creates an obvious need to establish local production, even in small markets and at inefficient scales, large markets have an independent attraction even under free market conditions. In activities like consumer goods or customized capital or intermediate goods, where close interaction with the buyer is important, many firms regard a production presence as a competitive advantage. Even for export-oriented projects, a large host country market can be important if it allows the investor to sell a proportion of its output locally or if it favourably disposes the government to allow it to set up a local market-oriented project.

Factor endowments include a number of things: the availability of natural resources (for extractive and processing investments); "raw" labour costs; the availability of skills at low costs and at various levels; the quality of a supporting infrastructure of *created* assets (standard, quality assurance, technology, information services, research laboratories); and the efficiency of the relevant suppliers of inputs and services. The first does not need explanation. The second and third are also clear, but it needs to be stressed that cheap "raw" labour is a locational attraction in only the simplest of activities. Even in garment assembly, a very low technology entry-level activity, a base of worker literacy and trainability, and of supervisory and technical skills, is essential for export-oriented investments. In more complex activities, the need for diverse and sophisticated skills is much greater. If production has to be internationally competitive (as it increasingly does under more market-oriented strategies), technologically demanding activities will gravitate to locations that can provide the skills, or at least have the capability to acquire them quickly (and at low cost to the investor). Some high level skills can be imported, but longer-term cost competitiveness depends on a local supply of most relevant technical and managerial skills.

The need for a good technological infrastructure rises with the sophistication of the technology involved, especially in engineering and other activities where a high level of precision is involved.[12] Many large investments can internalize the necessary technological activities, or draw on the parent company for the services needed (though this may be expensive). Smaller investments may be handicapped by the lack of technical services that are taken for granted in developed countries and NIEs. Similar considerations apply to the supplier system. In many process industries, there is little need to depend on suppliers of components and specialized inputs. In engineering industries, however, efficiency depends on specialization and a dense network of linkages between subcontractors, suppliers and service firms. In particular, where "just-in-time" inventory systems are becoming necessary for competitiveness, a highly developed supplier network becomes a precondition for foreign investment. The quality of the supplier network is also dependent on the efficacy of information flows and the services provided by the technology infrastructure. A dynamic financial system is also essential to industrial functioning.

These factors related to skills, technology organizational competence and the presence of suppliers can be broadly labelled the "technological capabilities" of the host economy. The level of such capabilities influences the nature of inward investment and TT (that is, which activities and technologies are attracted), and also the results of such investment (that is, how well the technologies are absorbed, utilized and further developed). The relevance of the *physical infrastructure* to all this is clear. Modern industry, especially if it is to compete in world markets, needs excellent transport and telecommunication facilities. More and more activities need constant contact with the outside world, both in physical inputs and outputs and in information and personal contacts.

These locational factors have to be put in the context of *current technological changes*, which have been more fully described in chapter 1. A whole set of interrelated and generic technological advances, together with the acceleration of technical change, is amounting to what is in the view of many analysts a new technological revolution.[13/] From this revolution will emerge massive changes in competitiveness, location of activity, skill needs, work organization and technology-support needs. While the ramifications of these changes are still difficult to define, and the process will take a long time to work itself out, some tendencies of relevance to TT to developing countries may be tentatively noted:

- First, industry is becoming increasingly globalized, with countries specializing in segments of industries rather than entire industries (for example, engines for cars rather than the whole automobile); the globalization process is being led by TNCs from the developed countries, and it is becoming increasingly difficult in many technology-intensive industries to develop independent dynamic comparative advantage.[14/]

- Second, international investments by the advanced industrial countries are increasingly focusing on technology-intensive activities, while the lower technology segments are being taken over by firms from NIEs.

- Third, even low technology activities are being affected by technological progress, so that competitive production requires higher levels of skill, specialized training and flexibility.

- Fourth, because of these forces (and assuming favourable government policies), it is likely that medium to high technology investments in the developing world will increasingly concentrate in locations that are already industrialized, have good infrastructure, and have developed a base of technological capabilities. Lower technology investments will go to less industrialized areas, but even here they are likely to concentrate on locations with relatively high levels of human capital and infrastructure.

- Fifth, the preconditions for higher "quality" foreign investment can only partially be created by the investors themselves. The bulk of the work will need to be done by the countries themselves, in terms of investing in education, technology and the like, and perhaps by intervening selectively to promote infant industries that embody their dynamic comparative advantage (see below).

- Finally, because of the increasing competition for IF and a widespread move to liberal economic policies, it is imperative to have an investment regime that is stable, welcoming, transparent and efficiently administered. An important part would be a strong intellectual property rights regime. It is widely accepted that intellectual property protection *per se* is a valuable stimulant to innovation and TT in only a few industries (pharmaceuticals and software being the prime examples), where the results of expensive innovation are easy to copy. In other industries, the proprietary nature of the skills and knowledge involved are the most important means of protecting intellectual property. Nevertheless, the "signalling value" of the intellectual property regime has become extremely important in recent years. In general, countries that seek to attract technology-intensive foreign investments also offer strong protection to those investments. The developed countries, in particular the United States, is putting strong pressure on developing countries to check intellectual property abuses, with trade access as a bargaining tool.

Contribution of transnational corporations activity to technological capabilities

It was noted at the start of the present chapter that there are several steps between the transfer of a technology, in the sense of providing the equipment, instructions and blueprints, and its effective absorption, deployment and subsequent upgrading; and on its effect on the efficiency and structure of economic activity. The same technology may be used at widely differing levels of efficiency in different locations, and its productivity may decline in one place while it rises sharply in another. Many of these differences can be traced to differing levels of technological capabilities. These capabilities are the skills, technical knowledge, organizational structures, and external (to the firm) linkages necessary to master an imported technology, adapt it to local factor and market conditions, upgrade it to maintain competitiveness in world markets and improve on it to allow diversification.[15/]

The initial transfer of a technology cannot lead to efficient operation if the necessary expertise, skills and technical and managerial know-how are not generated; and there are many "implicit" elements in technology that need a long period of learning by the recipient. That learning may be partly the automatic result of production experience, but in most activities it will also require purposeful investments by the firm in training, search for new technical and other knowledge, experimentation, and developing the organizational capacity to create, communicate and diffuse knowledge internally. In advanced industrial activities, the absorption of new technologies will also require the undertaking of formal research and development.[16/] There are many levels of capabilities that can be acquired in a given technology, with varying inputs of local, as opposed to foreign, knowledge and skills.

In developing countries, many of the low level absorptive skills that are taken for granted in the developed world may be lacking, because the complexity and scale of new technologies will tend to be far more in advance of existing technologies. Even mundane activities like plant layout, quality assurance, maintenance and process optimization may call for substantial capability-building. Thus, the acquisition of technological capabilities may often entail, apart from in-house efforts by firms, broader social investments in education, training and the provision of information. In addition, capability-building by firms does not usually take place in isolation. In most activities there is a need for a great deal of interaction between firms, and with technology service and infrastructure institutions like standards laboratories, extension services, research centres, quality control centres, and similar support institutions. Thus the promotion of linkages and the development of institutions to undertake activities beyond the scope of individual firms becomes a vital part of capability development.

Since the development of capabilities is analogous to investment in physical facilities, taking time and involving cost and uncertainty, it is highly sensitive to the incentive environment facing firms. Some capability-building is essential merely to operationalize a new technology, and will occur in all regimes. The achievement and maintenance of international competitiveness, however, calls for much more. The trade and internal competition regime thus has a powerful impact on the extent and direction of capability-building efforts undertaken. An environment that insulates firms from competition, especially world competition, has been found to promote less, and less efficient technological development.

Given the time, costs and external support needed by firms to master complex technologies, however, a full exposure to world competition may abort the learning process altogether, preventing a deepening of the industrial structure.[17/] The extent to which technological development can proceed with such exposure depends on the level of skills already present, the complexity of the technology involved and the indigenous mastery of the technology aimed at. In very simple industries, given a base of local manufacturing know-how, capability development may be best promoted by free trade backed by some institutional support. In more complex activities, a high reliance on foreign investment and skills can shorten the learning period, and also relieve the financial stress on local enterprises (which do not have the "deep pockets" of TNCs). This may, nevertheless, have other repercussions, that are noted below.

Where a developing country desires to enter a heavy, complex industry with a large element of local technology, there may be a strong case for promoting and protecting infant industries during the learning period. Given the deleterious effects of protection, however, offsetting measures may have to be undertaken, for example, limiting the duration of protection, forcing firms to compete internally and to enter world markets quickly. This has been the strategy pursued by the larger East Asian NIEs, and earlier Japan, to promote heavy industry under national ownership.[18/] It must also be remembered that most of the presently industrialized nations also protected and promoted entry into heavy industry in the last century and the earlier part of this century; and that these were years of more natural protection (from transport costs, differing standards, procurement practices etc).[19/]

What role then does foreign technology play in local capability development and industrial restructuring? As with any make/buy decision, the choice of whether to import a technology or to create it internally has to be decided on its economic merits: the direct costs and returns as well as the externalities and longer-term dynamic benefits. The decision is not usually a black-and-white one, in the sense that there are innumerable variations possible on how much, and what stages, of particular technologies are imported or created locally. Moreover, local efforts do not have to "reinvent the wheel" even if they do not utilize formal imports of technology - much of such efforts rely on imported equipment, information (via journals, visits, and so on), and reverse engineering. Given the level of local technological capabilities, therefore, the need for formal imports will rise with the sophistication of the technology: some technologies can be mastered relatively easily by importing equipment; some will need discrete inputs on licensing; and some will need (or only be available under) equity participation by the technology suppliers.

The relationship between local capability building and technology imports is therefore both complementary and competitive.[20] Inputs of knowledge from countries that already have a technology are clearly necessary to launch local efforts to master it. But too passive a dependence on imports of know-how can stifle the development of local capabilities, with three deleterious effects: first, the cost of absorbing and deploying a technology is higher if local capabilities are weak; second, the adaptation and further development of a technology, and its beneficial externalities, are reduced if local firms are unable to undertake these tasks; and third, the "quality" of investment related technology imports cannot be raised if the local economy is not able to offer higher levels of skills and technological effort. There is thus a clear policy choice to be made on the extent of technology imports. Whatever the choice, the developing country has to invest in skills, R&D, infrastructure and support systems, as well as providing a conducive policy environment for technological effort, in order to promote industrial and technological development.

There is, nevertheless, a choice to be made regarding the form of technology import. Given the need for foreign technology, how do internalized and other forms affect the development of local capabilities? A useful way to tackle this question is to classify such capabilities into four levels (see figure 2). At the bottom level are the simplest ones, needed for operating a given plant: these involve basic manufacturing skills, as well as some more demanding troubleshooting, quality control, maintenance and procurement skills. At the intermediate level are duplicative skills, which include the investment capabilities needed to expand capacity and to purchase and integrate foreign technologies. Next come adaptive skills, where imported technologies are adapted and improved, and design skills for more complex engineering learned. Finally come innovative skills, based on formal R&D, that are needed to keep pace with technological frontiers or to generate new technologies. Simplified as these categories are, they are helpful in illustrating the path of capability development within and across technologies.

Figure 2. Levels of technology transfer defined

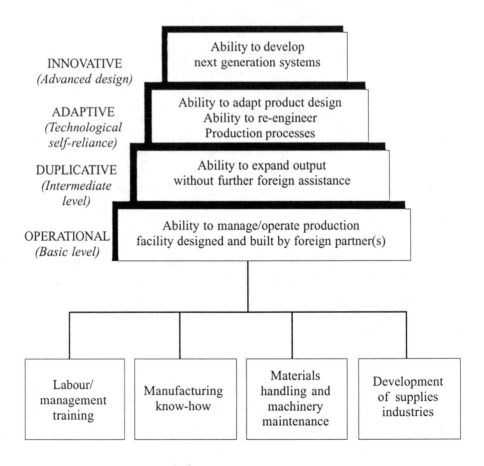

The transfer of foreign technologies may help progress at any or all of these levels, depending on the considerations noted above. The advantage of investment-related, internalized forms of TT over others lies, as noted earlier, in the long-term commitment of the foreign partner to the success of the project, its ability to provide many of the elements of the package needed to operationalize new technologies and its access to world class technologies and markets. At the lowest level, therefore, foreign investment may be one of the most efficient ways of transferring technology. Since all technologies need adaptation and improvement to keep them competitive, foreign affiliates, with their base of high-level management and technical skills, tend to be in the forefront of such activity in developing countries. In addition, TNCs enjoy the experience of other affiliates in the developing world to draw on, and can shift knowledge and personnel across countries to help with the upgrading of local capabilities.

As capability development progresses to the fourth level, where local innovative efforts become viable, there arises the possibility of a conflict of interest between the developing host country and the foreign investor. There are strong reasons for the investor to keep innovative activities centralized at home or in a few developed countries, for reasons noted above, and even the more advanced NIEs get essentially adaptive R&D investments from TNCs.[21/] At the same time, it is economically efficient for a number of the more advanced developing countries to invest in higher-level technological activity, and the success of exports of sophisticated products based on local R&D (as in car, television, aircraft and machinery sectors) testifies to their capabilities to absorb the relevant technologies and further develop them on their own. Transnational corporations tend to transfer the results of their R&D rather than the innovative process itself, at least until fairly high levels of development, whereas the sustained technological growth of developing countries calls for increasing investments in local innovation. There is, then, a case for restricting reliance on internalized forms of TT, and boosting local R&D based or other forms of TT.

At the same time, it should be remembered that there is considerable flexibility in investment-related forms of TT, and a developing country may be able to induce a higher level of innovative activity if it can offer the right skills and infrastructure. In addition, a foreign presence may have beneficial externalities by stimulating indigenous competition, helping local suppliers and providing linkages with international centres of technological activity. Where economies of scale in R&D are high, it may not be advisable to "go it alone" in innovation. The increasing trend to strategic alliances among the largest firms suggests also that local firms should strike deals with technology leaders that allow them some access to frontier technologies.

It is not possible to generalize on the optimal policies for choosing the extent and form of reliance on foreign technologies. Much depends on the existing and evolving levels of local skills and capabilities, on the nature of the technologies concerned, and on the alternative means of access available. Given the international conditions, what is desirable for a country like the Republic of Korea or Singapore may be inappropriate for Chile or China, and simply out of the question for a very poor developing country. The Republic of Korea has managed to reach many technological frontiers with relatively low reliance on internalized TT, by dint of its investments in human capital, institutions and technology, and by a combination of selective protection and the promotion of large domestic firms.[22/] Few other countries have managed this combination. The correct choice on TT thus depends on the choices made earlier on trade and industrial policies and on investments in capabilities.

Technological change and competitiveness

It is now widely accepted that competitive advantage in world markets for manufactures is determined only to a minor extent by national factor endowments (in the neoclassical sense of given stocks of labour and capital).[23/] Other factors, related to technological leads and lags, economies of scale and product differentiation, and the location decisions of TNCs have a far more powerful impact. Much of the empirical research on trade patterns supports the "neo-technology" or dynamic version of comparative advantage theory.

Apart from obvious advantages created by the possession of natural resources, factor endowments in a static sense affect trade patterns only in activities where technologies are simple, well diffused, small-scale and easily transferred and absorbed (for example, garment sewing). In most industries (including the design of garments) these conditions do not apply. Where technologies are difficult, specialized skills are required, and complex organizations are needed to handle large scales of manufacturing, sales or research, the ability to master these before competitors becomes the determinant of comparative advantage. This ability is, in turn, determined by government policies on trade and industry, investments in capabilities (human capital and technology), and the development of support institutions.[24/]

While the significance of technology factors is evident in explaining the trade patterns of advanced industrial countries, their role in developing countries is not so obvious. After all, the developing world accounts for a small fraction of the world's R&D expenditures (about 5 per cent), and of the innovating activities by TNCs (about 6 per cent) and the most successful exports of NIEs are not based on their own innovations. This interpretation is based on a view of technology as "major innovation", where a lead emerges from a new process or product that no one else has. The correct scope of technological activity is, in fact, much wider.[25/] It includes "minor innovations", the steady stream of small incremental improvements that accounts for the larger share of productivity increases in the developed world, and that explains much of the cost, design or quality advantages that drives competitive advantage. It also includes, for developing countries, the gaining of "technological mastery", the assimilation and adaptation of a given technology, which involves just as much technological effort as innovation, and often entails formal R&D. In combination with their natural factor endowments (a plentiful supply of labour), the gaining of mastery explains much of the dynamic comparative advantage of developing countries. Differences between countries are then explained by differences in their capabilities to master technology, and in their policy regimes (including the granting of infant industry protection) that promote national capabilities.

Technology thus has as large a role to play in determining competitiveness in developing as in developed countries. Within technological activity, the relative roles of simple learning by doing, experience-based engineering activity, more disciplined search and experimentation, and formal R&D, depend on the activity and the stage of industrial development concerned. There is a steady progression up the ladder with industrial development, with more formal technological activities taking precedence as the informal ones become more routine and widespread. As the complexity of the industrial sector rises, increased inter-industry specialization becomes imperative and greater interaction

251

among firms, and with technology institutions, becomes necessary: thus, the technological determinants of comparative advantage encompass mechanisms for technological diffusion, information flows and infrastructure support for training and research.

The impact of technical progress on the dynamic comparative advantage of developing countries is pervasive.[26/] All industrial technologies are subject to constant change and improvement, and the latest wave of information technology innovations are affecting practically every industry. This is affecting their locational advantages in developing countries, as discussed in the section on the determinants of technology flows. The competitiveness of any particular location is dependent on several factors, the nature and relative significance of each varying by the technology involved:

(i)   Its ability to furnish the minimum levels of skills (technical and managerial) that the efficient operation on the new technology requires; as technologies become more complex and science-based, this calls for a higher level of training in a wider spectrum of subjects;

(ii)   Closely related to the above, its ability to provide a labour force that is productive, flexible and low cost, one that is able to conform to very demanding quality standards, to operate across traditional work categories, and to accept the need for continuous retraining in new skills and attitudes;

(iii)   Its supplier system, to meet the needs of evolving "just in time" production techniques, and the support needed for information-based processes;

(iv)   Its technological infrastructure that feeds into the technological work of individual enterprises and promotes information flows within the country as well as into it;

(v)   Its ability to provide the physical infrastructure needed to keep the new activities running efficiently at world levels of efficiency, including transport of goods and services, communications, finance and information.

Until now, the impact of these factors has been unequal across the developing world. Countries that have built up a certain level of technological capabilities and adopted appropriate policies have gained far more than less industrialized countries. There is a spillover of activities evident from the more to the less advanced developing countries, but again the process is uneven and localized. At each stage, progress is determined by the ability to absorb technologies efficiently and by the nature of government policies.[27]

Policies play a dual role. First, they directly affect the inflow of technology, by direct investment and by other means. Here, the widespread liberalization that is sweeping the developing world means that, macroeconomic considerations apart, there will be fewer differences in the policy factors that attract investment flows. Second, policies affect TT indirectly, via education, training, science and technology, competition, trade orientation and so on. The pace and nature of technological progress is such that these indirect influences on TT and technological development will be more important than direct ones in the foreseeable future.

There are then close interlinkages between the technical change, technology flows, domestic capability development, competitiveness in trade, investment flows and government policies. These linkages have grown closer because of the internationalization of production and the growing significance of trade. Technology generation is now geared to global needs and aspirations, despite the concentration of innovation in a handful of countries and companies. Developing countries are increasingly conscious of the need to participate fully in world trade and production. The way that they can participate depends on the competitive advantages that their past investments in capabilities gives them, and the dynamic competitive advantages that they can build in the future by policies on incentives, skills, technologies, infrastructure and the relevant institutions.

The role of investment-based technology flows is increasing rapidly and, given the nature of the current technological revolution, is bound to grow in the future. This does not mean that domestic effort at capability development will become less important. On the contrary, the attraction of technology flows of higher quality necessarily involves continued investments in national technological capabilities (and the accompanying developments in managerial and organizational skills). And the development of national capabilities also requires a strong indigenous industrial sector that is complementary to the foreign-owned sector. The precise lines between these will vary from one country to the next, by their history, location, size, ideology, and capabilities themselves. What will be common will be the interlinkages between indigenous capability development, TT, investment and competitiveness, all depending on the adoption of the right policies.

Conclusions

The issues that arise for developing countries, seeking to benefit from a globalizing world economy, essentially concern the policies that they must adopt in order to benefit from emerging technologies and the potential for technology transfer by direct investment and other means. The world today is very different from that in which most industrial strategies were formed some three to four decades ago. This realization is leading to massive changes in most developing countries. In a reaction to over-interventionist, inward-oriented, public sector led industrialization, they are generally switching to policies that are more market-oriented, open to trade and foreign investment, and reliant on private enterprise. In general, there is a much greater belief in market as opposed to government efficiency.

As far as TT and investment flows are concerned, the speed of technical change and the desire to become trade oriented mean that developing countries will encourage both, but with a heavier emphasis on investment related inflows of technology and skills. Under ideal circumstances, FDI can become the engine of dynamic comparative advantage in developing countries, providing the "missing factor" to their industries in accordance with their emerging competitiveness. The main policy requirements will then be to provide a stable macroeconomic environment, a conducive regime for foreign entry and liberal trade policies, with investments in human capital and technology support institutions to encourage continuous upgrading of industrial activities (what the *1991 World Development Report* calls "market friendly policies").[28/]

This reading of policy issues may be somewhat disingenuous. While it is certainly the case that more market-oriented policies will benefit the industrialization process, and that much of past interventions have been misguided, the positive role of government interventions (apart from "market friendly" ones) should not be so easily dismissed. Many markets in developing countries, and in international capital and technology flows, do not work perfectly.[29/] The presence of externalities, information gaps, uncertainty, public goods, risk aversion and so on lead to market failures, when the lack of interventions may lead to sub-optimal results. The real policy issues then are the correct extent and nature of interventions that remain in a more liberal economic environment.

As far as international investment and technology flows are concerned, it has been suggested in the present chapter that the ultimate determinant of industrial success, regardless of the form of TT, is a sustained national effort to upgrade indigenous physical and human capabilities. This embraces interventions in education and training, the physical and technology infrastructures, and the development of supporting institutions (with which most analysts would agree). It also includes interventions in trade and industrial structure to promote the development of infant industries, the selected encouragement of externalized purchase of foreign technologies, and the focusing of education, training, technology and institutional efforts on areas of future comparative advantage (what is loosely referred to as "picking winners"). Here the recommendations are far more controversial. Yet, as long as the resources available for capability development are limited, and there are high learning costs associated with the indigenous mastery of complex industries (and beneficial externalities arising from such mastery), there is a strong case to be made on theoretical grounds for selective interventions. But the case is not merely theoretical. The experience of NIEs illustrates that different forms of intervention can lead to different results in terms of industrial depth, efficiency and indigenous technological capabilities.[30/]

Governments of developing countries should realize the interlinkages between capability building, technology transfer, investment inflows and competitiveness. In order to optimise their own development opportunities they should adopt a combination of market friendly and selective interventions that allow them to draw upon foreign know-how, while building their own ability to use and improve upon technologies, and ultimately to have a technological base that allows them scope to diversify and exploit the externalities that are inherent in such a base.

In some circumstances, this entails the free entry of foreign investors. In others, it means the promotion of indigenous technological capabilities and the competitiveness of their own firms in the global market place.

In conclusion, the economic prospects of developing countries in the contemporary globalizing economy are mixed. Those most industrially advanced and who are pursuing policies consistent with the needs of international markets would seem to possess the brightest prospects. These include most East Asian countries and China, whose forecast growth in the 1990s is well above average (World Bank 1993), and are attracting substantial inflows of foreign direct investment as well as generating their own TNCs. For those countries, now in the transition stage of their economic development, for example, India and many Latin American countries, the future is less certain, but the opportunities are scarcely less great than those faced by East Asian countries a decade or more ago. On the other hand, as shown in chapter 5, much of Africa seems likely to be marginalized in the globalization process - at least for the rest of this century. In particular much remains to be done in these countries to upgrade their indigenous created assets and to promote economic policies congenial to both domestic and foreign investors.

Notes

1. In 1994, IF to the developing world reached $83 billion, accounting for 37 per cent of world-wide investment inflows. In relation to international payments for technology in the form of royalties and fees, while global IF grew at similar rates until the 1980s, they began to diverge thereafter, with investments growing one and a half times faster than royalties for the world as a whole, and nearly two times higher for the developing countries. See UNCTAD-DTCI (1995) and UNCTC (1992).
2. On classic and new forms of foreign involvement, see C. Oman (1984) and Oman et al. (1989). UNCTC (1987) and Vickery (1986) provide analyses and data on different forms of technology trade.
3. See Dahlman, Ross-Larson and Westphal (1987), Enos (1992) and Lall (1990, 1992).
4. Only formal modes of TT, involving a contractual relationship, are considered here. There are many other modes, such as migration of skilled personnel, publications, symposia, visits, and so on, that often contribute to TT, but these are ignored here. The transfer of "embodied" technology in the form of sale of equipment, if not accompanied by other contractual arrangements, is also excluded. For a detailed analysis of the various modes of TT, see UNCTC (1987) and Oman (1984).
5. For this reason it is not possible to quantify technology flows by these categories. Data on royalty receipts and payments are available for many countries, but the bulk of royalty payments are for internalized TT, from one part of a transnational enterprise to another. See Vickery (1986).
6. See Dunning (1993) for a succinct and comprehensive review.
7. See UNCTC (1992), chap. VI.
8. See Dunning (1993) and Porter (1990).
9. See the classic article on this by Vernon (1966) and the update in Vernon (1979).
10. See Porter (1990).
11. Examples include the extensive subcontracting facilities of firms like Benetton and Nike in the Far East. For further details see Harrison (1994).

12. On the differences that arise from the nature of the technologies, see Pavitt (1984),
13. See for example Freeman and Perez (1988), Lazonick (1992) and Gerlach (1992).
14. See UNCTC (1992).
15. For a more detailed exposition, see Enos (1992) and Lall (1992).
16. See Cohen and Levinthal (1989).
17. See Lall (1992) and the World Bank (1992).
18. See ibid. and Amsden (1989), Pack and Westphal (1986) and Wade (1991).
19. See Vernon (1989).
20. See Chesnais (1986), Lall (1992) and Porter (1990).
21. There do exist a few instances of truly innovative work by foreign affiliates in developing countries like India, Brazil and the Republic of Korea, but these are rare and confined to a few industries like food, pharmaceuticals or transport equipment where local conditions differ significantly from those in other countries, and where import substitution policies have forced firms to find local substitutes for imported inputs.
22. See the World Bank (1992).
23. See Porter (1990) and Chesnais (1986).
24. On the role of incentives, capabilities and institutions in shaping industrial success, see Lall (1990).
25. See Nelson and Winter (1982) and Rosenberg (1976).
26. For a stimulating discussion, see Freeman and Perez (1988). See also Dunning (1993), chap. 10.
27. For a general analysis of policies towards technology development, see Dunning (1993), chap. 11.
28. World Bank, *1991 World Development Report*.
29. See the World Bank (1992) for a brief analysis.
30. See Lall (1992).

References

Amsden, A., (1989). *Asia's Next Giant: South Korea and Late Industrialisation*. New York: Oxford University Press.

Chesnais F., (1986). Technology and competitiveness. *STI Review: Science, Technology and Industry*, No. 1. Paris: OECD. pp. 85-129.

Cohen, W.M. and D.A. Levinthal (1989). Innovation and learning: The two faces of R&D. *Economic Journal*, vol. 99, No. 4, pp. 569-596.

Dahlman, C., B. Ross-Larson, and L.E. Westphal (1987). Managing technological development: Lessons from newly industrializing countries. *World Development*, vol. 15, No. 6, pp. 759-775.

Dunning, J.H. (1993). *Multinational Enterprises and the Global Economy*. Wokingham, Berkshire, and Reading, Massachusetts: Addison Wesley.

Enos, J., (1992). *The Creation of Technological Capabilities in Developing Countries*. London: Pinter.

Freeman, C. and C. Perez (1988). Structural crises of adjustment: Business cycles and investment behaviour. In G. Dosi et al.,(eds.). *Technical Change and Economic Theory*. London: Pinter.

Gerlach, M.L. (1992). *Alliance Capitalism: The Social Organization of Japanese Business*. Oxford: Oxford University Press.

Harrison, B. (1994). *Lean and Mean: The Changing Landscape of Corporate Power in the Age of Flexibility*. New York: Basic Books.

Lall, S. (1990). *Building Industrial Competitiveness in Developing Countries*. Paris: OECD Development Centre.

_____ (1992). Technological capabilities and industrialization. *World Development*. vol. 20, No. 2, pp. 165-186.

Lazonick, William (1992). Business organization and competitor advantage: Capitalist transformation in the twentieth century. In G. Dosi, R. Gianetti and P.A. Toninelli (eds). *Technology and Enterprise in Historical Perspective*. Oxford: The Clarendon Press.

Nelson, R.R. and S.J. Winter (1982). *An Evolutionary Theory of Economic Change*. Cambridge, Massachusetts: Harvard University Press.

Oman, C. (1984). *New Forms of International Investment in Developing Countries*. Paris: OECD Development Centre.

_____ et al. (1989). *New Forms of Investment in Developing Country Industries: Mining, Petrochemicals, Automobiles, Textiles, Food*. Paris: OECD Development Centre.

Pack, H, and L.E. Westphal (1986), *Industrial Strategy and Technological Change: Theory versus Reality*. Journal of Development Economics; vol. 22, No. 1, pp.87-128.

Pavitt, K. (1984). Sectoral patterns of technical change: towards a taxonomy and a theory, *Research Policy* (Amsterdam, the Netherlands), vol. 13.

Porter, M. (1990). *The Competitive Advantage of Nations*. New York: Free Press.

Rosenberg, N. (1976). *Perspectives on Technology*. Cambridge: Cambridge University Press.

UNCTAD (1994). *World Investment Report 1994: Transnational Corporations, Employment and the Workplace* (United Nations publication, Sales No. E.94.II.A.14).

_____ (1995). *Compendium of Documents and Reports relating to the work of the UNCTAD Ad Hoc Working Group on the Interrelationship between Investment and Technology Transfer* (United Nations publication, Sales No. E.95.II.D.12).

_____ Division on Transnational Corporations and Investment (UNCTAD-DTCI) (1995). *World Investment Report, 1995: Transnational Corporations and Competitiveness* (United Nations publication, Sales No. E.95.II.A.9).

UNCTC (1987). *Transnational Corporations and Technology Transfer: Effects and Policy Issues*, ST/CTC/86 (United Nations publication, Sales No. E.87.II.A.4).

_____ (1992). *World Investment Report 1992: Transnational Corporations as Engines of Growth* (United Nations publication, Sales No. E.92.II.A.19).

Vernon, R. (1966). International investment and international trade in the product cycle. *Quarterly Journal of Economics,* pp. 140-207.

_____ (1979). The product cycle in the new international environment. *Oxford Bulletin of Economics and Statistics*, pp. 255-267.

_____ (1989). Technological development: The historical experience. Washington, D.C.: The World Bank, Economic Development Institute, Seminar Paper No. 39.

Vickery, G. (1986). International flows of technology - recent trends and development. *STI Review: Science, Technology and Industry*. No. 1, Paris, OECD, pp. 47-84.

Wade, R. (1991). *Governing the Market.* Princeton, New Jersey: Princeton University Press.

World Bank, *1991 World Development Report.* Washington, D.C.: The World Bank.

_____ (1992). *World Bank Support for Industrialization in Korea, India and Indonesia.* Washington, D.C.: The World Bank, Operations Evaluation Department.

_____ (1993). *Global Economic Prospects and the Developing Countries, 1993.* Washington, D.C.: The World Bank.

9

Enhancing competitive advantage in technology-intensive industries

Yair Aharoni and Seev Hirsch

Introduction

In the absence of natural resources and unilateral transfers, economic growth development will sooner or later depend on an increase in the share of the technology-intensive sector of the economy, as has been so convincingly demonstrated, first by Japan, and later by the Asian tigers.

In the 1950s, it was believed that economic development could be achieved by capital infusions that would break the so-called vicious cycle of poverty. The mere transfer of capital, however, was found to be insufficient. While Europe was able to reconstruct itself once it received Marshall Plan funds, most developing countries were unable to use capital inflows in an effective manner. Clearly, technical and managerial knowledge was a crucial ingredient of economic growth.

A country's comparative advantage increasingly depends on its ability to use effectively technology, which is generally a function of the capacity of its population to command new technologies and incorporate them in production processes. Labour rate differences or proximity to sources of raw materials have become much less important considerations in determining location of manufacturing and service facilities relative to the availability of technology-supporting facilities and market considerations (Stopford and Strange, 1991).

The recognition that global industry and commerce are being reshaped by technological change has made both governments and business leaders focus on their ability to command technology and to enhance their capabilities to achieve technological sophistication as users if not as producers.

The custom of discussing international trade and investment in terms of the comparative advantage of countries could be misleading since it down plays the role of the firm.[1] This omission is particularly serious when international transactions in technology-intensive products are under consideration. In this case the role of individual firms is of particular relevance because of the central role they play in the creation, transfer and absorption of technology, which is an important determinant of competitiveness.

The impact of technology on economic development and the interaction between technology, trade and investment policies are among the least understood aspects of the economic development process. Until the 1980s, most research on economic development was based on neoclassical economic assumptions – namely, that technological changes come about because of reactions to changes in factor prices – while the firm was treated as a "black box". The discussion revolved around the labour or capital intensity of the production techniques – or the "appropriateness" of the technology.[2] Attention was also drawn to the comparison of purchasing "packaged" and "non-packaged" technology (Vaitsos, 1974).

The transfer of technology entails costs to the provider (Teece, 1977) and to the recipient (Dahlman and Westphal, 1982). Moreover, technology is not always codified in blueprints or patents. Much of the technology is tacit and can be transmitted only slowly between organizations. Intra-organizational transfers of proprietary knowledge tends to be less costly than transfers between independent organizations. Technology transfer requires a certain degree of technical know-how on the part of the receiving firm (Aharoni, 1991).

Factor substitution is not based on well-defined menus that firms can scan (Dahlman and Westphal, 1982). Countries differ widely in their ability to absorb technology, to deploy it efficiently, and to create it. Virtually all developing countries are currently seeking to increase their share of world output, employment and trade of technology-intensive products, which has been very small to date. Achieving this goal, however, depends both on macro-environmental conditions and on the strategy of business organizations. In the present chapter the characteristics of high-technology products and of the firms which produce them are examined, focusing on the processes which go on within the TNCs and their interaction with their domestic and international environments. It also spells out the main conceptual and policy implications of the interrelationship between technology acquisition, FDI and trade. In fact, the accumulation of knowledge may change the course taken by the firm by stimulating activities never before imagined. Several case studies of developing countries published in the 1980s (for example, Katz (1978, 1984), Teitel (1981, 1984), Lall (1980, 1981)) Westphal (1983)), allow a glimpse into the trials and errors of the innovation process.

Scholars who did not believe in the ability of developing countries to create technology and move away from the "periphery", articulated the "Dependencia" theory in the mid-1960s. It was argued that dependant economies either were growing poorer (Frank, 1967) or could only obtain marginal growth (Cardoso, 1972). When some of the "dependant" countries were able to deepen their industrial structure and achieve economic growth, these achievements were explained by the triple alliance between the state, foreign capital and domestic capital - and labelled "dependant development" (Evans, 1979). Yet in Brazil, about which Evans was primarily writing, there were significant indigenous developments in the aircraft industry (Ramamurti, 1987; Sarathy, 1985), the electronics industry (Schmitz and Cassiolato (eds.), 1992), and the computer industry (Tigre, 1983). Further, Joseph Grieco (1982) clearly demonstrated that dependant development and its assumptions about technological dependencies did not explain India's computer policies. In fact, several developing countries were able to develop their own technologies, often by adapting imported technologies and then upgrading the technologies used. The apparent success of countries adopting this kind of strategy, most notably the Asian NICs, undermined the views of technological dependence.[3/]

Despite the weakness of the dependencia theory, it made a significant contribution to economic development theory by drawing attention to the interaction of social, political, and economic characteristics and their impact on policy choices. As pointed out by Sanjaya Lall in chapter 8, technology policy cannot be achieved without the formation of suitable institutions, laws and organizational structures. Technology policy must also ensure the availability of both physical and human capital.

Available data indicate that TNCs control a high share of employment, output and trade in technology-intensive industries and of access to new technologies. TNCs possess firm-specific intangible assets, including outright control of proprietary technological knowledge, and accumulated expertise in the management of international operations. In the 1960s, foreign direct investments (FDI) grew at twice the rate of GNP. In the 1980s, FDI grew more than four times as fast as GNP, despite the economic recession in the early 1990s, and FDI has continued to grow over the past five years (UNCTAD 1996).

Among developing countries, 69 per cent of FDI inflows between 1981 and 1995 was direct to ten countries, seven of which are in South-East Asia. At the same time the least developed countries – especially those in sub-Saharan Africa – are receiving only a trickle. If the majority of developing countries continue to be a less attractive location for TNCs, they may experience lower growth. It is also possible that fiscal or regulatory measures that hinder the operations of TNCs may damage the developing countries' economies by restraining technological transfer, trade, employment and capital inflows. A key policy issue, therefore, is how to reduce the risk of developing countries being left in slow or no-growth situations.

In the first section of the present chapter, the operations are analysed of traditional and technology-intensive firms operating in domestic and international markets. It explores their interactions with the input and output markets, and with other economic actors. The examination of the relationship between firm characteristics, product characteristics and international operating modes shows how TNCs can acquire a competitive edge in technology-intensive products.

The following section outlines a conceptual scheme which analyses a matrix of different combinations of trade and technology policies, distinguishing between inward- and outward-looking trade policies, on the one hand, and policies designed to promote technology absorption, adaptation and creation, on the other. The conditions which enable countries to move from one box of the matrix to another and the role of TNCs in this process are discussed, as are the interactions between technology policy, foreign investment policy, trade policy, and elements of what is commonly termed industrial policy.

In a final section of the chapter, technology policy issues are examined for developing countries at different stages of development. It is shown that a meaningful expansion of an outward-looking technology-intensive sector is extremely difficult without the involvement of TNCs in the process. The choice is not between TNCs and domestic firms, but rather between foreign-based and home-based TNCs.

Technology and competitive advantages

Universal and firm-specific inputs

To appreciate the problems involved in increasing the share of the technology-intensive sector in the economy, it is necessary to understand what this implies for individual firms.

In the production process, firms use two kinds of inputs: universal production factors and technology.[4/] Universal production factors include inputs such as labour, physical and financial capital, natural resources, and other inputs generally available in the appropriate markets. Technology or "technological capability", as defined by Lall (1990), has entrepreneurial, managerial and technical components. Entrepreneurial and managerial capabilities encompass the knowledge required to mobilize the human, material and financial resources employed by the firm. Technological capability in the narrower sense was defined by Lall as the ability to "execute all the technical functions entailed in setting up, operating, improving, expanding and modernizing the firm's productive facilities" (Lall, 1990).[5/]

Knowledge possessed by a firm can be viewed as a distinct firm- or ownership-specific production factor. It is embodied in the managers, engineers, skilled workers and other employees. It takes the form of codified and un-codified operating norms and policies, as well as past investments in process engineering and in product research and development. Technological knowledge, according to Patel and Pavitt is often tacit and mostly specific to firms and to particular classes of products and production processes.[6/] To be sure, much of the so-called firm-specific knowledge is based on the application of universal knowledge, but, when this combination of universal knowledge with firm traditions and methods becomes immersed in the firm's culture, it becomes unique. This can be accomplished by indoctrinating the entire organization, by building what Carlsson and Eliasson (1991) termed "competent teams".

Firm-specific knowledge can be viewed as an intangible asset which, like a machine, can be employed to increase the value (or reduce the unit costs) of the firm's output. Like a tangible asset, firm-specific knowledge depreciates over time. Depreciation in this case takes the form of obsolescence. The knowledge possessed by the firm becomes diffused through the expiry of patents, reverse engineering and straightforward copying. In time, the products on which it is based may get copied by competitors, some of whom may have access to less costly universal production factors.

Depreciated physical assets must be replaced if the firm wishes to stay in business. The intangible assets constituting the firm's specific production factors must similarly be upgraded and even re-invented. New knowledge in the form of new products, new production methods, new marketing techniques, and new management systems must be continuously introduced and absorbed into the organization. Failure to do so will lead to a decline in market share and profitability.

The analogy between physical assets and firm-specific knowledge is, however, incomplete. The difference between the two types of assets is not limited to their tangibility; equally important are the methods used for acquiring these different assets. A critically important characteristic of firm-specific knowledge is that it is not obtainable in the market place. It must be "produced" by the firm which uses it. Parts of the technical components of firm-specific knowledge can be obtained through licensing, or through contract research. In either case, the knowledge obtained must be actively absorbed by the receiving firm. The process takes time and is cumulative (Cantwell, 1989).

Since each firm's technological capability is created over time, it is idiosyncratic and path dependent. It is, at least to some extent, unique to the firm and cannot be fully replicated, even by individuals who leave the firm and join other organizations. The basic knowledge which constitutes technological capability remains intact as long as the team which embodies the capability continues to function. To translate its capability into competitive products, however, the firm must update and upgrade its capabilities not only in absolute terms, but relative to potential and actual competitors.

Technology absorption by individual firms depends not only on internal decisions and on the firm's level of competence, but also on the level and quality of the country's technological infrastructure. The better the educational system, the research done by universities, the linkages between universities and firms, the diffusion of technical standards, availability of testing facilities and other institutions, the more productive the process of firm-specific knowledge-building and the less the cost incurred by the individual firms in the process of creating the required level of their specific knowledge.

Universal and firm-specific outputs

Universal inputs combined with firm-specific knowledge are employed to manufacture goods and services, which may be grouped on the basis of the intensity of the inputs which they contain into firm-specific and universal products.

Firm-specific products contain a significant element of proprietary knowledge - knowledge which is available to the firm and not to its competitors - which imparts unique characteristics to the products, which consequently command a premium price. In contrast, the manufacture of universal products does not depend on the possession of proprietary knowledge by the producer. The technology is easily acquired and absorbed, and its possession does not confer a competitive advantage on the firm which possesses it.

Competitive advantage in universal products is determined by the relative cost of the universal production factors such as labour, capital, raw materials and other inputs. Competitive advantage in firm-specific products is, by contrast, determined essentially by the ability of the manufacturer to differentiate her output from that of her competitors, and to convince potential customers of its uniqueness.

In services as in goods, one can distinguish between universal services and firm-specific services. Universal services – finance, insurance, and transportation – can be acquired in the open markets. Firm-specific services – instruction, installation, repairs etc – depend on proprietary knowledge originating with the manufacturer of the goods. Firms can produce either goods or services or combinations of the two, that is, goods with varying service intensities.

Super computers, medical scanners, telephone exchanges, laser equipment and robotics are examples of firm-specific goods associated with firm-specific services. Before a medical scanner can be used, operators must be trained, the scanner must be installed and run in, spares must be supplied and the provision of maintenance services must be assured. These firm-specific services must be provided either directly by the equipment manufacturer or by an organization specifically authorized by the manufacturer to provide them.

Video equipment and personal computers are examples of firm-specific goods whose associated services have become universal. In this case, some services have been embodied in the equipment, which has been designed in such a way as to minimize the need for repair and maintenance. The information required to provide the remaining services has been made public by the manufacturers, thus making it possible for the equipment to be serviced even by persons not specifically authorized to do so by the manufacturer.

Information tends to be diffused over time, and becomes public knowledge, regardless of the intentions of the manufacturer. Consequently, as firm-specific products mature, they become "universalized". Thus, the services associated with cars, household appliances and industrial equipment started out as firm-specific services, but have become more and more universal in their character (Hirsch and Meshulach, 1992).

The product characteristics described above influence the organizational modes employed in their manufacture and distribution both within a country's boundaries and internationally.

Considering universal products first, recall that the knowledge required for their manufacture and servicing is in the public domain. The production technology is easily available, and can be acquired together with the production equipment which several firms from different countries will be eager to supply. The associated services can be similarly obtained from universal-service providers, firms which specialize in the provision of the service, and which do not depend on outsiders for product-specific knowledge. This knowledge, as noted above, is in the public domain. Transactions in universal products can therefore be unbundled in the sense that the goods and associated services can be provided by different organizations.

Transactions in firm-specific products are likewise influenced by their characteristics. Since the process technology, final product and the associated services depend on firm-specific knowledge which is not publicly available, unbundling is difficult, if not impossible. Consequently, firm-specific product firms which internalize research and development

267

(R&D), manufacturing, distribution and servicing within their organization, tend to have a competitive edge over firm-specific product firms which control only part of the value chain.

Firm-specific product industries tend to be dominated by firms characterized by vertical integration. Manufacturing, R&D, distribution and servicing are thus undertaken by organizations owned or controlled by a single firm. The operating modes of universial product firms are likely to be more varied. Thus, contract research, subcontracting of key components, distribution and servicing by independent agents, are more prevalent in the universial product than in the firm-specific product industries.

Firms which have acquired an advanced technological capacity will presumably use it to manufacture what we termed firm-specific products. Note, however, that sophisticated and technologically advanced design and manufacturing processes can be employed to produce the so-called "low-tech" products, thus transforming the economic basis of their competitiveness. This is best demonstrated in "mature" industries, such as clothing and furniture making. Consequently, a high technology base can be utilized to produce all kinds of products ranging from universal goods associated with universal services, through specific goods associated with universal services to specific goods associated with specific services.[7] A low technology base, however, can only be employed to manufacture universal products.

International transactions in universal and
firm-specific products

The distinction between goods and services introduced above is particularly germane when we consider international transactions. Marketing across national boundaries requires a knowledge of foreign languages, familiarity with more than one legal system and "ways of doing business" in the target markets, as well as dealing with foreign exchange and specialized financial instruments. These activities tend to be more complicated and more costly than marketing in the familiar and close home market, giving rise to an export marketing cost premium. The export cost premium is also influenced by the characteristics of the products being traded.

The export marketing cost premium of firm-specific products is, *ceteris paribus*, higher than the cost premium associated with universal products. The difference is particularly critical for the service-intensive firm-specific products. The knowledge on which the service components of the product is based originates, as was noted above, with the manufacturer of the product.

Exporters of firm-specific service products must choose between providing the associated firm-specific services by organizations which they control (subsidiaries) or by independent organizations (agents, distributors), to which they transfer the requisite service-related knowledge. The second option is less costly and less risky, since it requires no up-front investments in foreign marketing affiliates. On the other hand, the exporter ends up sharing proprietary knowledge plus a higher proportion of the transaction value with independent organizations with which he might have conflicts of interest. It is not surprising, therefore, that, when firm-specific service firms are not operating under severe resource constraints, they prefer to be fully integrated.

Note that universal goods associated with universal services and firm-specific goods associated with universal services are less affected by the export cost premium discussed above than firm-specific service products. Universal services and firm-specific goods associated with universal services consist of goods associated with universal services which are as a rule provided by specialized service firms (banks, insurance companies, transport companies etc.). The manufacturer of the product need not invest scarce resources in risky foreign markets to make sure that the customers end up getting what they bargained for. Consequently, firm-specific service firms are expected to be characterized by higher degrees of forward integration than universal services and firm-specific goods associated with universal services firms in both domestic and international markets.

Turning next from the firms to the national economy, it can be noted that the product groups listed above are consumed in all economies regardless of their level of development. Typically, however, there is a significant difference between the industry structure of developing and developed economies, the output of the former being characterized by a high proportion of universal products and a low proportion of firm-specific products (see World Bank, 1992b). By the same token, analysis of the trade balance of different countries will usually reveal that developed economies tend to have a trade surplus in firm-specific products, particularly in firm-specific goods associated with firm-specific services, while developing economies tend to have a deficit in firm-specific products, financed by a surplus in universal products.

One of the apparent goals of economic development is to change this distribution, and to increase the share of firm-specific products in the industrial output of developing economies. Achievement of this goal requires an increase in the relative number and growth rate of firm-specific product firms, expansion and upgrading of their technological base, production techniques, and marketing capabilities. This transformation cannot be achieved by the efforts and initiatives of business firms alone. They must be accompanied by appropriate public policies.

Technology policy options - a conceptual scheme

Firms differ widely in their capabilities to deploy efficiently different technologies. These differences vary from one part of the value chain to another: a firm may possess enough knowledge to cope with the product and process engineering, but not the necessary skills to market the goods it can produce. The aggregate of firms' capabilities can be viewed in some sense as the national capability. These capabilities are also affected by public technology policy, which is based on certain basic choices, that are interwoven with choices regarding both trade and foreign investment policies. The following discussion indicates two main trajectories of technology policy: these are the market-orientation dimension and the technology dimension.

Market and technology dimensions

One can distinguish between inward (domestic market) and outward (world market) orientation by the indigenous firms. Inward or home-market orientation is considered inferior to world-market orientation for obvious reasons. The home market is more protected as a rule by both "natural" and man-made barriers. Firms sheltered behind entry barriers at the national level frequently fail to adopt the latest technologies and to manufacture "world-class" products. The horizons and economic prospects of the firms are limited - they cannot expect to benefit fully from economies of scale or scope, and they are unlikely to utilize the best available technology. Further, a protected market decreases customer welfare as customers are denied access to best quality or least costly products.

Outward orientation does not necessarly mean a free trade regime. It means that domestic firms must formulate their product policies on the assumption that they will not benefit from artificial trade barriers in the domestic market. The standard against which the firms measure their performance and target their policies should be the standard adopted by world leaders - in terms of quality, product specifications, delivery practices, service provision and price.

Inward market orientation is a characteristic of firms which shelter behind trade barriers, and which enable them to raise prices, downgrade quality, provide poor services, and generally offer products which cannot compete in the world market with the leaders. Natural barriers are frequently augmented by protectionist policies, such as import quotas, prohibitive tariffs, foreign exchange limitations, licensing requirements, discriminatory technical standards, or terms of access to public procurement, "voluntary export restraints", and a myriad of other non-tariff barriers. When such measures are adopted for the entire economy, firms increase their returns by orienting their products towards the protected domestic market and away from the competitive international markets. Frequently, however, this policy is inconsistent with the exploitation of economies of scale and of scope, due to the small size of the domestic market. Clearly, an economy-wide import-substitution policy is hardly consistent with the creation of world-class manufacturing firms. The exposure of the domestic market to international competition is advocated primarily because of the clear message it sends to the domestic business sector to adopt an outward-looking orientation.

Outward orientation is not synonymous with export orientation, and similarly, inward orientation is not the same as import substitution. Both terms focus on the nature of the competition and not on the target markets. Thus, while export-oriented firms will generally follow an outward orientation in the sense used here, firms engaged primarily in import substitution will not necessarily be inward oriented. A liberal import policy, for example, may force an import-substituting firm to adopt an outward-oriented technology posture.

The technology dimension pertains to the capabilities acquired by domestic firms to employ different technologies to manufacture goods and services. Acquisition of this knowledge progresses from the ability to absorb universal technologies embedded in equipment and coded in blue-prints, through the ability to absorb, upgrade and eventually adapt licensed technologies, engage in reverse engineering, adapt processes used by other firms, and manufacture products whose specifications are not in the public domain. The firm attains the highest level of technical knowledge when it acquires the ability to develop its own products, that is, to manufacture products based on in-house knowledge acquired through its own R&D efforts.

Technology levels, product characteristics and
market orientation - a micro-view

Figure 1 describes the process of technology accumulation taking place within individual firms. For illustrative purposes distinction is made between three basic levels - low, medium and high, which are represented by rectangles of different sizes. Technological capacity, which is assumed to expand in proportion of the size of the rectangles, has three components: absorption, adaptation and creation.

Technology absorption pertains to the ability of the firm to assimilate existing technological knowledge, and to utilize this knowledge in the process of manufacturing universal goods and services. The knowledge in question is embodied in engineers, technicians, and operatives employed by the firm, in production equipment, and in product specifications copied from existing products, or contained in blue prints provided by the customers.

Technology adaptation refers to the ability of firms to make changes to product specifications and established production processes. Firms which have attained this ability have the capacity to produce and marginally upgrade firm-specific goods and firm-specific services. Research and development (R&D) performed by these firms is not aimed at new innovations, but at product, process or material improvements or adaptations.

The highest level of technological capacity is represented by technology creation. Firms which attain this level have the capacity, as mentioned earlier, to engage in full-fledged product and process innovation of their own, and to produce the full range of universal and firm-specific goods and services independently of external organizations.

Figure 1. The structure and development of technological assets

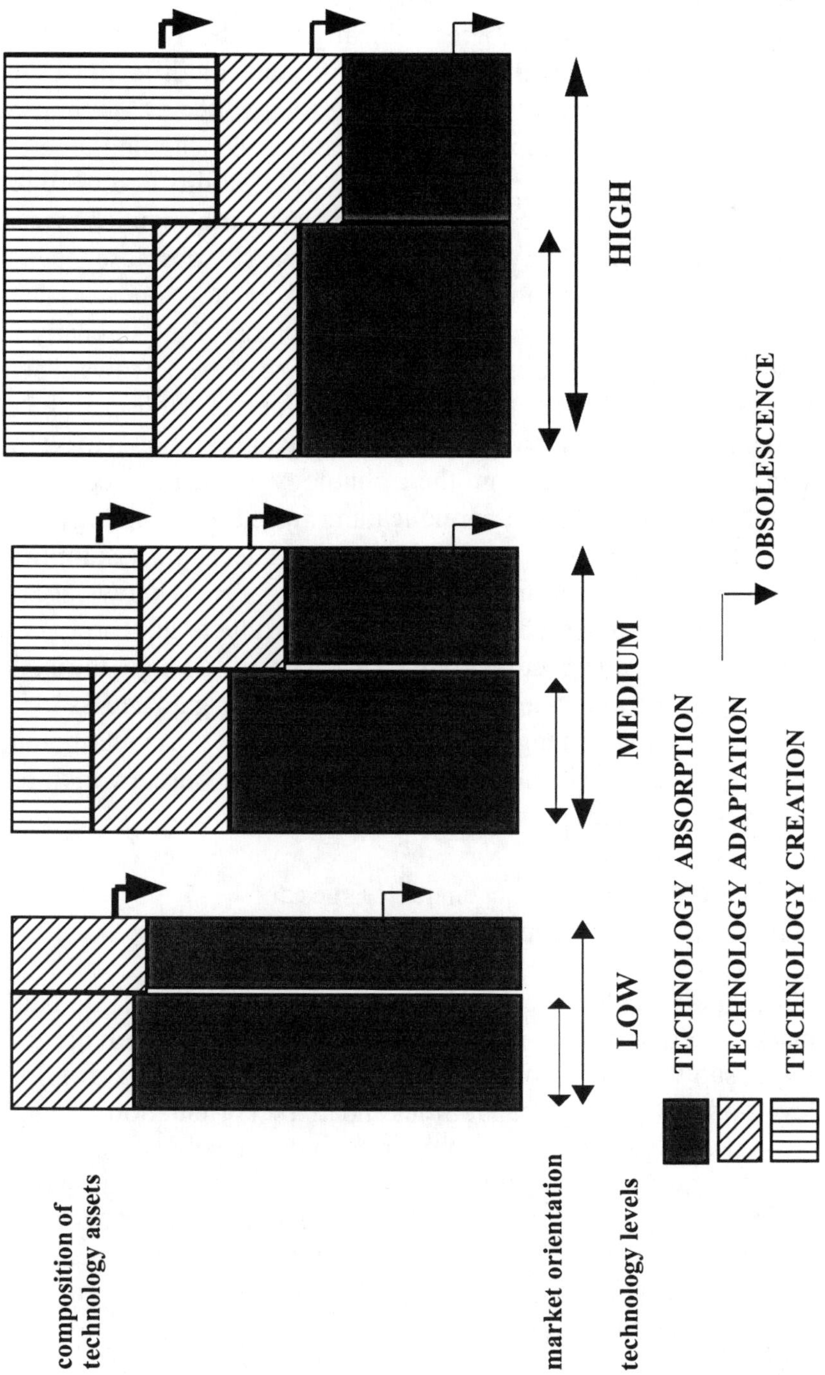

composition of
technology assets

market orientation

technology levels

LOW

MEDIUM

HIGH

OBSOLESCENCE

TECHNOLOGY ABSORPTION

TECHNOLOGY ADAPTATION

TECHNOLOGY CREATION

Technological capacity is best perceived as a continuum: firms may master existing technologies, then through learning by doing they may adapt the existing technologies to locally available raw materials or to other factors; they may then come up with some modification of design and so on until finally they are able to invent new technologies. Technological absorption also necessitates understanding; one cannot simply get the technology - one also needs the ability to absorb it.

The technological capacity built up by the firm should be viewed as a depreciable asset. The depreciation is caused by obsolescence, which takes place as old products are replaced by new ones, and as old production processes are upgraded or discarded. The intensity of the obsolescence process is represented by the size of the downward pointing arrows protruding from the rectangles in figure 1. Note that the arrow leading from the technology absorption rectangle is shown to be smaller than the arrow leading from the technology adaptation rectangle, and that the largest arrow is the one leading from the technology creation rectangle. The relative sizes of the arrows reflects the assumption that universal knowledge is more durable than firm-specific knowledge. While the former becomes obsolete when old products and processes are discarded, the latter becomes obsolete when it is no longer the exclusive property of the innovator, that is, when imitators gain access to it.

Each of the rectangles in figure 1 is divided horizontally into two segments denoted by the terms "inward" or "outward", which refer to the market orientation of the firm, as defined above.

Technology levels, product characteristics and
market orientation - a macro-view

The relationship between technology levels, product characteristics and market orientation at the macroeconomic level is shown in figure 2. The figure shows the options available to public policy makers at different levels of technological capabilities and market orientation.

At each given point in time, firms find themselves in one of the six cells of figure 2. In analysing a specific country, one may find a portfolio of firms operating in some or in all cells. Mapping out the distribution of firms in the six cells of the matrix allows an evaluation of a given country's position and accumulation of public policies intended to move the economy towards higher levels of development along the product-technology *cum* market-orientation vector described above.

Figure 2. Technology level and market orientation

Techology	Low Absorption	Medium Adaptation	High Creation
Product services[a]	U-U	S-U	S-S
Inward orientation	I	III	V
Outward orientation	II	IV	VI

[a]   U-U = universal products, universal services.
      S-U = specific products, universal services.
      S-S = specific products, specific services.

Different economies will be characterized by different distributions. The position of each country is characterized by the clusters of firms which dominate it. In turn, the locations of these clusters is determined by the capabilities of firms and by their resource availability and history, which includes the outcome of past technology policies. As pointed out by Lall it is the "complex interaction of incentives, endowments, institutions, and technological efforts" that explains the performance of a given country.[8/]

In the least developed economies almost all firms are found in the first cell. In an early phase of development, domestic firms possess only the technical ability needed to manufacture products labelled in section I as universal products, based on publicly available mature technology for the domestic market. The technical knowledge required for the manufacture of these products is readily available, and is frequently obtainable together with the production equipment. The goal of technology policy of economies in this development stage is to establish their capacity to absorb existing universal (mature) technologies developed elsewhere. Skills needed to market the products internationally are rarely available, and external inputs are also difficult to acquire. A major advantage of countries in cell I is likely be their low labour costs or abundance of certain natural resources.

Firms in the second cell, like those of the first, are universal-goods producers. They must, however, be internationally competitive since they compete by definition with world-class firms either in the home market or in third-country markets. The technology level in this case must be higher than that attained in the first cell. The products must be price competitive and conform to a consistent level of quality. Most important, while firms may enjoy government protection in the domestic market, they sometimes face intense competition in the international arena, increasing the incentive to master quickly operating methods.[2/]

Firms in the second cell may, in some cases, concentrate on one specific portion of the value chain. Thus, they may perform subcontracting work of labour-intensive parts of a product exported to or through a TNC. Firms may be able to export products based on mature technologies with or without the help of the TNCs. Developing countries such as Bangladesh or Pakistan are able to produce such goods as basic textiles or jute goods for local consumption and export.

Based on sustained efforts and learning by trial and error, economies may be able to upgrade their technological capabilities, still basing themselves on the same low labour cost advantage, thus moving to cells III or IV. Starting with absorption of universal technologies by equipment embodied diffusion, some firms in developing countries managed to learn and absorb more complex technologies and also to the innovation of new technologies. These firms acquired the necessary knowledge to produce high technology goods, but lacked the capabilities to market these goods and, in particular, the network needed for the supply of pre- and post-sales services. Thus, firms were able to produce electronic components for use by other firms, by mastering certain elements of the more complex technologies needed for the production of the components, the fastest way of gaining such mastery being to work with established TNCs.

Singapore's industrial development has been largely based on such a policy. In fact, 90 per cent of the island's exports are made by TNC affiliates. Such exports can be made if TNCs establish subsidiaries in the developing country, or if local firms act as subcontractors to TNCs. In recent decades countries such as Malaysia and Thailand have expanded their exports substantially, by combining their low labour cost advantage with enhanced skills that allowed them to export components. Some countries, in particular large ones, have adapted technologies for local consumption to create local industries. India, for example, has been able to take advantage of its growing numbers of skilled computer programmers by adopting such policies.

As knowledge and experience accumulate, firms are able to invent new technologies and supply the services associated with them. Thus, at an earlier stage of its development, the Japanese industry concentrated on technology acquisition, quality improvement, and productivity gains (Abbegglen and Stalk, 1985). Later the Japanese moved to the creation and mastery of advanced technologies. The same has been true for the Republic of Korea, where firms were established through the transfer of universal technology after building organizations capable of absorbing the technologies (Kang, 1989). Later the firms began to produce variations in the product, increasing innovation by a process of learning and adjustment (Kim, 1980), thus becoming technology-intensive.

Economies that have attained the sixth cell level boast a well-developed technological infrastructure which offers a wide range of services to the business sector. Firms produce world-class firm-specific goods and services developed internally, which compete in the global market. Firms belonging to this class have well-developed downstream operations which market their output and provide their customers in the home market and in the international markets with the required associated services. The economy is dominated by technology intensive industries, in which changes in the knowledge base are frequent and are transmitted rapidly to new processes and product specifications. Because of the need to couple tightly scientific knowledge and production, these industries employ a high percentage of scientific manpower and spend a high percentage of sales revenue on R&D.

An integral part of a firm's technology strategy at this level is the definition of its strategic technology domain, or the areas of technology in which it would strive to excel. Based on this definition, the firm will decide which technologies to develop on its own. Innovations necessary for the development of new products form an "envelope curve" encompassing different stages of technologies. As technology moves along the envelope curve, it becomes more sophisticated and requires much greater knowledge (as well as financial) resources. Often it creates specialized, firm-specific assets.

Clearly only a handful of countries have developed the capability to innovate in areas considered to be on the frontiers of knowledge, but many more countries are able to develop the necessary capabilities. The scientific and technical resources needed to develop new theories are heavily concentrated in a small number of countries, however, as are the engineering and managerial resources required to develop new products or processes and to carry out essential modifications in new products after their initial commercial introduction. In fact, at no point in time have technology and knowledge been equally distributed in the world. One or a few countries achieved technological leadership. Examples include ocean navigation pioneered by the Arabs in the late Middle Ages, modern textiles and steam engine technology developed in England, the chemical industry of Germany, the preeminence of the United States in aviation and computer technology and, more recently, the leadership position achieved by Japanese firms in copiers, semiconductors and car manufacturing.

The transition among cells

Past experience of the developed countries as well as of some developing countries, allows us to make some generalizations not only regarding the positioning of different countries in the matrix proposed in figure 2, but also on the transition from one cell to another. Clearly, the transition is associated with the elevation of the technological level of the economy.

In 1986/1987, developing countries accounted for only 4.3 per cent of world R&D expenditures. Moreover, the combined spending on R&D in these countries has been less than that of France alone. Research and development activities in developing countries are much more labour-intensive. They employ 12.6 per cent of the global workforce in R&D activities (National Science Foundation, 1989). As to patented innovations, the United States originated about 80 per cent of the major innovations in the world in 1970, but, by 1987, this share had been reduced to 58.5 per cent (National Science Foundation, 1989). Countries such as the Republic of Korea and Taiwan Province of China, however, are showing themselves to be increasingly able to change the production process or add some dimensions to the product, increasing the proportion of firm-specific products they produce and market.

Despite the obvious difficulties, some developing countries have been able to reach a high technological plateau, though only a handful have been able to develop new technologies. Governments in these countries helped local firms in carefully chosen areas by temporary import substitution policies. In large countries, such as India, Brazil and the Republic of Korea, subsidies for capital expenditures were important.

In Brazil, EMBRAER has successfully competed in the aerospace field not only by adoption of existing technologies, but also by the design of its own aeroplane. Other firms were able to develop high technology products in very difficult fields such as atomic energy - where the willingness of governments to spend substantial resources was justified on the grounds of national security. In countries such as Pakistan and India, the defence sector has been able to absorb and even develop indigenous technologies. The use of the funds for this purpose may be debatable, but the ability to achieve a high level of technological capabilities is indisputable.

The choices, however, between absorption of existing technologies, adaptation of technologies or the creation of new products through expenditures on R&D and on innovations, as well as the degree of reliance on the market, are unique for each nation and depend also on the level of initial development (Gerschenkron, 1962) or on the degree of modernization. They depend on several internal and external political and economic factors, including the ideology on the role of the state, the structure of domestic institutions and the degree of cooperation among different interest groups in the private and the public sectors (Johnson, 1985), the complexity of the technology and the amount of funds needed to master it; the willingness to allow foreign investment versus saliency attached to specific domestic ethnic groups; as well as the size of the country - and therefore the local demand, the incentives in the private sector, and macroeconomic conditions.

Generally a country may, in its early stages of development, concentrate on the production and sale of universal products. At higher levels of development the country may attempt to produce firm-specific products associated with universal services. At the highest level of development, the country acquires the capability of producing firm-specific goods associated with firm-specific services. Universal products are not, as a rule, associated with firm-specific services. Firm-specific goods associated with universal services products are, on the other hand, more abundant: Most consumer electronics require neither training nor maintenance, and even sophisticated video recorders require almost no maintenance. The progression along the output dimension is thus from universal services through firm-specific goods associated with universal services to firm-specific goods associated with firm-specific services. Note, however, that there may be legitimate disagreement about the path to be followed. While there is little doubt that cell VI is superior to cell I, there may be disagreement about whether an economy should seek to move from cell I to II or from I to III, as well as whether cell VI should follow cell V, cell IV or directly from cell III, or whether outward orientation should precede or follow the transition from universal to firm-specific products etc. The preferred policy depends on factors such as market size, relative abundance of natural resources and other universal production factors, and the public views regarding incoming and outgoing FDI. Clearly, the transition may be hastened, retarded, reoriented or accelerated by public policy, which ought to take into account the desired level of technology, while bearing in mind the level already attained by the business sector and other economic actors, as well as the availability of resources required to move the economy to higher technology levels.

The technological level required to acquire the capacity to develop new products and processes is higher than that needed to absorb existing technologies. More resources must be invested to produce domestic technology and to be internationally competitive. Closing the technology gap, however, can be economically rewarding. Countries were able to move from cells I or II to III or IV and then V or VI by increasing investments in education combined with subsidies to R&D.

The process of acquiring technological expertise is cumulative and involves interaction with the customers, suppliers and other factors in the environment (Cantwell, 1989). Moreover, the ability of a firm to participate in any given technology depends on whether it participated in an earlier generation of that technology (Teece, 1992). Thus, experience is almost an insurmountable barrier to entry for most developing countries. The establishment of firms in developing countries in certain high tech industries is therefore often dependent on substantial government support. For example, when the Indian firm BHEL started its production of heavy electrical equipment in 1956, it competed against firms that had been established many years before: Siemens in 1847, ASEA in 1883, Brown Bovery in 1891, General Electric in 1892, and a relative newcomer, Hitachi, established in 1910 (Ramamurti, 1987). It is unlikely that BHEL would have been able to enter successfully the industry without receiving large government subsidies and import protection.

Governments typically exert a strong influence on the choice of major technologies even in developed market economies. Airbus, the

European airliner, would never have been produced if this multi-country project had not been underwritten by the governments of the participating firms. The entry of firms from the Republic of Korea in the early 1980s into the semiconductor industry, and more recently into the much less costly liquid crystals display (LCD) industry, would have been similarly unthinkable without active government involvement.

Government help should take the form of assisting firms to improve their performance, rather than protecting them against more efficient international competitors, offering superior designs and/or lower prices. The rejection of protectionist policies as a means of promoting manufacturing industries is motivated by the realization that protection of the whole economy will lead to the development of the "wrong" industries, that it will divert the energies of business managers from the market to the government, and that it would be extremely difficult to redirect towards the international market the focus and policies established to run inward-looking businesses.

Targeted protection for a limited period can be compatible with outward orientation, as illustrated by the experience of Japan and the Republic of Korea (Pack and Westphal, 1986). For an economy endowed with a low level of human capital, some protection may be justified in order to create "highways of learning" needed to develop the capability of manufacturing exportable products not formerly manufactured in the country (Lucas, 1988, Lockwood, 1963). The drawback of such a policy is that it creates vested interests which make it difficult to discontinue when it has served its purpose. "Infant industries" have the habit of refusing to grow up when growing up implies changing their orientation from inward to outward looking.

Experience in successful developing countries points to different policies in attempting to get a more technology intensive economy. Singapore relied almost exclusively on foreign TNCs. Hong Kong tended to specialize much more in universal products, while the Republic of Korea aimed at creating its own TNCs by helping its *chebols*.

In theory, a developing country can create conditions that will nurture the creation of home-based TNCs. In reality, the process of learning and accumulation of expertise and know-how needed for the successful operation of a TNC is an extremely long one. Technology policy in most countries must be primarily based on the developed countries' TNCs as a vehicle which provides access to foreign markets.

Without these firms, it is almost impossible to reach higher levels in the technology-cum-market orientation matrix analysed in the present section. The choice of instruments capable of advancing this goal is the most important variable in formulating and evaluating alternative public policies. Government officials, however, must enhance their ability to negotiate with the developed countries' TNCs.

For those developing countries with a relatively large supply of scientists, such as India or Israel, one policy issue is whether or not one should leverage the limited amount of scientific skills, discouraging TNCs from operating only R&D laboratories and conditioning such a development on the establishment of production facilities that will create more high-value-added employment opportunities.

Market size

Market size is relevant primarily because of its effect on minimum efficient scale. Clearly, the smaller the domestic market, the more dependant are firms on export markets for the attainment of minimum efficient scale. Thus, in countries with small domestic markets, firms are more pressed to adapt their products to the more stringent conditions of the external markets than are firms in larger countries. Bearing in mind that market size is determined by purchasing power and not merely by the number of potential customers, one can conclude that market size has, *ceteris paribus*, a stronger effect on the attainment of minimum efficient scale in developing than in developed countries.

Since technology-intensive industries such as pharmaceuticals, aerospace and computers require very high investments in R&D and, therefore, a large scale of production and sales to reduce the average unit cost of the development, the introduction of these industries into developing countries may well be retarded not only because of the inadequate level of technological capabilities, but also because of the small size of the domestic market, on the one hand, and the entry barriers in potential export markets, on the other. The amount invested in a search for new technology depends on the anticipated profitability of the investment, but also on supply factors, such as the availability and quality of scientists and engineers. Market size and technological backwardness may thus feed on each other and create a vicious circle.

Size-related factors have two contradictory effects on firms. On the one hand, they increase the pressure on the development of outward (that is, export) oriented policies by the local firms. On the other, they increase the risks which they face, including the risk of producing technology-intensive products which depend on foreign markets. These factors may well reduce the number of firms which are ready to operate in markets for firm-specific goods and services. This, however, is not inevitable, as is amply demonstrated by the high-technology based economic achievements of small countries like Sweden and Switzerland in Europe and Hong Kong, Singapore and Taiwan Province of China in Asia. Leading firms in these countries adopted outward-oriented strategies despite the small size of the domestic market. Entry barriers into the export markets were overcome in some cases by outward foreign direct investment.

Transnational corporations and product characteristics

Industrial development implies, as shown earlier, an increase in the share of manufacturers of firm-specific goods and services in the economy, and this in turn requires that firms enhance their capacity to absorb, adapt and improve and ultimately create product and process technologies, and develop an international market orientation. Transnational corporations typically have these capabilities. They have multiple operating affiliates in different countries. Individual affiliates can engage in several activities - production of goods and services, servicing the domestic market and export markets, engaging in research and development and other activities leading to the introduction of new products and production processes. In each affiliate, production can be for the domestic, regional or global markets, depending on the competitive advantage of the location, and the cost of transferring outputs to different target markets.

Since the manufacture of many products is characterized by multiple stages, TNCs can minimize total production costs by sourcing primary and intermediate inputs in the least-cost location. Intra-company sourcing rather than arms'-length sourcing will be used when intra-company transactions are less costly, or more reliable in terms of quality, delivery time etc.

Affiliates of TNCs also engage in marketing, which implies interfacing with customers, product distribution and provision of pre - and post-delivery services. Multi-product TNCs are able to use their marketing affiliates to distribute products manufactured by both domestic and foreign affiliates. Affiliate marketing is superior to marketing by independent distributors when firm-specific goods associated with firm-specific services are involved, that is, when associated services depend on proprietary knowledge supplied by the product manufacturer. Marketing by independent organizations leads to loss in revenues and market power because it requires sharing of proprietary product information with outsiders.

By controlling the most important links in the value chain which extends from R&D through production to distribution and provision of pre- and post-sales services, TNCs not only minimize costs, but they also enhance market power in comparison with single-country firms which do not control their downstream operations. This point is particularly relevant to the technology- and service-intensive firm-specific products.

The role of public policy

Enhancement of technological capabilities of the economy in general and of business enterprises in particular, has been shown to be a major factor in achieving economic growth. Policy choices of governments play a pivotal role in shaping, stimulating or inhibiting growth rates and the technological capacity of the country. The drive towards higher technology levels must be supported by a build-up of skills at all levels and by extensive development of the scientific and educational infrastructure. In addition, developing countries face an urgent need to stop the haemorrhage of the brain drain, and to direct investments in both physical and human capital into areas considered to have a significant growth potential.

Technological infrastructure

Technology absorption and technology-creation capacities are enhanced by the development of the technological infrastructure, which includes technical schools, colleges, universities and research institutions. These institutions provide skilled employees and, in time, scientists who constitute the technological manpower employed by business enterprises. The investment in education is essential to develop cadres of people capable of understanding technology, absorbing and upgrading technology, and ultimately developing new technologies (Aharoni, 1991).

The accumulation of skills, knowledge and technological know-how is a very long and arduous process. Only a long-term effort to build institutions and develop capabilities can create a higher level of industrial competence. Not until educational levels have been raised, and a minimum number of engineers and scientists are available, do the import of technology and its assimilation become technically and economically feasible.

In many developing countries, the record up to now has been dismal. Even the mastery of mature and easily available technologies cannot be assumed to exist in all countries. Because of the length of the process, and the low level of technological accumulation possessed by these countries, they face a growing danger of marginalization. New information technologies and flexible manufacturing systems contain an almost untapped potential for developing countries to increase their productivity and to create new technologies based on local know-how. Yet an OECD report has concluded that, "despite the new technologies, and indeed, on account of their particular requirements in terms of resources and skills, the gap separating rich and poor nations is likely to increase".[10/]

The level of technological capabilities also depends on macro-environmental conditions, including government regulations, the level of patent protection and anti-trust laws, and the characteristics of the physical infrastructure. General macroeconomic policies must create an atmosphere amenable to the flourishing of entrepreneurs.

As has been argued in other chapters in the present volume, the role of public policy should not be confined to the creation of macroeconomic and appropriate environmental conditions, to legal and administrative frameworks, to law enforcement, and the provision of efficient public services. It can be, and often is, much more direct and active, ranging from direct funding of R&D activities, subsidies for capital expenditures and training, public procurement etc.[11/]

Subsidizing R&D in particular and innovation in general has been recognized in the economic literature as being consistent with neoclassical principles since it helps to neutralize "market failures" caused by the likelihood that the innovator will be unable to appropriate a sufficiently large share of the benefits generated by her innovation. Subsidies for R&D or for capital outlays may be employed to induce firms to overcome their reluctance to enter firm-specific products industries, by neutralizing the high risk burdens firms are required to assume.

Successful technology policies need not necessarily be directed to transforming the entire economy or even an entire industrial sector. They may be aimed at parts of the sector or even at only a handful of firms. Moreover, their effects may well vary among sectors, among firms, and over time. To be meaningful, however, the policies should be pervasive enough to affect the direction and vision of the economy's leading firms and public institutions. Obviously, the exact set of policies will be different for countries at different levels of development. The common denominator for all these policies, however, is that they must deal simultaneously with skill enhancement, institution-building and the attainment of stability.

Empirical work points to a complementary relationship between technology imports and local R&D efforts. Based on his case analyses of several Latin American economies, Katz (1982) asserted that foreign know-how stimulates local absoption of technology. Dosi claimed that domestic R&D units "recognize, evaluate, negotiate and finally adapt the technology potentially available from others".[12] Siddharthan (1992) demonstrated that domestic R&D is not in conflict with imported technology. Rather, they are complementary to each other.

Components of technology policies

Formulation of public technology policy involves difficult choices. Governments cannot rely on picking individual winners (Nelson, 1990). Even business firms cannot always make the right technological decisions, since such decisions are based on incomplete and unreliable information. It must be realized at the same time that even a decision to set up a department of computer science in an institution of higher learning and not, say, a department of chemical engineering, reflects a belief about future "winners". In due course, the abundance of computer scientists in relation to chemical engineers in the future will undoubtedly affect the competitive advantage of the economy and the sectorial distribution of business investments.

It is highly probable, however, that, in the absence of an active public policy, the business sector will underinvest in higher risk technology-intensive projects. In developing countries, where the risks are high, where the capital markets which elsewhere provide efficient instruments for allocating and sharing risks are often non-existent, the likelihood of underinvestment in technology-related projects is particularly high. Public policy in this case should substitute for the malfunctioning or non-functioning institutions which in the advanced countries help entrepreneurs with the complicated task of risk taking.

Public policies towards TNCs

Transnational corporations have been shown in the present chapter to be the most effective instrument for developing outward-oriented firm-specific product sectors in developing economies. Transnational corporations possess the ability to develop new products and technologies in one country, locate operating units wherever the universal factors of production are most abundant, and to transfer technologies and other resources between operating units. The advantage of TNCs relative to other modes is further enhanced when international marketing is considered. Control of downstream operations, including the sale and distribution of firm-specific products in the target countries, and the provision of associated firm-specific services, is an important determinant of competitive advantage in firm-specific products. The vertical integration normally practised by the TNCs, their control of the entire value chain, even when its links are internationally dispersed, endows TNCs with a most important competitive edge over single-country firms seeking to attain the same objectives. While there is no question that TNCs offer an efficient mechanism for expanding the firm-specific products sector, however, one must examine the extent to which TNCs' interests typically coincide or conflict with those of the developing countries.

Developing countries aim at maximizing the creation of wealth *within* their borders or, in the words of Stopford and Strange, "to maximize the share of world demand satisfied from their national territory".[13/] Assuming that natural resources are fully exploited, this

287

goal can best be achieved by expanding firm-specific sectors to the greatest extent possible (Porter 1990).

Transnational corporations, as stated above, constitute a highly efficient mechanism for creating firm-specific knowledge and for transferring this knowledge to different affiliates. Transnational corporations are similarly effective in integrating geogaphically dipersed and functionally separated markets and operating activities. It is hardly surprising that their share in world output, employment and trade has risen so dramatically after the Second World War in general, and in the last few years, which have been characterized by increasing liberalization of capital movements and of world product markets integration in particular (United Nations, 1993). Yet, both inward and outward FDI have been traditionally viewed with suspicion and mixed feelings by home-country and host-country policy makers and scholars alike. Many governments, even when they are ideologically committed to the market system, have often sought to restrict and control TNC activities.

Apparently there is after all a built-in conflict of interest between states, which seek to maximize the value of the wealth available to local economic agents, and the TNCs, which presumably seek to maximize the wealth of their shareholders.

The conflict may be not only over the distribution of net value (that is, profits) created by the TNCs, but also over the location of different activities performed by them, the rate of investment, direction of trade, deployment of local labour and managers etc. The home government wants high-value-creating activities to be located within its territory, even when this implies a diminution in total value created by the TNCs, and subsequent loss of income for the TNCs' shareholders or other stakeholders or other stakeholders located in third countries.

Formulation of national policies towards TNCs is a difficult and complex task. It requires the evaluation of both costs and benefits associated with the presence of TNCs within the national boundaries. The benefits of added wealth creation, of increasing the scale and scope of economic activity, of expanding the list of tradable goods and services to include firm-specific goods associated with universal services and firm-specific goods associated with firm-specific services, must be balanced against the costs involved in the diminution of sovereignty, and in sometimes receiving a smaller share of an admittedly larger pie. The outline of such an analysis as it relates to the potential role of TNCs in the enhancement of the technological base of developing countries is described below. Hopefully, the reader is by now convinced that such an analysis should encompass public policy towards both inward and outward FDI undertaken by home-country and host-country TNCs.

The matrix in figure 3 illustrates the interaction between inward and outward FDI policies, and indicates its likely effects on both firm behaviour and the composition and sequence of typical developing countries' industrial sectors. Inward policies pertain to foreign firms seeking to invest in the country, while outward policies concern the conditions facing home-country firms seeking to engage in foreign direct investment.

The matrix distinguishes between liberal and restrictive policies. These pertain to the terms and conditions of the initial establishment of TNCs and ongoing operations, as well as remission of profits and of capital. It should be possible in principle to order such policies along a

Figure 3. Interaction between inward and outward FDI policies

Inward FDI policies

	Restrictive	**Liberal**
	I	**II**
Outward FDI policies — **Restrictive**	* Diversify; U-goods * Licensing + local * Late export of U-goods * No FDI	* Focus: U&S goods * Licensing + TNCs + local * Early export of U&S goods * Limited export of service-intensive S-goods * Inward FDI
	III	**IV**
Outward FDI policies — **Liberal**	* Diversify: U&S goods * Licensing + local * Delayed export of S-goods * Early outward efficiency seeking FDI * Late outward market seeking FDI excluding service intensive	* Focus: U&S goods * Licensing + TNCs + local * Early export of U&S goods including service intensive * Early outward market and efficiency seeking FDI

continuum, ranging from highly liberal to highly restrictive, and to agree on a cut-off point between the two groups.

Each cell pertains to the interaction between inward and outward policies. The horizontal axis considers inward FDI policies and the vertical axis shows outward FDI policies. The inward and outward policies need not be symmetrical. Liberal inward policies may be combined with either liberal or restrictive outward FDI policies. Restrictive inward policies may likewise be combined with liberal or restrictive outward policies.

The United States, Britain, The Netherlands and Germany have traditionally pursued liberal inward and outward FDI policies. Other European countries, Spain, and Italy, for example, have until recently had liberal inward and restrictive outward FDI policies. Japan and the Republic of Korea were claimed until quite recently to have had restrictive inward and liberal outward FDI policies. Examples of countries pursuing restrictive inward and outward FDI policies abound, of course, among the developing countries. The late Soviet Union, Brazil, India and, somewhat more surprisingly, France, are frequently cited as examples of countries following such policies in the past. The outcomes, that is, the effects of the interaction between the two policy sets on firm behaviour are schematically illustrated in the four cells of the matrix.

The first cell in figure 3 depicts an economy where the government restricts both incoming and outgoing FDI - both foreign and domestic TNCs are unwelcome. The effects of this policy on domestic firms are straightforward. Indigenous firms pursue an inward-oriented, unfocused, product policy. Domestic market oriented firm-specific product manufacturers will base the development of their technological capacity on licences obtained from foreign firms, including TNCs. Firm-specific product manufacturers are likely to limit their product range to the firm-specific goods associated with an universal services category. Firm-specific goods associated with firm-specific services will have a strictly home-market orientation.

The inward orientation of the business sector is strengthened by both "market pull" and "supply push" factors. Lack of competition from efficient foreign-owned TNCs provides the "pull factor". Restrictions on outward-resource and efficiency-seeking FDI prevent the acquisition of the most suitable inputs, and retard the adoption of internationally competitive production processes which are essential components of the "push factor".

The combined effects of restrictive outward and liberal inward FDI policies are shown in the second cell. This policy is most frequently employed in the developing countries and in Eastern Europe in countries where the governments are seeking to achieve a transformation from command to market economies. These governments recognize the potential advantages which inward FDI can offer in the form of capital and technology inflows. Outward FDI tends to be restricted on the grounds that the economy lacks foreign exchange and managerial talent, and that the requirements of the home economy should be given priority over all alternatives.

If successful, the policy leads to inflow of capital and technology from incoming resource and market-seeking TNCs. Incoming TNCs may transfer advanced technologies to their affiliates, thus contributing to the establishment of a firm-specific products sector in the economy. The flow of technology to indigenous firms will be rather limited, since the most lucrative opportunies will presumably be exploited by incoming TNCs. Indigenous firms trying to enter the firm-specific goods markets will have to supplement their own technology development efforts with licensed technology. Prevented by the incoming TNCs from competing in their home firm-specific products market, the indigenous firms focus mostly on universal products which they sell in the home and export markets. Thus, the firm-specific sector is dominated by TNCs and the universal sector by indigenous firms.

Next, let us analyse the effects (depicted in cell III) of a restrictive, inward FDI policy combined with a liberal, outward FDI policy on the evolution and strategy of indigenous firms. This combination of policies is not as far-fetched as it might seem at first. In fact, it was pursued by the Government of Japan during the 1960s and 1970s and of the Republic of Korea during the 1970s and early 1980s. Both Governments were subsequently pressured into liberalizing their incoming FDI policies by the United States and the European Union, which complained about the lack of symmetry between inward and outward FDI policies.

Examination of the likely effect of the above on the product strategy of indigenous firms suggests that firms will tend to be more diversified when inward FDI is restricted. Relieved of the pressure of competing TNCs, indigenous firms will tend to focus their attention on the relatively lucrative domestic market, at least during the early phases of industrialization. In this market they will at worst be forced to compete with each other and with imported goods.

The role of licensing is expanded when compared with the situation where inward FDI is encouraged. Foreign firms, denied the opportunity to exploit their proprietary knowledge through FDI will prefer licensing to the "do nothing" alternative, especially if exporting too is restricted by tariffs, by administrative fiat, or by objective economic considerations. Consequently, the locally dominated firm-specific sector is expected to be larger than under a liberal, inward FDI regime.

Foreign suppliers of technology will, however, seek to limit the ability of the licensees to compete with them in their home markets and in third markets. Their ability to do so depends, of course, on their bargaining power *vis-à-vis* the potential licensees. The licensing option will presumably be chosen mostly by foreign firms motivated by market-seeking investment. Other firms, especially efficiency seekers, are less likely to be satisfied with licensing.

Efficiency-seeking FDI is concerned with the regional or even global optimization of TNC operations. The firms in question are more likely to insist on full control of their operation, a criterion which is not compatible with licensing. Consequently, they are likely to settle for locations which allow inward FDI, even when they offer fewer location advantages than the economies which restrict inward FDI.

Considering the effect of the restrictive, inward FDI policy on the indigenous firms, we recall that, *ceteris paribus*, the latter face less competition in the domestic market, and they have access to a larger supply of licensed technology, which will facilitate the earlier development of a home-controlled firm-specific sector. The lure of the more profitable domestic market, however, combined with the restrictions imposed by the licensors on exporting, will affect the market orientation of the firm-specific sector. The sector will be initially inward oriented. Consequently, universal goods will tend to dominate the export sector for a longer period than when inward FDI is permitted.

A successful liberal, inward FDI policy pursued by the Government of the host country attracts investments by TNCs in sectors in which the location bound resources for which they are responsible are comparatively advantaged. In a developing economy these might include an abundant supply of unskilled labour (the Philippines), semi-skilled labour (Mexico, Malaysia), or even skilled labour (Russia, the Republic of Korea), natural resources, a suitable climate, an attractive location (Hong Kong,

Singapore) etc. Combining their ownership advantages with the competitive inputs constituting the host country's location advantages, the incoming TNCs contribute to the establishment of relatively high-value-creating enterprises (Dunning 1993).

The price for local resources will rise due to the increased demand generated by incoming TNCs. This factor, combined with the effect of competition in the product markets, will force the hard-pressed indigenous firms to adopt a strategy of focus. Instead of diversifying into related and unrelated products, local firms will be forced to focus on a small range of core activities in which they can expect to develop and maintain a competitive edge.

Technology will be obtained primarily through licensing from foreign firms, the diffusion of technologies imported by TNCs and, to an increasing extent though in a small number of niches, by the in-house efforts of domestic firms. The latter will find themselves under strong pressure to engage in early internationalization, that is, exporting and FDI of two kinds: market- and efficiency-seeking. Market-seeking FDI is motivated by the narrow focus policy forced upon the firms by the competitive pressures exerted by the government's open door policy towards incoming FDI. The domestic market is rarely large enough to enable the home firms to benefit from economies of scale, and the narrow focus limits the opportunities of economies of scope. Hence the early dependence on international markets.

It is in this area where the home country's policy towards outward FDI is of crucial importance. When a restrictive policy is adopted, internationalization is limited to exporting. This in turn limits the range of goods exported to universal goods and possibly to firm-specific goods associated with universal services goods. When a liberal outward FDI policy is adopted by the home government, this facilitates the early establishment of firm-specific industries in the economy, and the expansion of its scope to encompass both firm-specific goods associated with universal services and firm-specific goods associated with firm-specific services. Like universal goods producers, firm-specific producers (admittedly only a small sector in typical developing economies) can survive in the presence of competition from incoming TNCs only by early internationalization. The range of products competitively manufactured in the home country will be wider if internationalization includes outward FDI. This operating mode enables the firm-specific producers to provide their customers with associated firm-specific services originating from affiliates which they control, and which must be located in close proximity to the customer.

Liberal, outward FDI policies adopted by the government will also enable the home country firms to enhance their competitive position by engaging in efficiency-seeking investments which will supplement the less competitive inputs available in the home market.

To summarize, by pursuing liberal, outward FDI policies, the home government can help domestic firms to counteract the inherent disadvantages which they suffer *vis-à-vis* their foreign counterparts in a number of ways. Their ability to exploit economies of scale is enhanced by increasing the geographic scope of their operations, either by exporting or by foreign production. Their ability to exploit economies of scope is enhanced by their access to complementary inputs supplied, when the economic considerations so dictate, by captive foreign affiliates. A wider scope is offered to firm-specific services producers. Provision of firm-specific services associated with their firm-specific products by affiliates which they control enlarges the value chain they control and their market power. Control of the provision of associated specialized services not only raises revenues per transaction accruing to the home firm; it also raises both entry barriers facing competitors and exit barriers facing customers.

The size of the domestic market has important implications for the determination of the appropriate policy towards inward and outward FDI. When the market is sufficiently large, economies of scale and of scope can be exploited and, as the local technological accumulation reaches some threshold, the indigenous industry is ready to change its orientation from inward to outward orientation. When the domestic market is small, the policy of restricting inward FDI, especially when combined with import restrictions, may retard the development of an outward-oriented industrial sector permanently.

Concluding remarks

The ultimate goal of technology policy is for the economy to attain the capacity listed in the sixth cell of figure 2, that is, to increase the share of the firm-specific products sector in the economy. The transition between the industrial development stages depicted by the six cells is not automatic. Neither is the path of transition necessarily predetermined. The industrialization process usually starts with import substitution based on universal technologies. From this early stage, depicted by the first cell, the economy may move in the direction of the second cell – outward-looking market orientation combined with universal technologies, or the third cell – inward-looking market orientation combined with firm-specific goods and universal services, and so on. The capacity of economies to accomplish the transition and its duration depend on their current level of economic development, their history, and resource endowment, as well as their political and economic leadership. Most important, it can be influenced by technology policy.

Few policy makers would argue against the idea of having an economy dominated by internationally competitive manufacturers of firm-specific products, to the extent such a policy is feasible. Public policy can undoubtedly contribute, first to the establishment, and then to the development and expansion of an outward-looking industrial sector manufacturing firm-specific products. In the last section some of the options available to policy makers were reviewed and the interaction of technology policies with trade policy, policies towards TNCs, and elements of what is commonly termed industrial policy.

Despite the obvious benefits which home-based TNCs can offer to their home countries, public policy makers often find it most difficult to accept their establishment. Objections are based on the notion that home-based TNCs export capital and jobs, and scare managerial talents. While these claims may be true, it must be recognized that, if small economies in general, and developing countries in particular, seek to possess internationally competitive firm-specific product industries, the choice is not between domestic firms and TNCs, but rather between home-based and foreign-based TNCs. The economy will have to do without some or even most of these industries if neither domestic nor foreign-based TNCs are acceptable to public policy makers.

The failure of the former Soviet Union and of other command economies to develop internationally competitive industries, producing civilian technology-intensive products, despite the fact that they had access to large pools of superbly trained scientists and engineers, clearly supports this view. Outward-oriented TNCs were simply not allowed to be established. In economies where enterprises were regarded as mere branches of a remote ministry, operating on a basis of rigid plans, the existence of companies with foreign operating subsidiaries, engaged in manufacturing, marketing and even R&D could indeed hardly be tolerated. The price of this policy was extremely high – the almost total absence of outward-oriented firm-specific goods associated with universal services and firm-specific goods associated with firm-specific services producing firms in the command economy of Eastern Europe.

Despite the inevitable conflicts between the TNCs and potential host countries over the division of costs and benefits associated with their operations, there is little doubt that there is no substitute for the TNC presence in economies seeking to develop an outward-looking firm-specific product sector. Public policy may nevertheless be employed to hasten the process of technology transfer, to reduce the costs of TNC involvement and to increase the benefits retained by the host country.

In conclusion, it is obvious that an active public policy has an important role to play in the process of industrial development. That role should not be confined to the creation of macro-economic and appropriate environmental conditions, to legal and administrative frameworks, to law enforcement, and the provision of efficient public services. Even when the environmental conditions are "right", there is no guarantee that the "invisible hand" will bring an outward-looking firm-specific products sector into being. The "invisible hand" ought to be helped by public policies which have clear objectives for the economy, and have the means to influence the behaviour of business firms in a manner which is consistent with these objectives.

Notes

1. A point also emphasized by Gray (1994) and Dunning (1995).
2. For a review see Cooper (1980); Stewart (1979); and Stewart and James (1982).
3. For a critique of the dependency theory, see Lall (1975) and Grieco (1986).
4. This nomenclature is broadly similar to that used by Dunning (1992) in his distinction between "natural" and "created assets".
5. S. Lall. *Building Industrial Competitiveness in Developing Countries* (1990). Paris, OECD Development Centre, p. 20.
6. Pari Patel and Keith Pavitt, "Is Western Europe losing the technological race?", *Research Policy*. Amesterdam, The Netherlands, vol. 16, 1987, p. 60.
7. We were unable to find examples belonging to the fourth category, United States products, that is, universal goods associated with specific services. This category is therefore not considered further.
8. S. Lall, op. cit., p. 59.

9. On the incentives created in export oriented situation, see Balassa *et al.* (1982); Porter (1990).
10. OECD (1992). *Technology and the Economy: The Key Relationships.* Paris, OECD, p. 21.
11. For a detailed review of technology policy in the leading OECD countries, see Henry Ergas (1987). Ergas distinguishes between "mission" oriented technology policies (United States, United Kingdom and France) and "diffusion" oriented policies (Switzerland, Sweden and Germany).
12. Giovanni Dosi (1988). "Sources, procedures and microeconomic effects of innovation", *Journal of Economic Literature*, September 1988, p. 1132.
13. John Stopford and Susan Strange, *Rival States, Rival Firms: Competition for World Market Shares.* New York: Cambridge University Press, 1991, p. 56.

References

Abbegglen, J.C. and G. Stalk, Jr. (1985). *Kaisha, The Japanese Corporation.* New York, N.Y.: Basic Books.

Aharoni, Yair (1991). Education and technology transfer. In Tamir Agmon and Mary Ann Von Glinow (eds.) *Dialectics of Technology Transfer in International Business.* New York: Oxford University Press, pp. 79-102.

Balassa, Bela and Associates (1982), *Development Strategies in Semi-Industrial Economies* (Baltimore, Johns Hopkins).

Cantwell, J.C. (1989). *Technological Innovation and Multinational Corporations.* Oxford: Basil Blackwell.

Cardoso, F. (1972). Dependency and development in Latin America. *New Left Review*, July/ August, pp. 83-95.

Carlsson, Bo and Gunnar Eliasson (1991). The nature and importance of economic competence. IUI Working Paper No. 294. Stockholm, Sweden: IUI (Industrial Institute for Economic and Social Research).

Cooper, C. (1980). Policy interventions for technological innovation in developing countries. Washington, D.C.: World Bank: Staff Working Paper No. 441.

Dahlman, Carl J. and G. Westphal (1982). Technology effort in industrial development an interpretative survey of recent research. In F. Stewart and J. James (eds.), *The Economies of New Technology in Development Countries.* London: Frances Printer, and Boulder, Colorado: Westview.

Dahlman, Carl J. and F. Sercovich (1984). Exports of technology from semi-industrial economies and local technological development. *Journal of Development Economics,* vol. 16, Nos. 1/2, September, pp. 63-99.

De Woot, P. and X. Desclee (1984). *Le management strategique des groupes industriels* . Paris: Economica.

Dosi, Giovanni (1988). Sources, procedures and microeconomic effects of innovation. *Journal of Economic Literature,* September, pp. 1120-1171.

Dos Santos, T. (1970). The structure of dependence. *American Economic Review, Papers and Proceedings,* vol. 60, No. 2, pp. 231-236.

Dunning, John H. (1988). The investment development cycle and third world multinationals. In John H. Dunning (ed.), *Explaining International Production*, chap. 5, pp. 140-168. London: Unwin Hyman.

———— (1990). Multinational enterprises and the globalization of innovatory capacity. University of Reading, *Discussion Papers in International Investment and Business Studies*, September, No. 143.

———— (1992). The global economy, domestic governance, strategies and transnational corporations: interactions and policy implications. *Transnational Corporations*, vol. 1, December, pp. 7-46.

———— (1993). *Multinational Enterprises and the Global Economy*. Wokingham: Berkshire, and Reading, Massachusetts: Addison Wesley.

———— (1995). What's wrong - and right - with trade theory?. *International Trade Journal*, vol. 9, No. 2, Summer 1995.

Ergas, Henry (1987). Does technology policy matter?. In Bruce R. Guile and Harvey Brooks (eds.), *Technology and Global Industry: Companies and Nations in the World Economy*. Washington, D.C.: National Academy Press, pp. 191-245.

Evans, P. (1979). *Dependent Development. The Alliance of Multinational, State and Local Capital in Brazil*. Princeton, New Jersey: Princeton University Press.

Foster, Richard N. (1986). Technology in the modern corporation: A strategic perspective. In Mel Horwitch (ed.), *Timing Technological Transitions*. New York: Pergamon Press, pp. 35-49.

Frank, A. (1967). *Capitalism and Underdevelopment in Latin America* . New York: Monthly Review Press.

Franko, Lawrence G. (1989). Global corporate competition: Who's winning, who's losing, and the R&D factor as one reason why. *Strategic Management Journal*, vol. 10, October, pp. 449-474.

Fransman, M. (1985). Conceptualizing technical change in the Third World. *The Journal of Development Studies*, vol. 21, No. 4 (July), pp. 572-652.

———— and K. King (eds.) (1984). *Technological Capability in the Third World*. London: Macmillan.

Furtado, C. (1970). *Economic Development of Latin America*. London: Cambridge University Press.

Gereffi, G. (1983). *The Pharmaceutical Industry and Dependency in the Third World* . Princeton, New Jersey: Princeton University Press.

Gerschenkron, A. (1962). *Economic Backwardness in Historical Perspective*. Cambridge, Massachusetts: Harvard University Press.

Gray, H.P. (1994). A Firm Level Theory of International Trade in Dynamic Goods. Newark, New Jersey: Rutgers University (mimeo).

Grieco, J. (1982). Between dependency and autonomy; India's experience with the international computer industry. *International Organization*, Winter, pp. 609-632.

_____ (1986). Foreign investment and development theories and evidence. In T. Moran (ed.), *Investing in Development: New Roles for Private Capital*. New Brunswick, New Jersey: Transaction Books.

Hirsch, Seev (1989). Services and service intensity in international trade. *Weltwirtschafliches Archiv*, vol. 125, No. 1.

_____ and Avi Meshulach (1992). Towards a unified theory of internationalization. Tel Aviv, Israel: The Israel Institute of Business Research, Working Paper No. 1/92 (mimeo).

Johanson, Jan and Jan Eric Vahlne (1977). The internationalization process of the firm -A model of knowledge development and increasing market commitments. *Journal of International Business Studies*, vol. 8, Spring/Summer, pp. 23-32.

Johnson, C. (1985). Political institutions and economic performance: The Government-business relationship in Japan, South Korea and Taiwan. In Scalapino, *et al*. (eds.). *Asian Economic Development - Present and Future*. Berkeley, California: Institute for East Asian Studies, pp. 63-89.

Kang, T.W. (1989). *Is Korea the Next Japan?*. New York: Free Press.

Katz, J. (1978). Technological change, economic development and intra and extraregional relations in Latin America. *IDB/ECLA/UNDP/IDRC Regional Programme of Studies on Scientific and Technological Development in Latin America*, Working Paper 30. Buenos Aires, Argentina.

_____ (ed.) (1982). *Technology Generation in Latin American Manufacturing Industries*. Oxford: Pergamon Press.

_____ (1984). Technological innovation and dynamic comparative advantage: Further reflections on a comparative case study programme. *Journal of Development Economics*, vol. 16, No. 12, September - October, pp. 13-37.

Kim, Linsu (1980). Stages of development of industrial technology in a developing country: A model. *Research Policy*. Amsterdam, The Netherlands, vol. 9, pp. 254-277.

Lall, S. (1975). Is "Dependence" a useful concept in analyzing underdevelopment?. *World Development*, vol. 3, Nos. 11 and 12, pp. 799-810.

_____ (1980). Developing countries as exporters of technology. *Research Policy* (Amsterdam, The Netherlands), vol. 9, pp. 24-52.

_____ (1981). Indian technology exports and technological development. *The Annals of the American Academy of Political and Social Science*, November.

_____ (1990). *Building Industrial Competitiveness in Developing Countries*. Paris: Development Centre of the Organisation for Economic Cooperation and Development.

Lockwood, W. W. (1963). *The Economic Development of Japan*. Princeton, New Jersey: Princeton University Press.

Lucas, Robert E. Jr. (1988). On the mechanics of economic development. *Journal of Monetary Economics*, vol. 22, No. 1, July.

Luostarinen, Reijo (1979). *Internationalization of the Firm.* Acta Academiae Oeconomicae Helsiniensis, Series A: 30. Helsinki, Finland: The Helsinki School of Economics.

Mansfield, Edwin (1968). *The Economics of Technological Change.* New York: Norton.

Mowery, David C. and Nathan Rosenberg (1989). *Technology and the Pursuit of Economic Growth.* Cambridge: Cambridge University Press.

National Science Board (1975). *National Indicators: The 1974 Report.* Washington, D.C.: National Science Foundation.

National Science Foundation (1989). *International Science and Technology Data Update , 1988.* Washington, D.C.: National Science Foundation.

Nelson, Richard R. (1981). Research on productivity growth and productivity differences in dead ends and new departures. *Journal of Economic Literature,* vol. 19, No. 3, September, pp. 1029-1064.

_____ (1990). Capitalism as an engine of progress. *Research Policy* (Amsterdam, The Netherlands), vol. 19, pp. 193-214.

_____ (1991). Why do firms differ, and how does it matter?, *Strategic Management Journal,* vol. 12, Special Issue, Winter, pp. 61-74.

Odagiri, H. (1983). R&D expenditures, royalty payments, and sales growth in Japanese manufacturing corporations. *Journal of Industrial Economics,* vol. 32, September, pp. 61-71.

Organisation for Economic Cooperation and Development (1992). *Technology and the Economy: The Key Ralationships.* Paris: OECD.

Ozawa, Terutomo (1992). Cross-investments between Japan and the EC: Income similarity, product variation, and economies of scope. In John Cantwell (ed.), *Multinational Investment in Modern Europe: Strategic Interaction in the Integrated Community.* Cheltenham: Edward Elgar Publishing.

Pack, Howard and Larry E. Westphal (1986). Industrial strategy and technological change. *Journal of Development Economics,* vol. 22, No. 1 June, pp. 87-128.

Patel, Pari and Keith Pavitt (1987). Is Western Europe losing the technological race? *Research Policy* (Amsterdam, The Netherlands), vol. 16, pp. 59-85.

Pearce, R.D. (1990). *The Internationalization of Research and Development.* London: MacMillan.

Porter, Michael E. (1990). *The Competitive Advantage of Nations.* New York: The Free Press.

Ramamurti, Ravi (1987). *State Owned Enterprises in High Technology Industries: Studies in India and Brazil.* New York: Praeger.

Sarathy, R. (1985). High-technology exports from newly industrializing countries: The Brazilian commuter aircraft industry. *California Management Review,* vol. 27, No. 2, Winter, pp. 60-84.

Schmitz, H. and J. Cassiolato, (eds.) (1992). *Hi-Tech for Industrial Development, Lesson from the Brazilian Experience in Electronics and Automation,* London: Routledge, for the Institute for Development Studies, Sussex University.

Servan-Schreiber, Jean Jacques (1967). *The American Challenge*. New York: The Atheneum Press.

Siddharthan, N.S. (1992). Transaction costs, technology transfer, and in-house R&D: A study of the Indian private corporate sector. *Journal of Economic Behavior and Organization*, vol. 18, pp. 265-271.

Stewart, F. (1974). Technology and employment in least developing countries. *World Development*, vol. 2, No. 3, pp. 17-46.

_____ (1977). *Technology and. Underdevelopment*. New York: Macmillan.

_____ (1979). International technology transfer: Issues and policy options, : Washington, D.C.: The World Bank Staff Working Paper.

_____ and J. James (eds.) (1982). *The Economics of New Technology in Developing Countries*. London: Frances Pinter Limited.

Stopford, John and Susan Strange (1991).*Rival States, Rival Firms; Competition for World Market Shares*. New York: Cambridge University Press.

Sunkel, O. (1969-1970). National development policy and external dependence in Latin America. *Journal of Development Studies*, vol. 6, pp. 23-48.

Teece, David J. (1977). Technology transfer by multinational firms: The resource cost of transferring technological know-how. *Economic Journal*, vol. 87, pp. 242-261.

_____ (1986). Profiting from technological innovation. *Research Policy*, (Amsterdam, The Netherlands), vol. 15, No. 6, pp. 286-305.

_____ (1992). Competition, cooperation, and innovation: Organizational arrangements for regimes of rapid technological progress. *Journal of Economic Behavior and Organization*, vol. 18, pp. 1-25.

Teitel, S. (1981). Towards an understanding of technical change in semi-industrialized countries. *Research Policy* (Amsterdam, The Netherlands), vol. 10, No. 2.

_____ (1984). Technology creation in semi-industrial economies. *Journal of Development Economics*, vol. 16, Nos. 1/2, September - October, pp. 39-61

Tigre, P. (1983). *Technology and Competition in the Brazilian Computer Industry*. Oxford: St. Martin's Press.

Transnational Corporations and Management Division, Department of Economic and Social Development (1992). *Transnational Corporations from Developing Countries: Impact on Their Home Countries* (United Nations publication, Sales No. E.93.II.A.8).

UNCTAD (1975). *Transfer of Technology: Technological Dependence: Its Nature, Consequences and Policy Implications* (TD/190).

_____ (1995). *World Investment Report 1995: Transnational Corporations and Competitiveness* (United Nations publication, Sales No. E.95.II.A.9).

_____ (1996). *World Investment Report 1996: Investment, Trade and International Policy Arrangements* (United Nations publication, Sales No. E.96.II.A.14).

UNCTC (1992a), *World Investment Report, 1992: Transnational Corporations as Engines of Growth* (United Nations publication, Sales No. E.92.II.A.19).

_____ (1992b). Foreign direct investment and industrial restructuring in Mexico. Current Studies No. 18, Series A. United Nations, New York.

_____ (1993). *Transnational Corporations from Developing Countries*, (United Nations publication, Sales No. E.93.II.A.8)

United Nations (1993). *Foreign Investment and Trade Linkages in Developing Countries* (United Nations publication, Sales No. E.93.II.A.12).

Vaitsos, C. (1974). *Intercountry Income Distribution and Transnational Enterprises*. Oxford: Clarendon Press.

Westphal, L. (1983). Empirical justification for infant industry protection. Washington, D.C.: The World Bank, Staff Working Paper No. 445.

World Bank (1992a). *World Bank Support for Industrialization in Korea, India and Indonesia*. Washington, D.C.: World Bank Operations Evaluation Department.

World Bank (1992b), *World Development Report*. Washington, D.C.: World Bank.

10

Access to networks

Albert Bressand

Introduction

To the extent that it is equated with a borderless world or with the end of geography (to use terms coined by Kenichi Ohmae and Richard O'Brien), the word globalization can be misleading. While it tends to be understood in geographic terms as the world-wide extension of markets, what is referred to as globalization is normally limited to certain parts of the world. As has been shown in chapter 1, the key features of present globalization patterns also relate less to market widening and more with the deepening of interactions among the more advanced economies, a process which goes well beyond trade and bordering on outright economic integration.

This does not mean that developing countries stand no chance to increase their role in the globalization process: on the contrary, the rapid development of the so-called emerging financial markets illustrates that newcomers can succeed not just as low-cost providers, but as magnets for capital in a highly competitive global economy. Similarly, a number of countries in East Asia have developed the productive and technological capacity to interact with developed countries, in a number of fields at least, on an almost equal footing. But as these success stories show,[1/]

globalization is an increasingly demanding process in which the relevance of comparative advantage as traditionally conceived comes to depend on a variety of other factors, including marketing channels, subcontracting relationships, real-time corporate link-ups, as well as overall political, administrative and managerial skills. The process at work is one of economic deepening, open yet centred on the more advanced parts of the world economy, rather than a natural process of market widening that would reflect arithmetic addition of customers and productive forces to the core economic zone. The term "deeper" is meant to contrast with the "shallow" arm's-length relationships that mainstream trade theory associates with the working of comparative advantage and with the ensuing process of trade specialization.[2/]

The present chapter deals with one important aspect of the deep integration agenda, namely, the role of networks in making possible closer structural relationships among economic actors. As many developing countries endeavour to accelerate the catching-up process by participating in deep integration and not simply in traditional trade specialization, the traditional strategies to seek greater access to trade will not necessarily bring about greater participation in globalization unless these strategies are rethought in terms of networking strategies which can help penetrate the linkages of deeper integration. In this respect, the policies behind Europe 1992 are a source of insights regarding the type of barriers that keep globalization less than global and the networking strategies that can help overcome them. After a brief review of the European experience, five types of networks are examined that appear central to that process, beginning with physical networks, but also encompassing financial networks, corporate co-production networks, co-regulation networks and human networks.

The European integration laboratory

The role of deepening economic integration is illustrated most vividly in the part played by regional agreements in shaping today's globalization patterns. The importance of regional agreements — in Europe, North America and parts of the Pacific Basin — reflects, in part, the complex nature of the issues that must be addressed in today's trade negotiations, as well as the "likemindedness", often necessary to address their political and cultural dimensions.[3/] While North Americans like to think of NAFTA as merely a free trade agreement, its passage has implied high degrees of convergence in the three areas that is, the environment, labour practices and judicial enforcement. Mexican policy makers have understood this need to go beyond traditional trade links and have accepted these deeper degrees of connection as a natural consequence of Mexico's entry into the OECD league. Other developing countries, notably in East Asia, have been reluctant to go much beyond shallow integration, but nevertheless are anxious not to be left out of critical networks such as computer reservation systems (for example, the Asian ABACUS network) global stock exchange quote networks and the various networks bringing world regulators together.

What makes Europe unique is the *explicit* way in which member countries have gone about addressing this new agenda. Europe is in the unique situation of having pursued political objectives at the same time as trade liberalization ones. Having learned the lessons of the failed European Defence Community in the 1950s, Jean Monnet and his followers were intent on setting, even if very gradually, the foundation for a federal Europe or, at least, for what the Maastricht Treaty now calls "an ever closer union". Trade liberalization measures have gone hand-in-hand with the development of a few common policies — over agriculture, but also over regional aid to the poorer regions, research, atomic energy and later electronics, as well as intergovernmental coordination on foreign policy. A turning point has been the Europe 1992 programme that began to be canvassed in the early 1980s. This programme extended liberalization efforts to a whole gamut of non-tariff barriers and regulatory policies.

The choice laid out in Lord Cockfield's 1985 White Paper was to base the internal market in highly regulated sectors on the principle of mutual recognition, namely, on the harmonization of a few essential parameters and the acceptance by each country of the ways in which other countries deal with the other regulatory parameters. Mutual recognition combined with the free flow of mobile factors of production launched a process of "competition between different regulatory systems ... which is free competition among different locations for internationally mobile resources, such as capital and entrepreneurship and also labour with a high content of human capital."[4/] As a result of this effort to address all types of barriers, from tax discrepancies to differing diploma requirements, "deep integration" in Europe goes well beyond the mere removal of trading restrictions to encompassing pro-active policies which foster closer relationships among actors in different European countries.

Networking is a good generic term for a number of the links that developed within Europe above and beyond the mere movement of goods. Indeed, a number the constituents of the Europe 1992 programme are specifically aimed at facilitating or fostering various types of cross-border networking strategies, whether in the technical sense of setting up pan-European communication networks or in the broader sense of fostering cooperative endeavours among actors. Five types of networks are especially relevant, as illustrated by the following examples.

(i)   *General purpose pan-European networks.* Closer interconnection of European road and railway networks has been one of the first tasks of the European Investment Bank and is now pursued in the form of the channel tunnel and of pan-European "TGV" train networks.

Since the mid-1980s, the development of a Europe-wide broad band Integrated Services Digital Network (ISDN) grid has been pursued notably through the RACE programme (Research on Advanced Communication in Europe). Geared towards the objective of a unified market for telecommunication equipment and information services, this effort was a formidable industrial policy objective in its own right, which is still far from achieved. Meanwhile, the Group Special Mobile (GSM) set up to promote a unified approach to mobile telephony has been extremely successful at making it possible to use the same portable phones from anywhere in Europe (and now in the many parts of the world that have adopted GSM standards).

Trans-European networks are described in the Maastricht Treaty as an essential foundation of the opening of each European economy to other European actors. The White Paper, presented by Jacques Delors to the European Council in Brussels on 11 and 12 December, 1993, puts forward common objectives, regarding the "information super highways" on the model of "National Information Infrastructures" put forward by Vice-President Al Gore in the United States.[5/]

(ii)   *Financial networks.* The London "big bang" of 1984 led to the creation of the SEAQ international network (Stock Exchange Automated Quote) that allows shares of blue chip companies from all major European countries to be traded on the same screens. The French futures market MATIF is connecting with its German equivalent, the

Deutsche Termin Börse (DTB) to lay the foundations of an integrated European market for derivative products.

(iii)   *Corporate networks to facilitate co-production.* The European Commission has given its blessing to the development of Europe-wide electronic networks bringing together market participants in sectors such as travel services, pharmaceuticals, chemicals, electronic banking services etc. The Amadeus and Galileo computer reservation systems are now at the centre of the restructuring and strategic alliance process reshaping the European airlines industry and influencing its transatlantic linkups, while the TEDIS programme promotes cross-border Electronic Data Interchange (EDI) among corporations in two dozen economic sectors, ranging from pharmaceuticals to insurance.

The European Commission had launched as early as 1984 the pace-setting programme followed by a number of similar, more specialized programmes to facilitate cross-border cooperation in precompetitive R&D. At the French urging, European Governments have followed suit with the more flexible, closer to market, EUREKA programme in which some non-European countries (Canada) are also involved. Hungary became the twentieth member of EUREKA at the Tampere meeting in 1992 and the June 1993 Paris meeting witnessed preliminary — and rather positive — discussions of the Russian candidacy.

(iv)   *Co-regulation networks.* The effort to eliminate regulatory obstacles has led to the creation of new standards-setting forums such as the European Telecommunications Standardization Institute (ETSI), in which telecommunication agencies (PTTs), manufacturers and users come together to develop common standards. The July 1987 Green Book set the stage for the development of Europe-wide intracorporate and transcorporate networks, as well as of value-added networks in general, with 1998 now the deadline for full liberalization of basic telecom networks.

(v)   *Human networks.* Meanwhile, the encouragement of cross-border, multilingual studies and research by students, teachers and scientists represents the counterpart for private citizens of these corporate networking programmes. Under the ERASMUS programme, students enrolled in a curriculum of three years or more can complete part of their home-country diploma in another country. Under the COMET programme, professors and researchers can pursue their work, and be credited for it, in other European countries.

Albert Bressand

Networks as relational management tools

As shown by these European examples, many different types of networks are involved to facilitate deep integration, from fibre optic links to cooperative R&D programmes. Yet, understanding what is implied by networks is a more complex task than one might imagine.

Indeed, the word network means something quite different to a geographer, a communication expert, an economist or an anthropologist, and yet all definitions are somehow relevant to the problem developing countries face in accessing supposedly global markets. Obstacles to full participation on their part can stem from poor access to efficient transportation networks, from being unable to plug into data networks, as well as from having no "connection" to the human networks in which creative ideas are shared and shaped. How can one go about analysing such a diverse challenge?

The role of networks is better understood if one looks at them not as infrastructures in the traditional sense, but as relational management tools.[6/] They are, indeed, an integral part of alliance capitalism, the nature and implications of which were dealt with in chapter 1. Their growing prominence reflects the role that closer relationships between customers, suppliers and partners play in the competitiveness of firms today. Defined as relational management tools, networks are equally relevant to the manufacturing and services sectors. More precisely, networks is define as a set of technical means — or infrastructures — combined with a set of strategic rules — or infostructures — enabling actors with rights of access to set up and manage value-creating relationships among themselves.

This definition covers informal cooperation arrangements, as well as traditional delivery systems and sophisticated electronic links. Its three components (infrastructures, infostructures, and initiatives) reflect the fact that three types of continuities are called for in the joint production of economic value, namely:

(i) *Physical communication* (contact) through delivery systems, telecommunication links or just interpersonal contacts;

(ii) *Organizational and legal continuity* (contract), whether through hierarchies, markets or formal contracts; and

(iii) *Strategic complementarity* (common goals), in the sense that actors must not only be linked, but must also agree on specific goals to be achieved in common.

308

Seen in this light, networks are a critical tool behind mass-customization — a word coined in 1987 to describe the combination of economies of scale and of tailor-made products — central to the search for competitiveness and innovation-led growth in many sectors of the advanced economies.[7] The move from mass-production strategies towards mass-customization reflects the lower communication and other costs at which actors are able to forge even more deepening relationships with one another.[8]

Networks are indeed the tools allowing actors to enter into deeper relations, and to do so with a level of effectiveness proportionate to present technological capacities. The five types of networks identified in the case of Europe 1992 can help us organize an analysis of the connections that developing countries need to establish so as to take part as full participants in the globalization process. For each of these five categories of networks, the global trends that developing countries should bear in mind will first be presented and, second, some of the direct implications of these trends for them.

General purpose networks

There is nothing new in the fact that infrastructures, as traditionally defined, are an indispensable support of economic interactions: the role of transportation networks, energy networks and telecommunications networks is almost self-evident. Yet, in the globalizing economy of the mid-1990s, the nature of these infrastructures and the links between them are undergoing significant changes. True, roads and ports still look like roads and ports, but it is clear, for instance, that the role of containers in present transportation techniques implies that port authorities around the world enter into much closer cooperation regarding, first, norms and equipment and, second, the information-processing activities that have become an integral part of moving containers around. Beyond the networks of port authorities themselves, cooperation must also develop with custom authorities (national and foreign) so as to allow the efficient and timely clearing of merchandise. Meanwhile, multimodal transportation — the seamless movement of containers on sea, rail and road links — calls for even other types of connection with trucking and rail companies. Eventually, being able to offer satisfactory docking facilities to foreign ships becomes only one small element in the far more complex challenge that countries face in order to connect to today's global transportation networks.

Information technology is clearly a central component behind this new generation of infrastructures. The greatly increased ease and reach of global communication calls for a reassessment of the ways in which both firms and markets in one country are structurally linked to those in other countries. At a time when companies follow zero-inventory techniques and leave no productivity stone unturned, "moving" goods is no longer enough. Goods must also be tracked, and providing real-time information about where they are and when they can actually be delivered is becoming an essential part of transportation. Increasingly, purchasers of components are operating their own plants under the assumption that their suppliers are able to guarantee delivery on schedule and can be brought into close partnership when needed. Information technology allows the creation of common production units from previously separated processing activities. Electronic networks combine their impact with that of other links, whether financial, physical or human. More generally, taking part in today's deep integration depends critically on a variety of networks that draw on electronic *and* non-electronic means, on public *and* private components.

To illustrate how these different types of networks combine their effects and change the nature of the barriers faced by developing countries, let us consider the case of an airline company from a developing country trying to gain market share in the air transportation market. First, and most obviously, that company needs to gain access to the physical infrastructure: landing rights are only the beginning of the story as time slots (when planes can land and depart from a given airport) and well situated gateways have become the scarce resources in major airports. Second, it must find ways to have its flights displayed on the computer reservation systems of the major companies, which may involve some form of alliance in addition to technical cooperation. Third, that same company needs to plug into a complex web of relationships involving maintenance, airport services, and training and, increasingly, agreements regarding frequent flyer programmes. Credit cards, mail ordering and airphones (which are in the process of becoming a standard feature on many routes) are additional loops in that intricate web. At a time when Western companies enter into code sharing agreements, in order to provide customers with single entry points into their complex

310

systems, it is not really possible to compete in the major markets without pro-active strategies within that network of networks.

Changes are as much organizational and financial as technical. Whereas developing countries are accustomed to thinking in terms of *national* networks that interconnect to one another, their trade partners in the North have begun to look for single entry points or "one-stop shopping" solutions, whereby one network operator can act as intermediary between them, other networks and their partners wherever they are. Developing countries need only look at the European scene to see that national network operators are now involved in ambitious alliances — such as *Eutelnet* in the case of FRANCE TELECOM and Deutsche Telekom or *Syncordia* in the case of BT and MCI — to provide their global clients with one-point shopping global solutions.

Beyond such alliances, a new generation of network operators are presently knocking at the door. An elite group of network operators are actually able to design and operate, truly global networks. Motorola and its Iridium project — a set of 66 satellites allowing subscribers to reach any other user from any point on earth — is the most spectacular example. In order to carry out this ambitious project (which draws in part on the Reagan period's Strategic Defence Initiative), Motorola has been able to bring together an international consortium in which five Japanese blue chip companies coexist with the Great Wall Industry Corp., the industrial arm of the Chinese army, as well as with Krunichev, the Russian rocket maker and with Veba, a German electricity company intent on competing with Deutsche Telekom. The 1992 ITU conference at Torremolinos has set aside frequencies for such low earth orbit (LEO) and medium earth orbit (MEO) satellite systems and a fierce competition is raging among half a dozen similar consortia, as well as the Inmarsat organization. In most of these global mobile communication projects, many developing countries seem to be considered as little more than exotic places where global-minded corporate travellers may happen to have to be reached. The exception is the *Teledesic* project put forward by multibillionaires Bill Gates and Craig McCaw. Rather than offering hyper-mobility to a few hundred thousand business travellers, *Teledesic* would draw on no less than 840 small LEO satellites to connect institutions in the developing world (such as hospitals, schools and public offices) to the global information highways.[9/]

Against that background, "missing links" are becoming increasingly apparent: in its seminal 1984 report, the Independent Commission for World-wide Telecom Development (Maitland Commission[10]) underlined that connection to the global world as primarily a matter of access to the basic telecom networks. Yet, 75 per cent of the 700 million phones were concentrated in only eight countries, while the developing world accounts for only 7 per cent of this number. To put it in demographic terms, 85 per cent of the world population had access to only 15 per cent of the phones meaning, for example, that there are fewer phones in the entire African continent than in the city of Tokyo. The discrepancy is made worse by the pronounced imbalance, in developing countries, between urban and rural areas: installing a traditional phone line is five times more costly on average in the village than in the city. Only 5 per cent of Indian villages have access to the national network, a situation closely parallel to that in Central and Eastern European countries, where those few phones that exist in rural areas have been described, at best, as quasi-phones, namely, phones shared among many and with only intermittent access to a working line.[11]

Correcting some of these imbalances in terms of access to information infrastructures should be a major goal of development policies. China for instance is now aiming to have 100 million phone lines in place by the end of the decade, a fivefold increase in the situation of the late 1980s. Developing countries and international organizations could reflect notably on the STAR programme, whereby the European Community helps accelerate the connection of less developed regions to the telecommunications grid. But this is only one aspect of the challenge as outward-looking companies will also be looking for a seamless connection to the rest of the world. Efficient trade relations depend on an increasingly complex "network of networks", of which traditional infrastructures are only one element.

Financial integration networks

The financial community has long been a prime user of advanced computer-related communication facilities – witness the creation in the 1960s of the SWIFT interbank network outside of the then almighty PTT monopoly, and the massive outlays of Citicorp to integrate operations across borders! Today, electronic networks continue to play an essential role in the development of financial integration and in the increasing autonomy of financial flows with respect to trade. Short-term foreign exchange trading worth 250 billion dollars, for instance, are channelled every day through the unregulated Reuters network linking 150,000 computer monitor screens around the world. More generally, the 24-hour round-the-world financial market rests on electronic networks for quote dissemination, as well as clearing and settlement and, increasingly, for transactions themselves. Repeating the quotation of Richard O'Brien, identified in chapter 1, global financial integration is bringing about "the end of geography". [12]

But, in addition, networks are now forging a new relationship between markets and territories, between domestic regulations and international politics. NASDAQ, the world's third largest stock market, consists of 160,000 terminals in the United States and 30,000 terminals in 45 other countries linking together a network of 370 American and British firms that have committed over 1 billion dollars in capital to act as market-makers. Its strength also lies in the computerized Stock Watch System programmed to refer any unusual pattern to analysts for review. Similarly, Reuters has now developed, at the request of the Chicago Mercantile Exchange (CME) and its partners, the GLOBEX network, on which French and United States Futures contracts can be traded during market closing time as if this were one single market. Agreements among the French and United States supervisory authorities allow GLOBEX to function above the Atlantic under joint supervision. Clearly, what is at stake are not just electronic "tools", but a different way to organize a market and to make it work across borders.

This creative interplay between computers, networks, rules and markets is not limited to Europe and North America, as it can be seen at work as far away as off the coast of Borneo where the island of Labuan — which few would cite as a hub in the world of financial markets — "is being transformed into an effective international offshore financial centre with liberal regulations and state-of-the-art communication" [13] or in the Stock Exchange of Thailand (SET) now drawing up its own software, in partnership with the United States Midwest market, to accommodate more than 100,000 transactions per day. [14] The Singapore financial and monetary authorities have been able to link the Singapore futures market, SIMEX, to the Chicago Mercantile Exchange through cross-trading agreements. Investors can therefore move Eurodollar contracts across the two exchanges in an almost seamless fashion, thereby giving Singapore a leading edge not just over other Asian exchanges, but also over the GLOBEX network set in place between the CME, its arch-rival the Chicago Board of Trade (CBOT) and the Paris MATIF.

Developing countries have begun to connect to the large international networks that have now become critical to financial back-offices world-wide. The trend, however, has still a long way to go and it was only, for instance, in the early 1990s that Latin American exchanges began to explore ways in which they could link to EUROCLEAR, one of the two global networks fulfilling clearing and settlement functions for international and domestic bond markets. At the present time, most of the EUROCLEAR membership is still to be found in the developed countries, a factor contributing to what is still a two-tier financial system.

Co-production and corporate networks

Globalization is not simply about flows of products and of money, it is also about the production process itself. In addition to "exchanging" value as embedded in products and in money, corporations are increasingly able to, and interested in, integrating their production processes closely enough to reduce inventories, combine skills and otherwise achieve the type of efficiency that could be realized previously only within a single production unit. Hence one of the critical differences between the TNCs of previous decades and today's global enterprises.

The TNCs of the 1960s were usually seeking a combination of (1) economies of scale through geographic concentration capitalizing on the product cycle (Vernon) and (2) access to less than fully open markets through the creation of foreign affiliates managed in a relatively decentralized or stand-alone fashion (UNCTAD 1993). By contrast, "globals" are integrated production systems in which the type of links among production sites in different countries does not differ from the links among production units inside a given national company. High-speed data links between plants, research centres and offices, as well as the diversity of inter-personal communication modes (fax, electronic mail, mobile communication), are critical to that level of globalization. In particular, private corporate networks like DECNET are one of the most rapidly developing part of the global telecommunication arena; the depth of relationship that they make possible gives global corporations a different profile and management style from that of TNCs. Their output can also be global in the sense that local customers are provided with complex combinations of software, services and/or material components assembled on a customized basis drawing on the whole network of plants and corporate facilities. Innovation-led growth and mass-customization often calls for in-depth corporate alliances allowing each company to specialize on exploiting its core competencies, as well as participate in standardization forums, in industry coalitions or even in joint R&D programmes to ensure the connectability of their advanced products.[15/]

Costs and benefits can be very large as the price tag for a major private or cooperative network is often in the half billion dollar range:

(i)   The Wal-Mart supermarket communication system cost $700 million;

(ii)   The Amadeus and Galileo reservation systems cost $150 to $350 million;

(iii)   The failed Taurus clearing and settlement network cost $ 800 million;

(iv)   Development of the Reuters 2000 network: $ 130 million per year.

Corporate strategies rely increasingly on the development of four different types of networks that need to be somehow internationalized for deep integration to be a truly global phenomenon.[16/]

(i)   *Intracorporate networks* (distribution and data management systems within a single firm): The main objective of these networks is to improve coordination of day-to-day activities by enabling end-users within the same company to share information and processing capacities irrespective of geographic location. Electronic networks allow real-time transmission, processing and distribution of information related to customers, as well as remote interaction between plants. They play a key role in making it possible to manage global networks of plants as integrated production facilities and in moving from the traditional product out vision (in which products are created and then marketed) to the market in vision in which production is a direct function of demand. As mentioned above, companies like Nissan, DEC, Citicorp have put such networks at the center of their search for higher productivity and better responsiveness to customers' demands.

(ii)   *Transcorporate networks* (data systems shared between firms): Transcorporate networking takes the form of electronic links between a company and its closest suppliers, customers and partners enabling them to coordinate around shared information, in a much more integrated fashion than used to be possible. In addition to reducing or eliminating paper transactions, extensive use of electronic networks makes possible the exchange of increasingly detailed and customized data flows. General Motors and Boeing have pioneered the use of Electronic Data Interchange (EDI) as a way to achieve higher integration with suppliers and/or clients. European car manufacturers and chemical companies are among those following suit.

(iii) *Inter-corporate networks* (joint ventures and strategic alliances): Corporate alliances of all sorts are a means of addressing the higher order information needs in a world where information on technology, customers and markets calls for increasingly sophisticated approaches. While cross-border corporate alliances are often perceived, notably by US companies, as a second-best strategy compared to direct exports or to the creation of a fully-owned subsidiary, they reflect the blurring of national and sectoral borders. They are also testimony to the fact that the higher level of specialization sought by many firms must be accompanied by alliances and cooperation arrangements of all types if final users are to be provided with the integrated solutions they are looking for. Inter-corporate networks of alliances such as the ones put in place by AT&T with Olivetti, Philips, Telefonica and others, help corporations meet the complex and demanding needs of accessing technological know-how and of customizing products to local demand, with greater timeliness, flexibility and efficiency.[17]

(iv) *Metacorporate networks* (business lobbies and private standards organizations): These networks aim to improve the political and market environment in which a group of firms operate. Lobbying associations are a traditional example. But metacorporate networks are now multiplying above borders as a response to the need to set and implement common information technology standards. In Europe, the ESPRIT programme has led not only to hundreds of specific R&D joint-ventures but also to information sharing among all participating companies, to specific rules of access to technological know-how and detailed rules governing intellectual property regarding research results.

Intracorporate and transcorporate networks allow the discharge of coordination functions central to the global management of the production process. Intercorporate and metacorporate networks, on the other hand, are set up to link up actors with complementary strategic roles: they serve to organize flows of higher-order information (knowledge) rather than data flows. Together, those four types of corporate networks allow firms to enter into relationships going well beyond arm's length relations.

Developing countries have only begun to explore the implications of these closer corporate link ups, with the obvious exception of traditional types of joint ventures that connect foreign firms with local partners. Being able to "plug" into many of these networks depends in part on the availability of adequate infrastructures. But the "missing links" are also a consequence of differences in corporate culture and of the difficulty to operate sophisticated links such as EDI networks across very different regulatory environments. Hence the importance of the fourth networking level, the one we refer to as co-regulation.

Regulatory networks and co-regulation

The advanced communication infrastructures, the global financial networks and the cross-border corporate networks that we have just described are major forces behind the blurring of the line between domestic policies and international relations. As a result, policy makers and regulators are also drawn into much closer cross-border relationships. In today's advanced economies, privately defined rules and standards are closely intertwined with public regulations. The "free market for free men" called for by the Chicago futures' exchange motto is now based on computer-assisted program trading and across the globe quote-dissemination networks like the Globex network that we briefly described above: such markets just could not exist in the absence of elaborate "infostructures" connecting through a diversity of domestic regulatory frameworks. Hence, national regulations in many fields need to be harmonized and they need to be developed by national authorities and constituencies with foreign regulations as a permanent reference. This process does not amount to supranational regulation of a "world government" type but, rather, to a diffuse process of convergence that we have labelled co-regulation.[18/] Co-regulation can range from complete harmonization to orderly procedures to facilitate dispute settlement. Somewhere along this spectrum, special attention is now given to mutual recognition, a principle pioneered by European banking authorities and by the world's securities industry.[19]

A number of developing countries are now taking this need for co-regulation into accounts through a number of formal or informal networks. An important forum in this respect is the International Organisation of Securities Commissions (IOSCO), which brings together regulators from a large number of stock exchanges. The 13 strong Technical Committee of IOSCO is a key place for the type of regulatory convergence now essential to the world financial markets, and developing countries like Mexico have recently begun to play a much more active role in these debates. Here again, however, there is still a long way to go before developing countries — leaving aside a few newly industrialized ones — are fully at home in such networks, but important initiatives are already underway.

In the fall of 1994, for instance, as part of NAFTA, the Mexican Stock Exchange (*Bolsa de Valores*) has begun to accept foreign securities firms as full members as long as they are incorporated in the United States or Canada (including therefore the United States affiliates of Deutsche Bank or Paribas Capital Markets). Mexican stock exchange authorities have also drawn a list of foreign exchanges with which interactions should be greatly facilitated from a regulatory standpoint: as a starting point, they have listed the exchanges from the 13 countries members of the IOSCO Technical Committee, illustrating the role of such networks in facilitating deeper integration. Not unrelated to these global networking strategies, the clearing and settlement arm of the Bolsa de Valores, INDEVAL, is leading a Latin American effort to upgrade and connect stock exchange back offices.

The challenge for developing countries

Hence, from a developing countries' perspective, access to networks is an important element in the move from traditional trade integration toward the complex patterns of competition and cooperation characteristic of todays globalizing economy. An initial tendency may be to deal with access to networks in a fashion similar to that of trade barriers: developing countries will tend to ask that such access be granted to them in the same way that they would ask for a quota to be dismantled. Such an objective, however, would be quite elusive — in some cases, almost futile. Gaining access to relation management tools is a complex undertaking as it involves taking part in an open-ended set of relationships that other actors have already set up among themselves. Electronic Data Interchange (EDI) networks, for example, require very specific skills, procedures and overall work organization on the part of the corporations wishing to take part. Non-electronic networks, such as strategic alliances or cooperative R&D arrangements, obviously cannot be accessed without in-depth preparation and agreements. The European experience shows that pro-active, cooperative policies are needed.

Companies from developing countries requesting access to a computer reservation system realize that physical operations must conform to a set of common standards. They also realize that taking advantage of the system assumes that they can define a whole new set of strategies with respect to types of tariff and links with customers through such things as frequent flyer programs: the movement of data is more than a passive image of physical movements as it leads to a new perspective on the physical operations as well as on the products, prices and strategies.

Similarly, banks were used to provide companies that engage in international trade with credits (documentary credit) anticipating the receipts expected from trade with foreign countries. Traditionally, this was one of the most paper-work intensive and least imaginative type of financing. As banks and companies now begin to interact through EDI networks, one can see a major change in the spirit presiding to the use of this traditional instrument. Because they are linked through an EDI network, because they have had to harmonize and to learn about one another's procedures, banks and companies have had to enter into a "club" type of relationship. In that case, trust is a by-product of steps taken in the mundane domain of data processing.[20] For developing countries, this is both a new barrier and a new opportunity. It is a new barrier because being accepted into the club assumes much more demanding and costly procedures in which cultural and geographic distance can be exacerbated rather than reduced. It is a new opportunity because participants able to overcome those barriers will gain access to another level of interaction, opening the possibility to offer new types of information intensive services (such as those related to corporate cash management). Banks from developing countries need therefore to develop the skills to use the EDI network to full potential rather than simply to gain access to the physical network itself.

So, altogether, what developing countries are really seeking to access involves not only some well defined networks, but also far more complex sets of networking tools and networking skills. Part of the difficulty of giving concrete meaning to the access to networks lies in the discrepancy between traditional concepts of trade barriers (obstacles that governments can remove at the stroke of a pen, at least in theory) and this complex, dynamic web of two-way relationships: "gaining access to" is often a short name for "entering into relationship with".

Figure 1 summarizes this more complex nature of "access" by showing the various levels that can be involved. The concrete process of "establishing" access to a given network needs to be analysed in terms of several successive steps, from mere physical connection to various levels of interaction, which range from discrete contributions to the creation of new products and to the definition of shared objectives among network members. Mutual expectations, common standards, compatible national regulations and a shared sense of purpose are some of the dimensions that can be addressed for network access to be more than a superficial connection.

Figure 2 illustrates both this critical role of global data networks and the fact that they are part of a broader network of networks (N^2) in

Figure 1. "Access" as Relational Ping-Pong
The shadow *give* behind the *take*

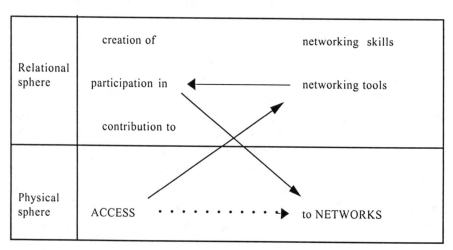

**Figure 2. Global Data Networks Shaping Interactions:
A Metaphoric Illustration**

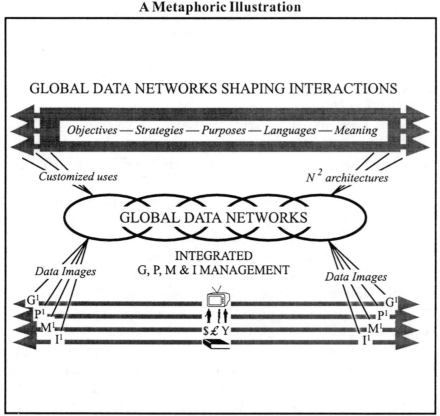

which the strategic positioning of actors calls for skills well beyond traditional comparative advantages.

An agenda for north-south re-linking

The real issue therefore is not access to networks per se, but the ways in which developing countries want to take part in deep integration, a stage in globalization that is qualitatively different from previous stages. Different countries will be inclined to give different answers to that question, and the European experience cannot be generalized into a universal model (indeed, within Europe itself, there are quite different views of what the model is). Four levels can be identified to help developing countries identify and articulate their own strategies.

Level one - Not to be excluded. The most basic imperative is to keep abreast of the restructuring under way in the advanced economies. While a few examples have gradually gained visibility (such as computer reservation systems), most developments take place within the private sphere, outside any public monitoring or oversight. The challenge is to create *transparency* rather than to define "codes of conduct" that would be seen as negating the market logic which brings economic actors into networking in the first place. The United Nations system would need to broaden the coverage of the reports and documents that it makes available to developing countries with a view to encompassing the networking process under way.

In some sectors, *registries* might be developed as a contribution by the United Nations system to enhance transparency. This could be done using the above typology with respect to:

(i)   Communication networks and computerized on-line value-added services of importance to developing countries;

(ii)   Financial networks (for example, cooperative networks and third-party networks that are used to track and/or take part in financial markets);

(iii)   Corporate co-production networks, to the extent that they define themselves as open and take the initiative to bring their activities to the attention of the United Nations (many franchise networks would do so, but a number of manufacturers might be enticed to use what could be a clearing house, or rather a "yellow pages directory" for subcontracting and partnerships;

(iv)   Co-regulation networks: in one sense, this would be the most easily done, although a clear and concise description of the work done and of the ways to access it would not be trivial; and,

(v)   Human networks, a much too broad category to be addressed as a whole, but, henceforth, a vast domain from which to select networks of special relevance to developing countries. Education, fellowships and exchange programmes come to mind, but the responsible United Nations outfit could look at this — and at the overall registry endeavour — with a mixture of imagination and discipline.

In recent years, the United Nations has become a source of insights into the globalization process. It should be encouraged to raise awareness of changing globalization patterns *and* to provide opportunities for member countries to develop consensual approaches on these emerging issues.

Level two - PGMI norms. Flows of people, goods, money and information (in short, PGMI) are increasingly managed through information processing. Norms and standards pertaining to these "electronic images" of people, goods, money and information, including rights of privacy, intellectual property rights and the like have therefore an important impact on a country's capacity to position itself and create value. Developing countries participation in PGMI flows increasingly depends on their capacity to keep track of those norms and to take part in the public and private processes behind them. The measures agreed upon as part of the Uruguay Round of multilateral trade negotiations are only a beginning: here again, there is an important agenda for the United Nations system, the World Intellectual Property Organization (WIPO) and specialized agencies.

One example of such norms has to do, quite straightforwardly, with custom systems. One of the first steps taken by developing countries embarking on the journey towards a free trade zone or a custom union (for example, countries of the Central American Integration System) is to harmonize custom typologies and definitions. Similarly, as a prelude between a possible free trade zone between the MERCOSUR countries (Brazil, Argentina, Uruguay and Paraguay) and the European Union, custom typologies and procedures are presently being compared and improved with technical support from the EC Commission. Similar efforts could be undertaken within the United Nations system to make custom typologies, procedures and tariffs more transparent for potential partners in all countries with a view to facilitating future trade agreements.

Another example could be the conditions under which securities (bonds and stocks) from developing countries can be considered as investment grade or "blue chips" by investors from any part of the world. Presently, this question is answered mostly in two ways: listing on the United States markets in the form of American Depository Receipts (ADR) and the rating that can be conferred by a few respected private entities like Moodies and Standard & Poor. A better connection of developing countries to the largest capital markets could be achieved if internationally accepted ratings could be granted, with greater room for initiatives by corporations and market authorities in the developing world. In this respect, developing countries may seek inspiration from the European debate around the *Eurolist* project. The objective of the project is, first, to draw attention to hundreds of companies that can be considered to be "European class" (or world class) by giving them, after appropriate audit the Eurolist label. Second, the objective is to facilitate the simultaneous listing of such companies on several European stock exchanges by using the same prospectus and by providing a discount on listing fees in case of multiple applications. The attractiveness of the "emerging markets" could be increased by a "worldlist" label to be granted by a private group of high standing (in which Moodies and Standard & Poor could well be represented, together with federations of stock exchanges). Such an idea could be further developed in a "Group of Thirty" type of report that the United Nations system could help commission.

Level three - Participation in global data network. Most data networks must be seen as private undertakings and there is little that can or should be imposed to establish access for developing countries. Yet, a small number of such networks are becoming global utilities all but in name. As figure 3 suggests, networks can go through a life cycle that sees them evolve from purely proprietary status to that of an "infrastructure" for a sector as a whole: in many ways, this is what has happened to the largest Computer Reservation Systems (SABRE) when the United States Department of Justice found it necessary to impose a code of conduct upon the companies (such as American Airlines) operating such systems. Rather than through abstract codes of conduct, developing countries access to these networks would probably be enhanced by engaging the network operators themselves in the type of dialogue that they understand to be in their best long-term interest.

The contribution of the United Nations system to this move towards "global information utilities" could reside in:

(i)   Helping to meet part of the cost and training involved in developing countries' participation in such networks; and

(ii)   Helping to develop competition rules to make sure that developing countries are not excluded from the interactions made possible by essential networks.

Level four - Participation in strategic networking. Obviously, there is little that can be done through international organizations to ease access by developing countries actors to the commanding heights of a global networked economy. Here, the European experience can be useful as a source of inspiration for similar endeavours among specific groups of

Figure 3. When Private Networks Become "Essential Facilities"

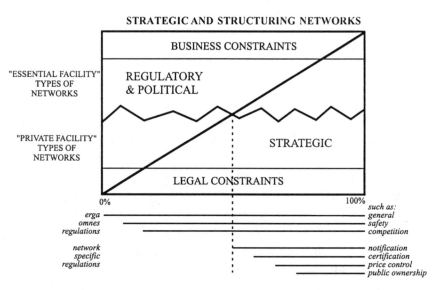

STRATEGIC AND STRUCTURING NETWORKS

The percentage on the horizontal axis refers to the proportion of actors in a given sector who need to use a given network in order to remain competitive. Overtime, some networks become indispensable tools that no actor can afford not to utilize. Hence, a tendency in the society at large to apply an increasing gamut of regulations to network operations as such trends develop. The above diagram is based notably on United States and European experience with Computer Reservation Systems.

countries. One can think of pilot projects — such as regional computer reservation systems on the ABACUS model or electronic banking applications — that could be the focal point of international cooperation. In particular, the European experience brings to light two different organizational models that developing countries may find relevant: the ESPRIT model, and the EUREKA model.

The ESPRIT programme is intended to foster cooperation among European companies. It was launched in 1984 around a set of R&D objectives in the information technology field. The European Commission provides a level of financial support intended to compensate for the added cost of cross-border cooperation as opposed to a purely national approach.

Originally ESPRIT had three concrete aims pragmatically determined in discussions between the Commission and industry:

(i)   To create a technology base designed to make European information technology competitive — now and in the future — with the United States and Japan;

(ii)   To promote cooperation between IT companies, research institutes and universities in Europe; and,

(iii)   To contribute to the development of standards.

The ESPRIT model is easily transplanted into the setting of an international organization, as it keeps at least one step away from market applications and as its focus is on reducing obstacles to cross-border networking. The contribution of industrial companies is essential — not only do they have the required knowledge, they should also participate in the projects and implement the results. ESPRIT also includes a deliberate financial and administrative effort to make Europe more competitive, with its focus on "pre-competitive" research, and the effort to stimulate participation by the less-industrialized regions of the Community, a feature most appreciated by Spain, Portugal and Ireland.

Wisse Dekker, the Chairman of Philips, in evaluating the results of the first eight years of ESPRIT in 1992 (before the launch of the third phase), emphasized that ESPRIT had indeed "a significant catalytic effect" on industrial restructuring and that it could contribute to a fuller exploitation of the promises of information technology. Such objectives are shared by developing and developed countries alike and United Nations agencies should be encouraged to put forward a global ESPRIT focused on sectors with strong public goods dimensions, such as health, the environment, software compatibility, advanced languages and the freer flows of scientific knowledge. In so doing, however, one should bear in mind the problems highlighted by Dekker, and notably the tendency of governments to give excessive prominence to "juste retour" (fair return) and other distributive principles (small versus large companies, universities versus companies etc). In his words: "non-technical criteria should be omitted as much as possible. Employees' technical merits, capabilities of the laboratories, organizational skills, and scientific and (in the end) industrial relevance should be the sole criteria in the selection of project partners and of the projects themselves."[21] In a sense, a global ESPRIT programme would serve the same "labelling" function for hi-tech corporations from developing countries as the "world list project" for corporate shares (indeed such projects would be mutually reinforcing).

The second model suggested by the European experience, EUREKA, does not lend itself to outright generalization as its objective is clearly to improve the competitive situation of European-based companies *vis-à-vis* Japanese and United States ones. EUREKA was set up in 1985 as a European answer to the R&D programmes triggered by the United States "Strategic Defense Initiative". Projects must be jointly submitted by companies or laboratories from two European countries at least, and they must embody concrete objectives regarding the production of advanced goods, services or processes for the international market. Between November 1985 and the end of 1993, more than 800 projects have been launched for a total of 15.3 billion ECUs. Each project involves between two and a dozen partners. Here again, the EUREKA label is considered an important help in itself for the research team and a facilitator of further administrative help. It can trigger co-financing by participating governments and the Commission, depending on each country's policy, with 35 per cent of financial support a frequent figure. While this description belongs more in the domain of regional or national industrial policy (with the United States Sematech programme another good example), an evaluation of actual programme results shows that participating companies' motivations are less easily contained within regional borders as the most widely quoted motivations were:

(i)   Risk sharing (38 per cent) and investment sharing (30 per cent);

(ii)   The need for complementary scientific and technical skills (32 per cent); and,

(iii)   Help (usually for smaller companies) in identifying foreign partners (32 per cent).

While only 20 per cent to 25 per cent of the participating companies mentioned new products or higher competitiveness as their prime motive for joining EUREKA, most of them looked at it as a way to establish potentially useful links with renowned companies and academic centres of excellence.

From a global perspective, what makes EUREKA interesting is the new type of cooperation that it embodies between the private sector (which must take the initiative, to a much higher degree than in ESPRIT), governments (which cooperate in subgroups of different membership on a case-by-case basis) and international organizations (in that case the

327

European Commission, which provides a minority share of the financing and organizational help). Also, such programmes have an important role to play in fostering the development of the human networks that play an invisible but essential role in globalization.

Both ESPRIT and EUREKA illustrate that the time is coming for international organizations to rethink their mode of operation in light of the more complex realities of deep integration in a world where public and private initiatives are increasingly intertwined and in which domestic and international policies can no longer be clearly separated.

The actions briefly sketched here cannot by themselves ensure access of developing countries to the many networks behind today's globalization patterns. Yet, taken together, they give a sense that international cooperation can and should adapt to remain relevant in the age of deep integration, the age of the global networked economy. The United Nations has played a significant role in addressing some of these complex issues — witness the importance of the EDIFACT norms in facilitating world-wide exchange of trade and production related data. A similar role should be explored in other areas.

Notes

1. See for example the World Bank (1993).
2. The difference between shallow and deep integration had been explored by the Integrating National Economies programme of the Brookings Institution. See also chapter 1 of the present volume.
3. Bressand, Devos, Raby and Woolcock (1994).
4. H. Giersch. *Europe 1992 in an Open World Order*, Hamburg, 1988. p. 5.
5. On information infrastructures, see C. Distler (1994).
6. See Bressand and Distler (1995).
7. See Bressand and Nicolaïdis (1989). The term mass-customization has since then been further developed by B.J. Pine (1993).
8. Such relationships are akin to inter-firm "deep" integration.
9. See Bressand (1994).
10. ITU (1984).
11. See Ehrlich (1993).
12. See R. O'Brien, *Global Financial Integration, The End of Geography*. London: Pinter Publications.
13. *Euromoney* (1992), "Labuan, an international offshore centre", September, Special Supplement.
14. Towie (1991) and interviews of Thai participants in the Vienna FIBV technology workshop of September 1992.
15. The significance of a firm's effective coordination of its own assets with the complementary assets supplied by other firms is analysed by Teece (1992).

16. See PROMETHEE (1989) and Bressand (1990).
17. For further examples see Gugler and Dunning (1993).
18. For an example of co-regulation in the financial field, see Saint-Geours (1992). Jean Saint-Geours is the Chairman of the French Commission des Opérations de Bourse and of the Technical Committee of the International Organisation of Securities Commissions (IOSCO).
19. Under mutual recognition, countries need to agree upon a limited number of important common regulatory principles on the basis of which they can accept that economic actors develop their activities under the regulatory oversight of their home country. For example, the international consensus regarding prudential ratios for banks, developed in the framework of the Cooke Committee of the Bank for International Settlements (BIS), provided a foundation for the creation of a truly open internal market in banking services in Europe through the Second Banking Directive. Under that directive, any bank licensed to operate within one of the 12 European Union countries can provide the same services in any of the 11 other countries, without having to establish a separate affiliate or subsidiary, under its home country regulation.
20. See notably Perdrix (1991).
21. Wisse Dekker, "Refining ESPRIT", *European Affairs*, No. 5, 1992, p. 52.

References

Bressand, A. (1990). Beyond interdependence: 1992 as a global challenge, *International Affairs*, vol. 66, No. I, pp. 47-65.

_____ (1994). Sécurité nationale et réseaux électroniques globaux. In *Défense nationale*, November, pp. 61-73.

_____ and C. Distler (1995). *Sous le signe d'HERMES : la vie quotidienne à l'ère des machines relationnelles*. Paris: Flammarion.

_____ and K. Nicolaïdis (1989). Vers une économie de réseaux. *Politique industrielle*, Hiver, pp. 155-168.

_____ S. Devos, G. Raby and S. Woolcock (1994). *Regional Integration Agreements and the Multilateral Trading System: The Risk of Divergence, and the Quest for Convergence*. Paris: Report to the OECD Trade Committee.

Dekker, Wisse. Refining ESPRIT. *European Affairs*, 1992, No. 5, p. 52.

Distler, C. (ed.) (1994). Télécommunications et espace, *Politique internationale*, No. 65, Fall, special issue.

Ehrlich, E. (1993) Knocking at the door of the communication age. *European Reunification in the Age of Global Networks*, Institute for World Economics of the Hungarian Academy of Sciences. Paris: PROMETHEE, 1993.

Euromoney (1992). Labuan, an international offshore centre. *Euromoney*, September, Supplement.

Giersch, H. (1988). *Europe 1992 in an Open World Order*, Hamburg.

Gugler, P. and J.H. Dunning (1993). Technology-based cross-border alliances. In R. Culpan (ed.). *Multinational Strategic Alliances*. Binghamton, New York: International Business Press.

International Telecommunication Union (1984). *The Missing Link*, Report of the Independent Commission for World-wide Telecommunications Development, December.

Lawrence, R. (forthcoming). *Regionalism, Multilateralism, and Deeper Integration*. Washington, D.C.: The Brookings Institution.

O'Brien, R. *Global Financial Integration. The End of Geography*. London: Pinter Publications.

Perdrix, M. (1991). Les forces de changement dans les systèmes de paiement des pays européens. *Revue banque*, No. 518, July-August, pp. 688-700.

Pine, B.J. (1993).*Mass Customization, the New Frontier in Business Competition*. Boston, Massachusetts: Harvard Business School Press.

PROMETHEE (1989). 1992: the Global Challenge. *Project PROMETHEE Perspectives,* No. 9, March, Paris.

Saint-Geours, J. (1992). Global financial networks and the governance imperative. *In Networks and Markets: More Than a Marriage of Convenience. Project PROMETHEE Perspectives*, No. 21, December, Paris.

Teece, D.J. (1992). Competition, cooperation and innovation: Organizational arrangements for regimes of rapid technological progress. *Journal of Economic Behavior and Organization* (Amsterdam, The Netherlands), vol. 18, pp. 1-25.

Towie, M. (1991). Thai exchange set to automate. *Banking Technology*, December. UNCTAD (1993).*World Investment Report 1993: Transnational Corporations and Integrated International Production* (United Nations publication: Sales No. E.93.II.A.14).

Vernon, R. International investment and international trade in the product cycle. *Quarterly Journal of Economics*, vol. 80, 1965, pp. 190-207.

World Bank (1993). *The East-Asian Miracle: Economic Growth and Public Policy*. Washington, D.C.: Oxford University Press for the World Bank.

Contributors

Yair Aharoni, Professor Emeritus, Tel Aviv University, Faculty of Management, The Leon Recanati Graduate School of Business Administration.

Albert Bressand, Managing Director, PROMETHEE, Paris.

John Cantwell, Professor of International Economics, University of Reading.

Daniel Chudnovsky, Director, Centro de Investigaciones para la Transformación, Buenos Aires and Professor of Development Economics, University of Buenos Aires.

John H. Dunning, Professor of International Business, University of Reading and State of New Jersey Professor of International Business, Rutgers University.

Khalil A. Hamdani, Senior Economist and Chief of Investment Policy Reviews, Division on Investment, Technology and Enterprise Development, UNCTAD.

Seev Hirsch, Jaffe Professor of International Trade, Tel Aviv University, Faculty of Management, The Leon Recanati Graduate School of Business Administration.

Louka T. Katseli, Professor of Economics, University of Athens.

Sanjaya Lall, University Lecturer in Development Economics, Queen Elizabeth House, University of Oxford.

Robert Z. Lawrence, Professor of International Trade and Investment, Center for Business and Government, The Kennedy School of Government, Harvard University.

Linda Y.C. Lim, Research Director, Southeast Asia Business Program of the Center for South and Southeast Asian Studies and Adjunct Associate Professor of International Business, School of Business Administration, University of Michigan.

Nathaniel Siddall, School of Business Administration, University of Michigan.

Stephen Thomsen, Research Fellow, The Royal Institute of International Affairs, Chatham House, London.

Index